# New Labour in power: precedents and prospects

The election of a New Labour Government with an
unprecedented majority is one of the most exciting
developments in British politics for decades. At the same
time, the new Government faces a world very different from
that which was faced by the last Labour Government. The
Labour Party itself is also radically changed. *New Labour in
Power* combines historical, political and practical approaches
to the questions raised by the Labour election victory. It
analyses the central question: how new is New Labour?

Through addressing core themes such as Europe, the
economy, the State, welfare, education and the constitution,
this volume provides a range of assessments of this new era.
It explores the resonance of Mr Blair's victory through
analysis of the historical context and also through the words
of contemporary media commentators, journalists,
economists and politicians.

*New Labour in Power* includes essential analysis of the
current state of the party and invaluable insight into the
context of longer-term trends.

# New Labour in power:
# precedents and prospects

## Edited by Brian Brivati and Tim Bale

London and New York

First published 1997
by Routledge
11 New Fetter Lane, London EC4P 4EE

Simultaneously published in the USA and Canada
by Routledge
29 West 35th Street, New York, NY 10001

Typeset in Palatino by the Institute of Contemporary British History
Printed in Great Britain by T. J. International Ltd., Padstow, Cornwall

British Library Catologuing in Publication Data
A catalogue record for this book is available from the British Library

Library of Congress Cataloging in Publication Data
A catalogue record for this book has been requested.

ISBN: 0-415-17972-6 (hbk)
ISBN: 0-415-17973-4 (pbk)

This volume is dedicated to
the Rt Hon Michael Foot
on the occasion of his 84th birthday

# Contents

# Contributors

## Editors

**Dr Brian Brivati** was deputy director of the Institute of Contemporary British History from 1992 to 1994 and is now Reader in History at Kingston University. His publications include *Hugh Gaitskell: A Biography* (Richard Cohen Books, 1996) and, as co-editor,*What Difference Did the War Make?* and *From Reconstruction to Integration: Britain and Europe since 1945* (Liverpool UP, 1992 and 1993), *The Contemporary History Handbook* (Manchester UP, 1996) and *Anatomy of Decline: the political journalism of Peter Jenkins* (Cassell, 1994). He has recently edited and written an introduction for Michael Foot's *Aneurin Bevan* (Victor Gollancz, 1997) for a single volume centenary edition.

**Dr Tim Bale** studied history at Cambridge University in the UK and Northwestern University in the USA. He did his doctorate at the Department of Politics at the University of Sheffield, where he now teaches. He is the author of articles on the Labour Party and politics more generally in journals such as *Twentieth Century British History*, *Contemporary British History*, *Labour History Review*, *Politics* and the *Journal of Legislative Studies*.

## Contributors

**Dr Gerard Alexander** is an Assistant Professor of Government at the Woodrow Wilson Department of Government and Foreign Affairs, University of Virginia. He specialises in European politics and his current research interests concern democratic consolidation in western Europe and models of voting, campaigns and elections.

**Professor Vernon Bogdanor** is at Brasenose College, Oxford. His recent publications include *The Monarchy and the Constitution and Power* (Clarendon Press, 1995) and *Power and the People: A Guide to Constitutional Reform* (Victor Gollancz, 1997).

**Dr Nick Ellison** is Lecturer in Sociology and Social Policy at Durham University. His recent publications include *Egalitarian Thought and Labour Politics: Retreating Visions* (Routledge, 1994) and 'Consensus here, consensus there...but not consensus everywhere', in H. Jones and M.

Kandiah (eds.), *The Myth of Consensus* (Macmillan, 1997).

**Edward Pearce** is a political journalist and author. His recent books include *Election Rides* (Faber and Faber, 1992) describing the 1992 election in 18 different constituencies and *Machiavell's Children* (Victor Gollancz, 1993) on Florentine theory in Hitler-Thatcher practice. His next book, *Winning Near the Goal*, contains long biographical essays on unachieved Prime Ministers, Butler, Healey and Macleod.

**Dr Jim Tomlinson** is Reader in British Politics and Head of the Department of Government, Brunel University. He has written widely on economic history and on the history of the Labour Party. His most recent book, *Democratic Socialism and Policy: The Attlee Years*, was published by Cambridge University Press in 1997.

**David Walker** is the chief leader writer of *The Independent* and Visiting Professor at the School of Public Policy, University of Birmingham. He is co-author of *The Times Guide to the New British State* (Times Books, 1995) and *Sources Close to the Prime Minister* (Macmillan, 1984).

**Dr John W. Young** is Professor of Politics at the University of Leicester. His publications include *Winston Churchill's Last Campaign: Britain and the Cold War 1951–5*, (OUP, 1996) and *Britain and the World in the Twentieth Century* (Edward Arnold, forthcoming 1997).

## Commentators

**Professor Joe Bailey**, Head of the School of Social Science, Kingston University. His publications include *Social Europe* (Longman, 1992) and *Pessimism* (Routledge, 1988).

**Rt Hon Edmund Dell**, Labour MP 1963–79, Secretary of State for Trade, 1976–78. His publications include *The Politics of Economic Interdependence* (Macmillan, 1987), *A Hard Pounding: Politics and Economic Crisis 1974–76* (OUP, 1991) and *The Chancellors: a History of the Chancellors of the Exchequer* (HarperCollins, 1996).

**Professor A. H. Halsey**, Nuffield College, Oxford. His publications include: *Change in British Society* (4th edition, OUP, 1995) and *English Ethical Socialism* (Clarendon Press, 1988).

**Peter Jay**, Economics and Business Editor at the BBC, Ambassador to the USA 1977–79. His publications include *The Crisis of the Western Political Economy* (Deutsch, 1984).

**Austin Mitchell**, Labour MP for Great Grimsby since 1983, journalist and broadcaster. His publications include *Can Labour Win Again?* (Fabian Society, 1979), *Four Years in the Death of the Labour Party* (Methuen, 1983) and *Election '45: Reflections on the Revolution in Britain* (Fabian Society, 1995).

**Michael Phelan**, general secretary of the Christian Socialist Movement.

**William Plowden**, Central Policy Review Staff, Cabinet Office, 1971–77; Under-Secretary at the Department of Industry, 1977–78. His publications include *Inside the Think Tank: advising the Cabinet 1971–1983*, with Tessa Blackstone (Heinemann, 1988).

**Christopher Price**, editor, *The Stakeholder*, Labour MP 1966–70, 1974–83, PPS to Secretary of State for Education and Science, 1966–67 and 1975–76.

**Professor Patrick Seyd**, Chair of the Department of Politics, Sheffield University. His publications include *Labour's Grass Roots: the Politics of Party Membership* (OUP, 1992) and *The Rise and Fall of the Labour Left* (Macmillan Education, 1987).

**Rt Hon Peter Shore**, Labour MP 1964–97, Trade Secretary 1974–76, Environment Secretary 1976–79. His publications include *Leading the Left* (Weidenfeld and Nicolson, 1993).

**Dr Martin Smith**, Sheffield University. His publications include *Pressure, Power and Policy* (Baseline, 1995) and, as editor, *Contemporary British Conservatism* (Macmillan, 1996).

**Professor Geoffrey Warner**, Brasenose College, Oxford, formerly at the Open University.

# Acknowledgements

The essays in this volume were discussed at a conference at the end of May 1997 held at the Institute of Historical Research and sponsored by the Kingston University Centre for the Study of Society and Politics, the Institute of Contemporary British History, the Department of Politics of the University of Sheffield and the Fabian Society. The editors would like to thank the IHR and the ICBH for their assistance with this conference and acknowledge the financial support of the Kingston University History research fund. We would also like to thank the contributors and commentators for meeting very demanding deadlines. The text was copy edited and typeset by Virginia Preston, with her customary speed, efficiency and brilliance and the history editor at Routledge, Heather McCallum, was a pleasure to work with. Jackie Bale transcribed and prepared the commentators' remarks with extraordinary speed and accuracy.

# Chapter 1

# Introduction

*Brian Brivati and Tim Bale*

In an influential essay on politics in the United States, Stanley Greenberg summed up the confused state of the relationship between the analysis of politics and the actions of the electorate thus: 'Those who rush to overinterpret are as likely to be surprised by the future as those who assume that the old rules still apply. Every election now is an expression of this new era where revolt is commonplace.'[1] The two ideas wrapped up in this quotation are at the heart of the purpose of this volume: it is the first academic attempt to stand back from the slightly intoxicating atmosphere of Labour's landslide victory in the general election of 1997 and ask: what does this mean? Its central methodological assumption is that contemporary historical and political science analysis, coupled with the experience of practitioners, is the best way of trying to find an answer to this question. The danger of rushing to overintrepret is very real, as is the danger of falling foul of the bias amongst historians against the notion of 'relevance' and the tendency amongst some political scientists towards 'presentism'.[2] However, the historical and political moment seemed of such significance to the editors that we felt it was worth attempting to challenge a little the notions which limit contact across disciplines. The second part of Greenberg's quote, on the volatility of contemporary electorates, highlights the central political question of this volume: What are the prospects for New Labour in power and what are the ideological underpinnings to the policies it will be pursuing? We have not attempted to rival the Nuffield and other general election studies and analyse the content and spread of Labour's vote, but have rather asked three central questions: What can we learn about the New Labour Government from the last three periods of Labour in power? How will changes over the last 20 years in national and international political economy and in the role of the state make this Government different? Which lessons and battles from the past are relevant and which can the party afford to leave behind?

The historical record is the most concrete basis we have for exploring both questions based on precedent and those about prospects; as Aneurin Bevan once put it: 'why look into the crystal ball when you can read the bloody book?'. After a period of rapid political change and in the face of the challenges represented in the global and national shifts of the 1980s and 1990s, understanding the historical context of the new Labour Government is crucial. This context can only be grasped by assessing the ideological distance between new and old Labour and the evolution of the British body politic in the years since the Winter of Discontent. Without an historical depth to political analysis, judgements will be limited in their usefulness, and without a sense of the way in which this past is reflected in current changes, there is little utility in trying to map the future. This is not to say that history is an efficient predictive tool, but it is to say that thinking about the future can be improved by reflecting on the past, if only to unlearn and escape from some of the old battles the better to engage with the new. However, academics, whether they are historians or political scientists, should not work in isolation from those who actually made the decisions that shaped the record they analyse. Therefore this volume combines the historical, political and practical approaches to the question of New Labour in power and attempts to produce a range of responses to the core themes. Moreover, it fits into an emerging literature which considers the response of European left-wing parties to the resurgence of neo-Liberalism and the ways in which left of centre parties have changed their ideology and electoral strategy in response to the general movement away from collectivism towards market economics over the last three decades.[3]

As some of the chapters in this volume are concerned with the search for precedents it is important to be clear about the usefulness of such an exercise, both in terms of electoral history and in terms of the history of the Labour Party. It is largely meaningless to look for precedents before the First World War, indeed before 1928. Much was made in the press coverage of the 1997 result of the last Tory defeat of a similar magnitude, the Duke of Wellington in 1832: given the difference in the voting franchise, party and electoral system, this is, of course, utterly bogus. Indeed, it contributes to the underlying Whig notion of British political history that somehow continuity of language in things like party names constitutes a timelessness in values and constitutional practices. This is a dangerous and highly misleading fiction. The label on the jar might be the same but it is critically important to understand the change in the nature of jar's contents. As with the electoral and political system, so with the Labour Party.

Tony Blair's project to reform the Labour Party has achieved its primary objective: office. This was achieved by harnessing the reforms in party democracy of the early 1980s to an economic programme more sensitive to electoral politics than the Bennite ideology these reforms had been designed to enable. The nature of this new political party is not a throw back to a type of Gladstonian liberalism, which supposedly reunites the strands of British radicalism like some kind of Siamese twin separated at birth. We have not seen the coming together of liberalism and socialism, and these are not the

1890s, for a number of different reasons. First, the notion that Gladstonian liberalism represented a united strand of radicalism is profoundly mistaken. The discrete radical tradition that gave birth to the Labour Party is much older and more defined than that. Chartism had little in common with the timid notions of Gladstonian liberalism and the socialist strand which formed a part of the coalition that started the Labour Party was never very interested in tinkering with the edges of social problems. So there was never a unity on the left in the way that some writers have imagined, and the earlier Labour pioneers used liberalism much as the new right used the Conservative Party: as a vehicle to get Parliamentary representation. In response the liberals adopted a form of radicalism in their New Liberalism of the Edwardian period that fell well short of the most basic reformist programmes of the Socialists. But the notion of a return to a supposed unity of the left is wrong for deeper reasons than this. The notion is bad history in terms of the story of the Liberal Party, and it is profoundly dishonest intellectual opportunism in terms of the history of the Labour Party.

### Labour and landslides: the record

Labour's record win of 1997 – in a general election that had all the characteristics of a national by-election – is the third substantial or landslide win that the party has enjoyed since 1945. Neither of the two previous wins directly compares with Labour's 1997 achievement of comprehensively defeating an incompetent Conservative Government. In 1945 Labour was coming from opposition to Government but many leading party members had been part of the wartime coalition. In 1966 Wilson had governed for 18 months with a slender majority. In 1997, Tony Blair was rather wide of the mark with his oft-repeated (anti-Sheffield rally) line that this country is not a country that gives parties landslides: there have actually been rather a lot since the introduction of universal suffrage. But an examination of 20th century election results reveals that the Labour Party has not done very well in the elections which take place *after* they have won a landslide. If we date universal suffrage from 1928, then the general elections that are significant for an analysis of the record are 1929, 1931, 1935 and the post-1945 elections: a total of 18 national polls. Of these, 1931, 1935, 1945, 1959, 1966, 1983, 1987 and 1997 produced substantial or landslide victories. The expectation at most of these elections was that the Government would win the following contest. In 1931 and 1935 the composition of the national Government made this expectation the most realistic, but in each of the other cases there was a confidence in the Government about being in power for the foreseeable future. This proved well founded in all but two instances, 1959 and 1966, both seeing substantial majorities overturned in one election after by-election defeats had nibbled into the majority. Each of these substantial or landslide victories that were not overturned had impacts similar to a stone in a pool of water: the elections which followed were ripples from the original result. Thus 1950, 1951, 1964 and perhaps even 1992, were elections that owed their character and content to previous results. British elections conducted using universal suffrage have been dominated by landslides: out of 18 elections 12 can be said to have been conditioned by such a result.

Perhaps Tony Blair just meant that this country does not give the Labour Party convincing victories as often as it gives them to the Conservative Party: only two in the party's history before 1 May, namely 1945 and 1966. In 1945 the Labour Party won 393 seats on a popular vote of 11,995,152 (47.8 per cent) in an election with a turnout of 72.7 per cent. Fifty-six months later in February 1950, the Labour Party secured 315 seats on a popular vote of 13,266,592 (46.1 per cent) in an election with a turnout of 84 per cent, the highest turnout in the period since 1945. The 1945 result gave the party an overall majority of 145, the 1950 election reduced this to 5. In 1966 the Labour Party won 363 seats on a popular vote of 13,064,951 (47.9 per cent) in an election with a turnout of 75.8 per cent. In June 1970, 51 months later, the Labour Party won 287 seats on a popular vote of 12,179,341 (43 per cent) in an election with a turnout of 72 per cent. The 1966 election gave the party an overall majority of 96, the 1970 election resulted in a majority for the Conservatives of 30. That, at its simplest, is the record of Labour re-election from a landslide position.

The 1945 general election is frequently called Labour's high tide. Though 1997 surpasses it on some measures (though not share of vote) and recent scholarly work has questioned the notion that this election represented the formation of a new political hegemony by examining popular attitudes to politics, the result remains both actually and symbolically, the most important in Labour's history. Comparatively speaking, 1966 is neglected by historians as an election result; for example the chapter in Hennessy and Seldon's *Ruling Performance* does not actually mention the general election of 1966 except in the chronology at the end.[4] However, as a piece of election management and an indication of the direction in which electoral politics seemed to be moving, 1966 was a fascinating result. The period 1964–66 also illustrates the pressures created when permanent campaigning clashes with government. A comparison of 1945 and 1966 highlights the difference between being in office and being in power. The landslide election is the beginning of the process and not the end; in this sense, the most interesting question about 1997 is what Tony Blair will do with power. The 1945 result suggests how much can be achieved with such a majority, while 1966 and the record thereafter question both the ambition of the 1964 programme and the idea of a landslide: such a result does not always lead to profound changes commensurate with the size of the majority. At the time of writing it looks as though the scale of the Blair Government's ambition is not less than that of the Attlee or Wilson Governments at the same point in their lives, but differently focused and communicated. The focus in 1945 and 1966 was on differing visions of economic modernisation with remarkably little interest in constitutional radicalism. Blair's Government has begun in some senses where the Labour Government of 1974–79 left off and is pursuing a radical constitutional agenda coupled to a moderate macro-economic programme.

**Structure of the book**

Each of the main challenges faced by the new Government is covered in an overview chapter. These are followed by shorter commentaries by academics or politicians. The final chapter draws some of the arguments together in a conclusion. In chapter 2, Jim Tomlinson considers the economic record of Labour Governments. He is highly sceptical about the impact and even the reality of globalization, and draws parallels between the 1990s and the 1960s. Then as now, a Labour Government placed its faith in the ability of a combination of stabilisation policy and supply-side reform to put an end to what in the earlier period was called *stop-go* or *boom-bust* – the tendency of the UK economy (notwithstanding the evanescent Thatcher 'miracle') to overheat almost as soon as it begins to grow, forcing Governments into deflationary policies which, among other things, discourage the sort of long-term investment that is the key to sustained economic success. Now as then, there is the possibility that the Government's intentions may be dashed by its simultaneous desire, pursued for a variety of reasons (not all of them economic) to maintain the UK's exchange rate at a predetermined – and perhaps harmfully high – fixed level: for the need to preserve 'parity' with the once-mighty dollar, read the assumption that, all things being equal, membership of a single European currency may well be in the nation's best interests. Yet, as Tomlinson notes, the parallels can be too tightly drawn. Old Labour was never the tax and spend party of Tory mythology, but it did believe (at least in principle) that public spending, when it could be afforded, was the way to offset poverty and inequality. New Labour's rigid stance on public (especially in the sense of welfare) spending is not simply a matter of dampening expectations – or of 'getting its betrayal in first' as some like to put it – but of a loss of faith in the capacity of such spending to realise the goals set for it, and perhaps even a loss of faith in the goals themselves.

In chapter 3, Nick Ellison considers welfare and education and argues that, if anything, Labour was stuck on, if not stuck in, the past. During its periods in Government between 1951 and 1979, Ellison stresses, Labour did at least try to achieve the classic social democratic balancing act, attempting to marry social justice and even some incremental redistribution with competent economic management. But its sense of achievement in the Attlee years – and more particularly the need to defend those achievements against the increasingly open attacks of the Conservatives – condemned it to a kind of collectivist stasis and prevented it from realising fully the need to adapt to and move into the 'post-welfare' era. The period 1964–70 is a case in point: moves towards using benefits to promote labour market flexibility and targeting or selectivity (as it was then called) jostled uneasily with memories of the means test on one side and the vague desire to complete the unfinished business of the Attlee years on the other. The first Wilson Government spent, not least because it inherited big plans from the Conservatives (who had hoped to buy their way to election victory in 1964), but it did not spend as much as it said it would, thereby disappointing its supporters and creating, wrongly or rightly, the impression of failure. During that period, education as well as welfare saw notable reverses, not least the failure to raise the school leaving age as planned and to 'destroy every fucking grammar school in England', as Tony Crosland once colourfully put it. Yet progress was made, and it was not until the mid-1970s under Jim Callaghan that education became less about equality (or at least equality of opportunity) and more about boosting the economic competitiveness of the nation – the theme that arguably dominates New Labour's presentation of the issue. Ellison goes on to show that, after a period in Government between 1974 and 1979 which witnessed the virtual 'implosion' of the Party as external constraints forced the rhetorical abandonment of the doctrine that higher public spending was either possible or conducive to prosperity or welfare, Labour took some time to learn its own lessons, concerned as it was to defend its historic settlement against Thatcherite attack. Indeed it was not until after the defeat of 1992 that it began seriously to reconfigure its social policy along the lines of a 'stakeholding' approach that would stress that rights entailed responsibilities and that the facilitation of individual effort and encouragement of 'social capital' would take pride of place over the collective provision of state benefits. Whether this reconfiguration – necessary though it might be and short on details as it is – represents an adequate response to the challenges of the future on the part of a transformed social democracy or instead the effective end of that ideology, Ellison is less sure.

In chapter 4, David Walker argues that just as Labour evacuates the traditional ideological content of 'socialism' (central among its elements an appeal to fraternity, community and equality), it seems to have discovered 'morality' (meaning a strong externally enforced sense of right conduct). This chapter seeks to explore the contradictions in this older vision which underlay previous Labour Governments and the new vision which underlies the current Government by examining traditional Labour morality, including its almost complete silence on sex and gender relationships; by noting the uncomfortable position liberals have always had in the Labour firmament and by examining the nature of New Labour's conversion to the New Rectitude and by considering the prospect for Government-ordained morality, for example in the educational curriculum and crime policy. The chapter concludes that the prospects for a moral revival are slim in the absence of new ideology for Labour which is explicitly anti-capitalist and/or anti-liberal.

Gerard Alexander, in chapter 5, argues that when it comes to the state, Labour managed to confuse means with ends. In so doing it condemned itself, first, to being associated with a not necessarily overmighty but often inefficient state and then, second, to feeling obliged to defend that state against reforms (running from clear privatisation to contracting out and the purchaser-provider split) which it should perhaps have recognised might afford it a better chance of achieving its goals when in Government. In fact, Alexander argues, this reputation for strong statism was unjustified: the record of Labour Governments suggests that their attitude to and use (and organisation) of the state was characterised by contingency and flexibility. The types of state action undertaken between 1964 and 1970, for example, were strikingly diverse, particularly when it came to economic policy but also across a broad range of areas encompassing everything from construction to culture. The years between 1974 and 1979, however, marked a crisis of confidence in the capacity of the state to respond to the changing international political economy and incorporate the various interests which hitherto had, more or less uneasily, coexisted as part of the post-war settlement. Losing office, as it so often did, however, provoked a sort of short-term memory loss which encouraged Labour in opposition – at least until the late 1980s – to fight Conservative moves to shrink or change the state – fights which were inevitably lost, which did little for Labour's electoral popularity and which blinded it to the fact that many of its core values (such as support for a welfare state wherein Government pays for even if it doesn't directly provide services) still survived intact in an admittedly more mixed economy. Despite misgivings as to the extent to which the means by which state services are delivered may actually militate against the kind of cross-class alliance vital to the continuing success of social democracy, then, Alexander is largely optimistic about the Blair Government's chances of making the machine it inherited work in its favour.

The analysis of the constitutional reform agenda of the Blair Government is divided into two parts. In 'Labour and the constitution, Part I: the record', Vernon Bogdanor considers the background relationship between the Labour Party and issues of constitutional reform. In 'Labour and the constitution, Part II: the Blair agenda', Edward Pearce analyses the prospects for reform under the current Government. The contributors share a certain scepticism about the new Government's motives for and commitment to wide-ranging reform. Vernon Bogdanor addresses Labour's traditional conservatism in this area. He locates this at a general level in the Party's conviction that it could both win office and wield real power under the existing settlement. More particularly, he points to the suspicion of judicial influence that has dampened enthusiasm for a Bill of

Rights, to the threat posed to executive power by a possibly elected second chamber that has undermined attempts to reform the House of Lords, and to the way in which devolution has been caught up in the conflict between support for local democracy and the feeling that national institutions are better guarantors of equality across the regions. Bogdanor goes on to suggest that the abandonment of traditional positions may indicate not so much a desire to transform the system by democratising it, but rather a loss of faith in many of Labour's basic convictions and its capacity to deliver change. Yet he is not altogether pessimistic: although he points to the fact that, when it comes to the enactment of what is easily labelled constitutional reform, the devil is very much in the detail, he also notes that such measures often develop a logic of their own which can take those who first framed them further than they may originally have intended to go. The same point is made by Edward Pearce, who is likewise impressed with many of what we might call the 'normative' arguments for reform both in terms of the electoral system and to Parliament itself. Pearce's main argument, however, is that constitutional reform is likely to play a major role in the programme of the new Labour Government because of what might be thought of as its purely political attractions. Hemmed in, largely of its own volition, by constraints on its ability to raise revenue and spend it, the new Government needs to be seen to make a difference but to do it without splashing out. On the other hand, Pearce suspects that the current leadership's centralising tendencies, and its concern to ensure more than merely one or even two terms, may conflict with its desire to make some sort of mark in this area.

When it comes to foreign, European and defence policy, John Young, in chapter 7, explores the way in which Labour has somehow allowed the Conservatives, whatever the historical truth, to pose as both the more patriotic and the more realistic of the two main parties – something which is all the more strange given the Tories' often catastrophic performance in office and Labour's record, whatever its ideology and promises in opposition, of standing up for very conventional national interests in international negotiations and sticking to very traditional positions on matters such as nuclear weapons and Britain's world role. He also points to the obvious, but all-too-easily overlooked fact that the familiar pattern whereby internationalism and idealism are forgotten once power is achieved owes less to Labour Governments succumbing to some underspecified Foreign Office seduction than to the fact that this particular policy environment is just much less easy to control than any other. Possibly, he suggests, the very idealism that led Labour Governments to suppose that their arrival would in itself somehow be enough to make a difference was – because it was a substitute for a strategy rather than a strategy in itself – a recipe for drift rather than decision, for reluctant retreat rather than the sort of bold moves required to adapt to (if not offset) the UK's decline. On the other hand, he notes that since the late 1960s Labour, although motivated by enthusiasm for free trade rather than a desire to pool sovereignty in order to facilitate peace and prosperity for all, does have a claim, despite internal disputes in the 1970s, to be the party of Europe and that this might be a fruitful way forward for the Blair Government – providing, of course, it can shrug off, in this post-cold war era, the kind of conventional thinking that has so dogged its predecessors.

Tim Bale argues that many of our received ideas about party management under Labour Governments are misleading. True, the Party's federated structure does facilitate internal strife, but it does not necessarily explain it – especially if we remember that relationships within, as well as between, Labour's component parts are often far more complex than the familiar caricatures suggest. Things have gone wrong in the past because fairly mainstream ordinary members have been disappointed by the failure of their parliamentary representatives in office to deliver the often very limited promises that they made in opposition. Trade unions caused Labour Governments problems because those Governments demanded sacrifices which union leaders – even where they were sympathetic to the Government line – were simply not in a position to oblige their rank and file to make. Attempts to bring them to heel were often undermined not just by the unions themselves but from within the right as well as the left of the PLP and indeed the Labour Cabinet. Indeed, more generally it is a mistake to blame left-wing MPs for all of the trouble the new Government's predecessors have had to put up with from their own side. Labour's parliamentarians of whichever ideological persuasion are an independent lot, whose good behaviour (especially when the Party has a large majority) has always depended less on enforcement of discipline and more on sympathy with the general direction of the Government – and, it must be said, on its perceived popularity. In any case it is issues – Europe, the constitution and (to a lesser extent) welfare and defence spending – rather than factions or organisational shortcomings that have brought past Labour Governments to grief. Given all this, and in spite of the changes of the last 18 years, Bale treats with some scepticism the idea, seemingly prevalent amongst commentators and politicians, that this Labour Government will escape the problems that have dogged its predecessors – unless, of course, it has the maturity not to indulge in self-mutilation at Cabinet level and manages to remember that the creation (and slaying) of enemies without is always more important than the demonisation of the enemy within. The volume ends with Brian Brivati, who attempts to draw the contrasting conclusions and debates together.

The diverse approaches and backgrounds of the authors and commentators in this volume have produced a range of tones and a variety of styles. The editors have not attempted to impose an overall voice but hope that the range of opinions and ideas contained here will help kickstart the debate on the meaning of New Labour in power.

# Notes

1 Stanley B. Greenberg, *Middle Class Dreams, The Politics and Power of the New American Majority*, Yale University Press, 1995, p.17.
2 Dennis Kavanagh, 'Why political science needs history', *Political Studies*, Vol. 39 No.3, 1991.
3 See for example, David S. Bell and Eric Shaw, *Conflict and Cohesion in Western European Social Democratic Parties*, Pinter, 1994.
4 David Walker, 'The First Wilson Governments, 1964–1970', in Peter Hennessy and Anthony Seldon (eds), *Ruling Performance: British Government from Attlee to Thatcher*, Blackwell, 1987.

# Chapter 2

# Economic policy
## Lessons from past Labour Governments

*Jim Tomlinson*

### The relevance of the past

Every generation since the industrial revolution has believed that it is living through a period of unprecedented economic change. Such a view is a commonplace today, and if it were true it would render discussion of past Labour Governments of little interest to today's policy-making. Yet evidence for such a view of today is scarce. At the most general level, we would surely expect 'unprecedented change' to be accompanied by particularly rapid growth of productivity, yet there is no sign of this. The trend in productivity growth in all OECD countries has been slower since the 1970s than before, even if, as seems sensible, we ignore the 1974–79 period as a distinct and unique crisis period, inclusion of which distorts long-run patterns.[1]

Perhaps the theme which is most in evidence amongst those who emphasise the pace at which contemporary economies are changing is that of 'globalisation'. Are we not living in an age when global economic integration is fundamentally altering the economic world, and in particular the capacity of national Governments to influence that world? The short answer to that question is 'no': internationalisation of economic activity is proceeding rapidly, but the novelty and scope of this process are much exaggerated. Ever since national economic management was invented in Britain, it has had to be conducted in an economy with extensive international linkages. Indeed, one could argue that the dominant intellectual force in creating British national economic management, Keynes, spent almost all his policy-oriented writing trying to argue how British economic management could be reconciled to difficult international economic conditions.[2] In addition, the concept of globalisation masks the extent to which economic integration in many areas is still predominantly regional (American/European/Asian) in scope. Globalisation, in sum, is a term which should be treated with great scepticism, as a disabling and misleading generalisation, which inhibits action in the present, and unreasonably implies that we live in such a changed world that nothing from the past can be of much relevance. National Governments, whilst weakened in some respects, still have substantial capacity to affect economic events, including, of course, by collaboration with other national Governments.[3] Finally, the concept of globalisation is commonly linked to an exaggerated emphasis on competitiveness as a policy goal, a point returned to below.

### The irrelevance of the 1970s?

Devotees of the comparative method dispute whether more is to be learned from comparisons of similar or dissimilar periods.[4] Certainly, too much dissimilarity seems likely to make comparison somewhat tortured. This is probably true for the case of comparisons between the 1970s and today. When Labour came to power in 1974 they inherited an inflationary boom seriously exacerbated by OPEC I. Whilst this boom had been encouraged by the Tories' expansionary policies after 1972, it was primarily an external force against which national policies were extremely weak. In all industrial countries this unprecedented problem led to a period of stagflation, even if by most standards this was worst in Britain.[5]

Second, the core of Labour's response to this crisis, once it became apparent that no international agreement on a Keynesian package was possible, was an incomes policy (the social contract) which put insupportable strains on the trade unions, which eventually cracked under the pressure. The problem was not, as commonly asserted, that unions in this period were too powerful, but rather that they were asked by the Government to play a role for which they were unsuited, and which contradicted their whole structure and ethos.[6]

Third, economic strategy was dominated by a combination of a Party commitment to the Alternative Economic Strategy (AES) which, whatever its economic and political logic, represented a violent break with the whole of post-war British approaches to economic policy; and a Government position which was virulently hostile to the AES, but which had little in the way of a coherent alternative, except reliance on the unions and a desperate attempt to maintain private sector confidence.[7] None of these key features of the 1970s are likely to recur. Inflationary pressures in the world are muted and OPEC is a dead duck. For good or ill, the trade unions have lost any likelihood of being treated (or expecting to be treated) as central to any Government's strategy. And, whether we like it or not, the Labour Party under Blair has been fundamentally reshaped to prevent the extraordinary depth of division between Party and Government being repeated in the future.

### The relevance of Labour's golden age in the 1940s

By common consent, the most successful Labour Government so far was that of 1945–51. After 50 years, is anything to be learnt from that period, when the economic and political environments were so different? Because of these differences, specific lessons are likely to be few, but recent writing on this Government has brought out features of the Attlee period which still have resonance today. Traditionally, these years have been celebrated by Labour supporters for the creation of the welfare state, the extension of public ownership and the pursuit of full employment. These remain major achievements, but contemporary analysis of the period has sought to refocus attention on the extent to which Labour in this period had a substantial agenda of industrial efficiency. Alongside its other goals, Labour was determined to underpin its welfare goals with strengthening the economy – what may be called Mr Attlee's supply-side socialism in modern terminology.[8]

Stressing this aspect of Labour's past, especially in the glory days of the 1940s, may serve to suggest that seeking to combine the watchwords of efficiency and fairness is no new dilemma for Labour. Rather, it has been the defining characteristic of Labour through most of its history. In that general sense, there is perhaps little that is new in New Labour.

## 1997 = 1964?

Comparisons may be most fruitful when two situations are not too fundamentally dissimilar. From this point of view the experience of the 1964 Wilson Government may be more instructive than that of the 1970s or 1940s. In 1964 the external economic environment was relatively benign, without the shocks working through from the commodity price rise of the early 1970s or OPEC I. The economy was overheating, and generating a serious balance of payments problem (see Table 1), but there was not the same intractable inflation/unemployment (stagflation) dilemma which haunted Labour in the 1970s. Similarly today, we are in the upswing of a cycle which has so far moved at a sustainable pace. (And where the lagging behind of Germany and France is likely to make the upswing sustainable for a long period.) The major problem of the cycle is the fiscal deficit, huge for this stage of the recovery, but there is no obvious reason why dealing with this should severely limit the possibility of that recovery continuing. The implication is that, whilst the unemployment problem is closer in magnitude to that of the 1970s than the 1960s, in other respects the context for Labour's policies now is more like 1964 than 1974.

There is a strong parallel too in the stance of the incoming Governments. In the 1960s the macro-economic promise was of an end to stop-go and a movement to economic and financial stability, though the 1964 manifesto is strikingly thin on how that new stability is to be achieved. Similarly, the 1997 manifesto promise is one of ending the instability of the previous 18 years, with a promise of a tough anti-inflationary stance and tight fiscal controls,[9] and at the time of writing, this policy has already begun to be pursued by the announcement of much greater independence for the Bank of England in the conduct of monetary policy.

*Table 1*    The legacies for 1964 and 1997

|  | 1964 | 1997/98 (forecast) |
| --- | --- | --- |
| Unemployment | 413,000 | 1,700,000 |
| Inflation (RPI) | 3.4% | 2.5% |
| Growth of GDP | 5.4% | 2.6% |
| Current account deficit | 1.1% | 0.03% |
| PSBR (% of GDP) | 2.8% | 3.1% |
| General Government Financial Deficit | 1.0% | 3.3%* |

*estimate

Sources: 1964: *Economic Trends Annual Supplement*. 1997/8: *National Institute Economic Review*, No. 160, April 1997.

The standard history of the 1960s is of how this promised end to stop-go was aborted by the adherence to an overvalued exchange rate, which for three years meant policies of prolonged stop. Some have seen a possible re-run of that scenario, with the Blair Government adhering to an overvalued exchange rate as part of a move towards monetary union.[10] This appears an unhelpful comparison on a number of grounds. First, it is part of a tradition of writing about the history of Labour's economic policies which sees Labour Governments as always fatally undermined by financial pressures to maintain an overvalued exchange rate.[11] This story is much too one-dimensional, and over-generalises from perhaps two episodes (1929–31, 1964–67) to Labour's whole history. (It also reflects the pessimistic, what went wrong style of writing about Labour's history that is in need of serious redressing.) Second, it draws on a mistaken understanding of the British adherence to the ERM in 1990–92. Of course Euro-sceptics in all parties present this as part of the Conservatives' European folly, whereas in fact it had little to do with Europe. Adherence to ERM in 1990 was fundamentally about the Conservative Government seeking to reassure financial markets about its anti-inflationary credentials in the wake of the failure of money-supply targeting in the 1980s. Adherence to (an overvalued) exchange rate was the chosen means to that end, rather than an end in itself. Exchange rate policy is usually the result of Government priorities, and it is those priorities which should be scrutinised, rather than the exchange rate position itself. Third, whilst the pound is probably slightly overvalued at the moment, the current account problems caused by this bear no comparison with the situation in 1964, as the figures in Table 1 make clear. Finally, and most importantly, whether adherence to a fixed exchange rate under ERM/EMU would in the medium term be more deflationary than any alternative policy is debateable – there are good reasons for thinking the opposite. Given the absence of an option of go-it-alone Keynesianism, adherence to EMU may prove to be the best foreign exchange framework there is available.[12]

This is not to say that the exchange rate policies of the 1960s do not have lessons for today. First, the over-politicisation of economic policy-making is strikingly evident in the devaluation saga of the 1960s. This is not to argue that economic policy can ever be wholly de-politicised (even with an independent central bank) but it was plainly excessive in the mid-1960s, with political concerns about American pressure and Labour's reputation given too much weight compared with the needs of economic management. Second, and linked to this over-politicisation, was the extraordinary declaration of devaluation as the unmentionable in official discussion of economic policy, which didn't, of course, stop it being mentioned, but hindered a sensible debate on the issue.[13]

### Problems of declinism

Perhaps the most interesting lessons from the 1960s may be learnt from the area of growth and 'modernisation'. Since the end of the 1950s Labour has adopted the declinist view that the British economy suffered from some long-term fundamental problems which have retarded growth.[14] Such 'declinism' tends to generate the production of panaceas; the key area of reform that can 'turn the economy round'. Rhetorically, the 1960s Government found such a panacea in technological change, with the idea both of expanding Britain's R&D effort, and focusing it away from the military and prestige science sectors to more commercially oriented civilian production. This, it should be emphasised, was not just empty rhetoric. The Government via Mintech made serious efforts to pursue this programme, but found a fundamental problem as well as operational obstacles. There is little evidence that more R&D spending *per se* necessarily generates faster technical progress, and indeed, as Edgerton points out, this basic point was coming to be accepted in Government circles by the late 1960s. By the end of the 1960s Mintech had come to recognise that it was the capacity of British companies effectively to deploy R&D resources, rather than simply the quantity of those resources, which was crucial.[15]

Today a similar declinist perspective seems to animate Labour – hence, for example, the emphasis on league tables of economic growth, a device invented in the 1950s at the beginnings of the first wave of declinism. Today, unlike the 1960s, the panacea is not R&D but education and training.[16] Are there similar dangers to those accompanying the emphasis on R&D 30 years ago? It should, of course, be said that a case can be made for emphasis on the expansion of education and training quite separate from arguments about their impact on economic growth. Labour itself emphasizes the importance of training for employment, given the collapse of demand for unskilled labour. But one could also advance social mobility arguments here, and, in relation to university education especially, the need in modern democracies for a large educated population to scrutinise and challenge Government policy effectively. But the danger is that education and training will be tied too closely to growth, where the evidence for any direct relation between educational inputs and economic performance is as problematic as that between quantities of R&D and subsequent output growth. It is easy to demonstrate that Britain has serious educational deficiencies (though not across the board), much harder to link these to productive failures.[17] As with R&D in the 1960s, too much emphasis on maximising an input glosses over the failures at the corporate level about the deployment of those inputs.

Adherence to declinism in the 1960s and 1990s raises broader problems. First, an emphasis on Britain's place in league tables of GDP is high-risk, given that (a) *vis-à-vis* western Europe the countries are all close together in terms of per capita GDP, so small movements can shift a country's league position quite sharply, and (b) recent overtakers of Britain in these tables have been Asian countries who are clearly on a different playing-field from Britain, and which it would be foolish to suppose could be easily overtaken. (For example, much of their growth stems from very high levels of capital accumulation and increases in hours worked which are implausible in Britain.) Second, there are a range of doubts about whether growth *per se* as an objective makes either economic or political sense. Recent attempts to measure economic welfare other than by GDP growth have emphasised such issues as transportation, pollution and inequality in real welfare, and how changes in these measures may diverge substantially from GDP trends.[18] What is interesting is how far such concerns seem to chime with opinion poll evidence about popular concerns, and how, therefore, too much emphasis on growth measured in traditional ways may be politically misplaced.[19]

The issue of inequality is of special interest to analysts of Labour Governments. Some of the problems of this objective are returned to below, but in the context of the growth argument, it can be noted that one of the most interesting features of recent economic argument is that which seeks to displace the age-old idea of an equality/efficiency trade-off.[20] If this were well established then it would cut across many of the arguments traditional in Labour circles (perhaps especially in the 1960s), which assumed that this trade-off was a central aspect of Labour's economic policy judgements. Finally, it is notable how in recent economic cycles, fluctuations in output are less closely related to GDP movements. Employment has become as much a question of how growth is distributed as how fast it takes place, so that rapid growth does not of itself deal with the unemployment issue.

All this suggests that, at a minimum, the league table of GDP growth rates is not a sensible device with which to demonstrate that Labour Governments can perform better than the Conservatives.

## The issue of competitiveness

Linked to the previous set of arguments is one about the place of competitiveness in Labour's goals. Competitiveness has become one of the buzzwords of the decade, and the previous Conservative Government began an annual series of competitiveness White Papers in the mid-1990s. However, as Krugman emphasises, this focus on competitiveness can easily be misplaced.[21] The living standards of the population, measured in traditional GDP terms, depend fundamentally on productivity, not directly on competitiveness. In a country like the USA, where only about 10 per cent of GDP is exported, the focus on competitiveness ignores the fact that most of output is not produced in competition with foreigners, so that competitiveness is not the key issue. The same point may be made, with qualification, about Britain, where about 25 per cent of output is exported. Focusing on competitiveness may have a number of unfortunate implications. Krugman highlights the protectionism which may flow from a pessimistic assessment of how a country is performing in competitive terms. This does not seem a danger in Britain, but other problems arise here. First, competitiveness is commonly measured in relative unit labour costs (RULCs), which inescapably highlights an agenda of wages as the problem in competitiveness, however much economists may emphasise that RULCs are a function of productivity as much as wage levels. This helps to create the underpinnings for an emphasis on lowering wage costs which was often linked with the Conservative approach to competitiveness, but which Labour should avoid.

Second, the competitiveness issue raises problems about the attitude to the balance between manufacturing and services. In the 1960s Labour's attitude was clear. In a fully employed economy, the belief was that workers should be transferred from service to manufacturing employment in order to raise average productivity. This was based on the belief that a substantial part of the higher productivity growth of western European countries in the 1950s had been the result of the transfer of large numbers of workers from agriculture to industry, and that Britain, lacking that source of labour, should squeeze workers out of services. This was the basis of the Selective Employment Tax, which provided an incentive for the service sector to reduce its employment levels.

The debate about the place of manufacturing in the economy has moved through several stages since the 1960s. In the 1970s deindustrialisation became a popular concern, especially on the left. The most persuasive accounts of the problem related it to the balance of payments, given the disproportionate importance of manufacturing to Britain's international trade. In the 1980s, with the rapid decline of employment in manufacturing in the early Thatcher years, the employment aspect was stressed, especially the collapse in numbers of traditionally male full-time manual jobs which were concentrated in manufacturing.[22]

In the 1990s the issue seems to have lost some of its prominence, with an acceptance that manufacturing employment is in decline in all advanced countries, and is now quite a small proportion (16 per cent) of total jobs.

Two points may be made on this. First, the 1970s concern with manufacturing because of its impact on the balance of payments is still broadly right – about two-thirds of Britain's export receipts (excluding returns on foreign investment) still come from manufacturing. So a concern with manufacturing for that reason seems quite appropriate. The difficulty here is that the gains in competitiveness in manufacturing over the last 15 to 20 years have come largely from labour-shedding with almost stagnant output – an example of how focusing on competitiveness may be unhelpful. Manufacturing employment has been falling more slowly in other countries because rises in productivity have been accompanied by faster growing output.

On the other hand, too much attention to manufacturing because of its balance of payments aspect takes attention away from the majority of the economy which is not internationally traded, which means most of the service sector. Contrary to Thatcherite claims, Britain's service sector is inefficient by international standards. A study of marketed services recently showed that on average the US, Germany and France all have productivity levels over a third higher in this sector than in Britain.[23] If this was the result of a Japanese-style absorption of low productivity labour into employment it could be argued to be a desirable feature of the British economy. But this does not seem to be the case, as job growth has been slow, and the service sector, if anything, is even more the home of macho, labour-cutting styles of management than manufacturing. The general point is not that these parts of the economy are not internationally competitive – rather the point is that most of their output is not internationally traded, so competitiveness is not the nub of the issue. The problem is best thought of as one of productivity, which, interestingly, was a buzzword of the 1960s, evident, for example, in the creation of the Department of Employment and Productivity. This focus on productivity is one which should be reasserted.[24] In the service sector the problem is not one of labour costs, but of low investment in infrastructure, poor management and inadequate training levels. All of these are problems which cannot be fully dealt with at company level – most obviously the issue of infrastructure investment.

## Investment

As in the area of employment, so in the area of investment, the presumption of the 1960s was that the low level of manufacturing capital was the central problem to be addressed. This focus arose from a long-standing argument that stop-go had inhibited British investment, and that Britain had a significantly lower proportion of investment to GDP than was typically the case in western Europe. The concentration on manufacturing investment arose from the standard 1960s assumption that it was investment shortfalls in this area that were most damaging to long-run growth performance. As with the issue of employment, the crucial role of manufacturing investment has been hotly debated over subsequent decades. Even in the 1960s some economists emphasised that British investment yielded low returns in output, and that this was a major inhibition, rather than the supply of investment funds which leftist accounts of decline have tended to stress.[25] The debate continues, and proponents of the deficient manufacturing investment thesis can certainly point to low levels, both compared with the past, and compared with other industrial countries in the present.[26]

However, two points may be made about this issue which mean that parallels with the 1960s should be treated with caution. First, the most striking long-run change in British investment since the 1960s has not been in manufacturing, but in the public sector, not so much the utilities (where investment has been much affected in recent years by privatisation), but in other infrastructure such as housing, schools, hospitals and transport.[27] It is important to emphasise that investment in these areas is very important for productivity, and we should not put too much emphasis on investment in directly productive equipment, which is always quite a small proportion of total investment in a modern economy.

Second, the desire to raise industrial investment in the 1960s was linked to the aim of raising profits, given that profits in the corporate sector had been squeezed since the 1950s. The Labour Government of the 1960s carried on the long-run policy of trying to offset cuts in pre-tax profits by cutting the tax burden on companies, though it reinvented the 1940s policy of trying to discourage the distribution of profits by taxing these at a higher rate than retained profits.[28] But in the 1980s and 1990s, even setting aside the effects of the economic cycle, profits have been high and rising. The pre-tax rate of return for industrial and commercial companies more than doubled between 1980 and 1993 to 8.3 per cent. This reflected above all the shift in the balance of power in the labour market.[29] Here there would seem to be scope for not allowing fears about the effects on investment to inhibit taxes on the corporate sector from rising, especially if that can be combined with a more stable macro environment which would be good for corporate profitability and would simultaneously reduce the risk premium investors in Britain demand because of past instability.

## Public expenditure, borrowing and taxation

The fiscal policies of the 1960s followed from the overall economic strategy. Initially the aim was steady as she goes, as devices like import controls were used to try to improve the balance of payments without a big deflation of demand. By 1966 this policy was running out of plausibility, and a severe stop phase in policy was inaugurated, involving public spending cuts, although most of the fiscal squeeze was by raising taxes. Only after devaluation in 1967 did the fiscal stance become severely deflationary, as the aim was to reduce domestic demand to make room for the exports made newly competitive. Eventually this policy worked – exports rose sharply, and the public finances moved into surplus. It is important to emphasise here that this movement to fiscal responsibility was not preceded by the kinds of fiscal extravagance that Thatcherites and their allies attribute to policies in the Keynesian era. As the figures in Table 1 suggest, the fiscal policy of the mid-1960s was conservative, with adherence to the golden rule that Governments should only borrow to finance investment spending. On the other hand, it undoubtedly is the case that, while the growth of public spending slowed in the years from 1964 compared with the preceding Conservative years, it was still faster than the growth of GDP – it was growing at the rate GDP would have grown at if the National Plan had not proved abortive. Only from 1968 did the Government impose a real slow-down (and this is possibly an important element in why they lost the 1970 election). This time round, as left critics of the Blair Government say, Labour 'has got its betrayal in early'. The new Government has tied itself for two years to spending targets which every commentator believes to be exceptionally tight, and unless they find cuts in programmes elsewhere, it is difficult to see how a tight and damaging squeeze on areas such as the NHS can be avoided.

The standard left criticism of past and present squeezes on public expenditure by Labour Governments raises a number of difficult issues. First, why has the left traditionally so strongly supported maximum public spending? Central to this idea has been the belief that public spending has an equalising effect, especially insofar as the money is spent on welfare. In fact this point can be exaggerated – Labour has never been as committed to a strategy of equality as some commentators have maintained.[30] It should be noted that the Labour architects of the 1940s welfare state put as much emphasis on establishing a national minimum as on egalitarian ends.[31] Similarly the Labour manifesto for the 1964 general election put little emphasis on equality, with concerns about growth and the balance of payments seemingly crowding the issue out.[32]

Second, is the view that welfare spending is egalitarian in effect accurate? Evidence rapidly accumulating since the 1970s shows that the welfare state has complex effects on the distribution of income, with those areas involving the provision of services in kind being especially far from unambiguously redistributive. In the case of the NHS, for example, it seems that the better-off gain significantly more per capita, partly because of their ability to find their way around a complex system. Of course, when we look at the redistributive aspects of welfare provision we need to take into account how the system is paid for. This is also a complex matter, but there is the well-known general point that the tax system as a whole has in the 1980s and 1990s become less redistributive compared with the 1960s. In combination, these two factors should make us wary of any simple equation between welfare spending and egalitarian outcomes. The past patterns of spending on welfare in Table 2 show two important points. First, historically, at least until 1979, welfare spending has tended to grow faster under Conservative than Labour Governments, though this overall result for Labour comprises very rapid initial growth followed by severe cutbacks later. Second, within those overall totals, Labour has tended to favour income maintenance programmes over provision of services in kind. This latter feature has increased the redistributive effects of welfare spending, especially as British income maintenance programmes seem to be quite efficient at achieving their goals.[33] But these very redistributive benefits are a cause of political problems: health and education tend to be the politically popular parts of the welfare state, with income maintenance, especially for the unemployed, the least supported by public opinion.[34]

Table 2    Patterns of welfare spending: growth of expenditure on categories of spending under different Governments (% real growth per annum)

|         | Income maintenance | Education | Health | Housing | Social services | Total |
|---------|--------------------|-----------|--------|---------|-----------------|-------|
| 1951–55 | 5.9                | 3.3       | -0.2   | -0.3    | -               | 2.7   |
| 1955–59 | 6.2                | 4.3       | 1.7    | -2.1    | 1.3             | 3.4   |
| 1959–64 | 4.9                | 6.3       | 3.3    | 11.0    | 7.1             | 5.7   |
| 1964–70 | 6.1                | 4.1       | 3.2    | 4.1     | 11.8            | 4.7   |
| 1970–74 | 4.3                | 3.8       | 3.4    | 18.3    | 13.3            | 6.4   |
| 1974–79 | 6.2                | 0.6       | 2.5    | -6.2    | 4.1             | 1.9   |

Source: R. Middleton, *Government versus the Market. The Growth of the Public Sector, Economic Management and British Economic Performance, c. 1890-1979*, Cheltenham, 1996, p.506.

Because of the levels of unemployment as well as the ageing of the population, the income maintenance programmes make up a far larger share of public spending on welfare than they did in the 1970s, let alone the 1960s. The problem is then quite clear – to allow income maintenance programmes to expand as they have done under previous Labour Governments is to invite major political problems, given the constraints on aggregate public spending. Here it should be noted that in some respects this problem can be exaggerated. There is no longer a public finance problem arising from the effects of an ageing population on the demand for pensions. This has been solved by the linking of pensions to prices rather than wages. This, of course, is not a solution to the problem of inadequate pensions, but it means the problem will not make itself felt directly by a crisis in public finances. The crisis in public finances arises from the huge rise in benefits paid as a consequence of unemployment (which includes much of the benefit paid for under sickness and disability pay, which in part at least reflects the weakness of the demand for labour) and secondly the rise in payments to those in work which reflect the enormous expansion of these kind of price-related subsidies in the recent past, as low wages have been compensated for through the public purse. Neither of these problems existed on anything like the current scale in the 1960s, and few parallels can therefore be drawn. But to the historian of Labour Governments it seems clear that dealing with the latter through minimum wage laws and welfare to work programmes is vital if the current Government is to escape the fiscal crises of its predecessors. On the former policy, it is of interest to note that the 1960s Labour Government did examine the issue of low pay, but only at the very end of its period in office, and without any result. Rightly, this has got to be much more central to economic and social policy than was deemed possible in those years.[35]

### Industrial policy

For much of its history Labour has been a party of industrial modernisation and economic efficiency.[36] Within that concern it has had a quite consistent view about the roots of efficiency. In summary terms, these have been seen as consisting predominantly of large-scale, high investment, high technology conditions. Conversely, the belief that competition is the key condition for efficiency has always been a minority view in Labour circles. The 1945 Government introduced the first legislation on monopolies, but it was half-hearted and ineffectual, and not many amongst Labour's leaders cared enough to make it any more than that. In the 1960s Labour introduced the first legislation on mergers, as well as strengthening the rules on monopoly. But again, this was a limited effort, both in design and execution.[37] The basic problem in the 1960s was that tough controls on mergers and monopolies would have conflicted with the desire to achieve economies of scale. Mergers aimed at this end were actively encouraged by the Labour Government via the creation of the Industrial Reorganisation Corporation (IRC). The results of this body were dramatically more evident than those of the strengthened Monopolies and Mergers Commission (MMC). Whilst the Government did not originate merger mania, it encouraged the process with few hesitations, most famously acting as midwife to the creation of British Leyland, ICL and GEC. The lesson from this episode is not necessarily that encouragement of mergers was inappropriate, although the approach of 'find an efficient company and merge everything with it' seems inherently not a good idea. What were clearly not useful were the conflicting messages sent out by Government policy, which demonstrated no understandable criteria of judgement about what a desirable merger might look like, or what characteristics might lead to it being referred to the MMC. In this climate uncertainty abounded, and

Government policy fell into disrepute. This time around it is hoped a more consistent policy will be developed, and a consistent message given to the corporate sector. One interesting possibility that has been suggested is compensation for workers made redundant following a merger, which would tend to reinforce the need for such changes to have a powerful economic rationale, which has not always been there in the past.

## The making of economic policy

When Labour came to power in 1964 they created the Department of Economic Affairs as a counterweight to the Treasury, in the belief that this would give a higher priority to long-term economic growth than was given by a Treasury allegedly obsessed by the short run. This was part of the criticism of stop-go, but also linked to the alleged amateurism of the Treasury with respect to industrial matters. In retrospect this division appears bizarre, given that the ending of stop-go precisely required changes to macro-economic policy which remained the responsibility of the Treasury. Even if devaluation had come earlier, it seems doubtful that this division of responsibility was tenable.[38]

A further highly problematic aspect of the economic policy-making apparatus in these years was the diversity and uncoordinated character of economic advice at the highest levels in the Government. The Government brought with them four senior advisers, to put alongside the advice offered by the Economic Section headed by Alec Cairncross. This was a recipe for confusion, and confusion seems to have followed.[39] What is striking about the Blair Government is not the number of senior, academically established economists from outside government involved in giving advice, but the apparent paucity of such figures. Since the 1960s faith in the usefulness of economic advice seems to have plummeted, probably to an excessive extent. As suggested above, the crucial decision not to devalue was taken on political-cum-moral grounds by senior ministers, against the almost unanimous advice from the economists. There would seem to be a danger that without the presence of powerful economic advisers in the Government, such over-politicisation of economic policy-making could occur again. The issue of Europe would seem a candidate for such treatment.

## Conclusions

The policies of the Labour Government of 1964 showed a strong initial faith in the capacity of structural policies to deliver more rapid growth, whilst avoiding the need to revert to stop-go strategies to deal with the balance of payments problem. Ultimately this approach failed, and there was a complete change of direction, under crisis circumstances, towards deflation. This in turn failed, and was succeeded by a devaluation coupled to deflation which finally delivered the economy from the balance of payments constraint, albeit at the cost of higher unemployment and a reversal of previous public spending plans. But output growth never recovered from the policies of the first four years, and the promise of modernisation appeared to have been undelivered. In fact some significant improvements had occurred. R&D spending had been redirected away from prestige and military projects, coupled eventually to a reduction in overseas military ambitions. Industrial Training Boards, introduced by the Conservatives, had been built up and were starting to deliver an improved supply of trained personnel. On the welfare front, despite the cutbacks of the end of the period, benefit levels had at least kept pace with prices. The period was by no means one of unrelieved failure. Equally, while the execution of policy had many faults, the basic idea of trying to create a more stable economic environment seems to be appropriate. Commentators at the time probably exaggerated the damaging consequences of stop-go for economic performance. In retrospect the cycles in activity in the 1950s and early 1960s appear extraordinarily mild in comparison with those in recent years, and indeed were no greater than those in faster growing western European countries.[40]

However, recent cycles in Britain have been much greater than those of earlier decades, and much greater than those in other western European countries.[41] In that context, an emphasis on maintaining stability seems eminently sensible. This is likely to give the biggest boost to investment, stabilise the public finances, and be most likely to avoid the crises of policy-making endured by previous Labour Governments. Macro-economic stability is not a panacea. Unemployment has to be tackled as a distributional as well as a macro issue, and the tax and benefit system requires fundamental reform if any reversal of the last 18 years of encouraging inequality is to be reversed.[42] But all of Labour's tasks become immeasurably more difficult in an unstable macro-economic environment. This is the enduring lesson from the 1960s.

# Notes

1  N. F. R. Crafts, *Britain's Relative Economic Decline 1870–1995*, Social Market Foundation, 1997, p.51.
2  D. Moggridge, *Maynard Keynes: an Economist's Biography*, Routledge, 1992.
3  P. Hirst and G. Thompson, *Globalization in Question*, Polity, 1996.
4  T. Mackie and D. Marsh, 'The Comparative Method', in D. Marsh and G. Stoker (eds), *Theory and Methods in Political Science*, Macmillan, 1995, pp.173–88.
5  A. Boltho, *The European Economy, Growth and Crisis*, Oxford University Press, 1982, pp.21–37.
6  W. Brown, 'Industrial Relations', in M. Artis and D. Cobham (eds.), *Labour's Economic Policies, 1974–79*, Manchester University Press, 1991.
7  M. Wickham-Jones, *Economic Strategy and the Labour Party: Politics and Policy-Making 1970–83*, Macmillan, 1996.
8  N. Tiratsoo and J. Tomlinson, *Industrial Efficiency and State Intervention: Labour 1939–51*, Routledge, 1994; J. Tomlinson, *Democratic Socialism and Economic Policy: the Attlee Years*, Cambridge University Press, 1997.
9  Labour's 1964 manifesto is reprinted in F. W. S. Craig, *General Election Manifestos*, Dartmouth, 1990, pp.43–60. The stability emphasis is most evident in the 1997 manifesto, *Britain Will Be Better*, pp.11–13
10  A. Mitchell, 'Older but no wiser', *New Statesman*, 7 March 1997, p.35
11  S. Pollard, *The Wasting of the British Economy*, Croom Helm, 1984.
12  D. Corry and J. Michie, 'EMU: the Left Debate', Political Economy Research Centre, University of Sheffield, Policy Paper No. 4, 1997.
13  A. Cairncross, *Managing the British Economy in the 1960s: a Treasury Perspective*, Macmillan, 1996, p.105; Cairncross, *The Wilson Years: a Treasury Diary 1964–1969*, Historians Press, 1997, pp.17–18.
14  J. Tomlinson, 'Inventing Decline: the Falling Behind of the British Economy in the Post-war Years', *Economic History Review*, Vol. XLIX, No. 4, 1996, pp.731–57.
15  D. Edgerton, *Science, technology and the British industrial decline*, Cambridge University Press, 1996.

16 Education, education, education.
17 T. Cutler, 'Vocational Training and British Economic Performance: a Further Instalment of the British Worker Problem', *Work, Employment and Society*, Vol. 6, No. 2, pp. 161–83.
18 Crafts, *Relative Decline*, chapter 1.
19 *British Social Attitudes*.
20 The efficiency/equity trade-off is a staple of most orthodox economics textbooks, e.g. D. Begg, S. Fischer, and R. Dornbusch, *Economics*, 4th edition, McGraw Hill, 1993, chapter 15.
21 P. Krugman, 'Competitiveness: a Dangerous Obsession', *Foreign Affairs*, Vol. 74, No. 2, March/April 1994, p.28–44.
22 T. Cutler, J. Williams, K. Williams, *Keynes, Beveridge and Beyond*, Routledge, 1986, chapter 4.
23 M. O'Mahony, N. Oulton and Jennet Vass, *Productivity in Market Services: International Comparisons*, National Institute of Economic and Social Research, Discussion Paper 105, 1996.
24 J. Tomlinson, 'Mr. Attlee's Supply-Side Socialism', *Economic History Review*, Vol. XLVI, No. 1, 1993, pp.1–23.
25 N. F. R. Crafts, 'Productivity Growth Reconsidered', *Economic Policy*, No. 15, 1992, pp. 388–414.
26 M. Kitson and J. Michie, 'Britain's Industrial Performance since 1960: Underinvestment and Relative Decline', *Economic Journal*, Vol. 106, No. 434, pp.196–212.
27 P. Wallace, 'Investment alone will not solve Britain's problems', *The Independent*, 3 March 1997.
28 M. Artis, 'Fiscal Policy for Stabilization' in W. Beckerman (ed.), *The Labour Government's Economic Record, 1964-1970*, Duckworth, 1972, pp.262–99.
29 *National Income and Expenditure of the UK*.
30 J. Le Grand, *The Strategy of Equality*, Allen and Unwin, 1982; B. Hindess, *Freedom, Equality and the Market*, Tavistock, 1987.
31 J. Tomlinson, *Democratic Socialism and Economic Policy*, Cambridge University Press, 1997, chapter 12.
32 M. Stewart, 'The Distribution of Income', in Beckerman (ed.), *Labour Government's Economic Record*, p.78.
33 D. Mitchell, *Income Transfers in Ten Welfare States*, Avebury, 1991.
34 *Social Trends 1996*, HMSO, 1996.
35 P. Townsend, 'Social Planning and the Control of Priorities' in Townsend and N. Bosanquet (eds.), *Labour and Inequality*, Fabian Society, 1972, p.291.
36 N. Tiratsoo and J. Tomlinson, *Industrial Efficiency and State Intervention: Labour 1939–51*, Routledge, 1994.
37 A. Graham, 'Industrial Policy', in Beckerman, *Labour Government's Economic Record*, pp.191–94.

38  Cairncross, *Managing the Economy*, pp.96–99.
39  Ibid, pp.145–8.
40  T. Wilson, 'Instability and the Rate of Growth', *Lloyds Bank Review*, No. 83, 1966, pp.16–32.
41  'Economic Instability – the UK's Biggest Barrier to Faster Economic Growth', *Lloyds Bank Economic Bulletin*, No. 13, February 1997, pp.1–6.
42  P. Johnson and S. Webb, 'Explaining the Growth in UK Income Inequality', *Economic Journal*, Vol. 103, No. 4, pp.429–35.

# Commentary

*Edmund Dell*

Should we really conclude that, while there may be some lessons from the 1960s, there is nothing to be learned from the last Labour Government because the instability of 1974–79 was supposedly too exceptional? And should we also conclude that economic stability, even if it can't be a panacea, must at least be the overriding goal and measure of success? This may be a mistake. As my old friend Harold Lever used to say: 'Anyone who wants to live in a stable economic climate should first find another world in which to live.' Remember that in 1992 there had not been a devaluation within the ERM since 1987 – a more or less stable five years. Then we had 1992 and 1993 and so on. Now, who knows whether things are going to be stable or not? We certainly should not rely on it: instability may well be a fact of life for the new Labour Government as it was for many of its predecessors.

This is all the more likely because of globalisation – something which it is as easy to underplay as overplay. Think simply of the question of the sheer speed of market reaction nowadays to economic announcements and events. Had things been the same in times past, devaluation under Attlee could not have waited in 1949 between February and March, when the Americans decided it was necessary, and September, when it occurred. Nor could it have been delayed under Wilson during the three-year period between 1964 and 1967. We could not today have the sort of protracted and semi-public debate that we had in the Callaghan Cabinet in 1976 over the IMF terms. The market would nowadays make it much clearer much sooner that something had to be done.

As for competitiveness, it is likewise as easy to underplay as to overplay its importance. But perhaps the opposite goes for governmental intervention to improve things. What MinTech learned in its short existence between 1964 and 1970 was what everyone in industry knew in 1964. The real lesson from the experience of MinTech is how innocent Governments in this country typically are of what industry and industrial activity is like. Jim Callaghan admits in his memoirs that he and his colleagues just had no conception of the problems that would arise in implementing the policies which Labour were committed to when they came in in 1964. They thought they could avoid devaluation because Labour policies were going radically to improve the performance of the economy. Arguably that sort of innocence exists still today, but in a subtly different way. Whereas previous Labour Governments – or at least some within them – have hoped to dictate to industry, now the opinions of industrialists are almost overvalued. The unfortunate, miserable, truth is that industrialists have no better perceptions of what is required to manage an economy than any other intelligent person. They swing from one thing to another. They are in favour of going into the ERM and, when they are in, they are in favour of coming out of the ERM. For anyone to rely on a consistency of view emerging from the CBI or the Institute of Directors, or even from an individual industrialist, is to put hope above experience.

Then there is the problem of growth, and how to stimulate it. One of the problems of Labour Governments – and this is perhaps as true of 1997 as it was of 1964 and 1974 – is that they believe that they know how to do this, when the truth of the matter is that they do not. Labour Governments are much better – indeed Governments generally are much better – at *reducing* growth than at stimulating it. But the belief that suffuses the present Government – that they know how to stimulate growth, that there is something they can do about it – is an extremely dangerous belief. It is particularly dangerous if you are aiming for stability.

One of the effects of your belief that you can stimulate growth is that you raise public expenditure higher than you ought to. Now, this Government has started with one sensible decision, namely that it will not raise public expenditure at least in the sense that it will accept the existing programme for two years. But will this really work? They can hardly do anything in two years anyhow. Nor is it certain that Labour has 'got its betrayal in first' on this occasion. The expectations of the movement are enormous, and although people might be prepared to wait two years, after that who knows? That is going to be the test of this Government: whether at that stage they are going to be able to control the pressures that will exist and to handle the expectations that, perhaps through no fault of their own, they have created.

One thing is certain, and that is that, on past experience, no-one should rely on Labour being helped by economic advisors. Either these advisors are not listened to or they are wrong. The outside advisors brought in by Labour in 1964, for example, were actually rather good. But when nearly all of them told Chancellor Callaghan to devalue, he ignored their economic advice. Unfortunately, 1974 provided an example of the opposite: all the economic advisors – with Nick Kaldor being the one major exception (and he was ignored) – were in favour of this country conducting an absolutely untenable economic policy. We already had an enormous balance of payments deficit, and we already had a frightening level of inflation, and yet they said that we must do our international duty and expand the UK economy in order to prevent the world as a whole running into recession. That advice was nonsense, but it was followed because it was politically convenient to follow – though, of course, it only proved possible to follow for about a year, while those who had accumulated the funds from the oil price increase, who would normally put their money into sterling, decided to invest them somewhere else and inevitably the whole framework of policy collapsed. Let there be economic advisors, by all means, but let there also be common sense.

# Commentary

*Peter Jay*

The best advice anyone can give to any Labour (or indeed non-Labour) Government of any country, anywhere, at any time, is never, never, never, never fix the exchange rate! There are two completely different reasons why, but both are borne out by British history in general and Labour history in particular. One is a matter of political science and political common sense, while the other is a matter of economics. Both are sufficient in and of themselves, but together they make the argument irrefutable.

To focus first on the political reason. Nobody ever, anywhere, at any time, entered politics because they had a burning desire to ensure that, come hell or high water, £1 should equal $4.03, or $2.80 or DM 2.90, or any other mysterious arithmetical equivalents in the foreign exchange markets. It is just not the kind of proposition that turns people on politically. Aspiring politicians don't go to meetings, they don't decide to take political careers, they don't seek nominations and get elected (sometimes to their surprise) to Parliament because they have a burning, life-long, deep desire to ensure that a certain relationship between one currency and another should be upheld. Yet, whatever the qualifications we may put on it, it seems undeniable that the attempt to uphold and enforce some such relationship has dogged, and to a large extent sapped, the political energies of, and accounted for a large part of the perceived failure of, one Labour administration after another.

It cannot make sense for a Labour Government (a group of people in a political party who have come together for all sorts of complicated motives, including personal ambition, but also including idealistic and virtuous purposes as well) to swallow the argument of people who never themselves run for election that some completely artificial, technical relationship is of such overriding national strategic importance that it must take precedence over all other goals – especially when the historical consequence of so doing has been to sap the energy and morale, to consume the time, to erode the reputation, and ultimately to ensure the defeat of both their predecessors in Britain and their fellow social democrats (for example in France in the 1980s) abroad. It is quite extraordinary that elected politicians, some of whom are supposed to be motivated by a desire for power, should be willing to acquiesce in these crazy doctrines and then to take the blame for them, leaving those really responsible – economic advisors, central bankers, civil servants and the like – entirely unscathed and able to give the same advice to those who will inevitably replace them in office, only to be kicked out of it for precisely the same reason a few years later.

But it is not simply that it would be foolish for the members of the new Labour Government to lay their political lives on the line for something which they cannot be sure they can deliver. It is also the case that even if they could, they are likely to find that the economic benefits of so doing are more than debatable. This is because successful economic management requires, amongst many other things, that different economies can adjust to each other as they are affected by shocks and differential rates of productivity, of inflation, or all the other things that enter into relative competitiveness. There are only two mechanisms known to man for enabling this adjustment process to work: one is changes in the real – or at least the nominal – exchange rate; the other is movements of population.

It is this, as much as anything else, that demonstrates that the argument against monetary union has nothing necessarily to do with a more general Euro-scepticism: in fact any Euro-sceptics would be well advised to advocate EMU on the grounds that it is a bomb implanted in the foundations of the European Union which could be guaranteed to blow it out of the water and to destroy its chances of success and harmony forever. This is because the predictable and inevitable consequence of ending the ability to adjust exchange rates is that people in tens of millions will be forced, on pain of destitution, to move away from the places to which they are tied, to move across frontiers of language and culture, law and history, and to go to places where they are simply not wanted by the indigenous inhabitants. To make such movements of population the primary mechanism of adjustment between the component economies of a political social and economic union, seems to me to be an act of transparent lunacy which only those who were determined to see the destruction of the wider European vision would really want to work for.

The *habeas corpus* of economic self-determination and of economic survival is to have an exchange rate which can adjust and correct serious competitiveness imbalances which develop between your economy and others – all the more so when one is steering an economy which, like the UK, has a long-running historic tendency, at any given exchange rate, to become uncompetitive over time. It is not a question of whether or not you enter at the right rate. Nor is it a question of whether or not there is today the same kind of fundamental disequilibrium in the exchange rate which characterised the period 1964–67. Of course there is no such disequilibrium today; but that is precisely because we have a floating exchange rate which – not every day or week or even month or quarter, but nonetheless progressively over time – will tend to maintain the equilibrium. The moment you fix the exchange rate, as the socialist Government in France did in 1983, you start the clock running to disaster. Once you have locked yourself into a single currency you are in the same position that Scotland has been in for two centuries, the same position that the southern states of the United States were in after that nation's civil war, the same state that any region is in which has neither the political sovereignty nor the economic machinery to enable it to correct the fundamental competitiveness imbalance that is the root cause of its weak performance and low standards of living.

For both economic and political reasons, then, you should never fix an exchange rate. Any commonsensical British Labour leader, having regard to the history of the Labour Governments in 1929–31, 1945–51, 1964–70 and 1974–79, would not, after 18 years of waiting, put the whole future of his administration in jeopardy for the sake of a commitment to something which has nothing whatever to do with why the Labour Party, or anybody else in politics, came into existence. What the exchange rate will be will change from time to time: it will either be left completely to market forces, or be nudged – not perhaps wisely – by the Government through various forms of intervention. But there should be no commitment to a particular rate or parity: the new Government should not allow itself to be set up to be destroyed in the way so many previous Governments (and since 1992 Conservative as well as Labour Governments) have been destroyed before.

# Chapter 3

# From welfare state to post-welfare society?

## Labour's social policy in historical and contemporary perspective

*Nick Ellison*

This paper is concerned with the Labour Party's approach to the welfare state in the post-war period and beyond. Labour Governments, operating within the broad framework of Keynesian economic management, created and developed the welfare state according to a dominant ethic of 'welfare collectivism' derived from a mixture of pre-war Labour thinking, 'blueprints', like the Beveridge Report, associated with wartime reconstructionism, and the practical implementation of welfare legislation by the Attlee Governments in the late 1940s.[1] As the first part of this paper suggests, Labour in power was continually confronted by the dilemmas created by this welfare collectivist legacy, prime among which was the persistent need to reconcile economic and social priorities. If in opposition the Party tended to assume sufficiently strong growth levels to ease the pain of increased social spending commitments, the experience in office in the 1960s and 1970s was rather different. Although Labour Governments attempted to maintain high levels of spending even in adverse economic circumstances, not only were they forced to make cuts to proposed increases, thus breaking manifesto promises, but they were also forced to rely on a combination of high levels of progressive taxation and incomes policies to make up the 'gap' created by falling productivity and an ever-increasing Public Sector Borrowing Requirement (PSBR). Because Labour was reduced to pursuing what amounted to little more than a pragmatic economic and social 'strategy', in which proposed socialist goals seemed increasingly elusive, Labour Governments alienated key elements of the wider labour movement, creating in the process an air of instability and crisis which the electorate hardly found appealing.

While Marxists and supporters of the new right have, for different reasons, always regarded this social democratic balancing-act with disdain, the post-war Labour Party, both intellectually and practically, remained committed to its pursuit. Reasons for such dedication have much to do with the legacy of the Attlee Governments to which Labour has until very recently been in perpetual thrall – these issues will be explored below in the context of a general account of Labour's social policies, particularly in the 1960s but in the 1970s as well. Now, of course, with a 'new' Labour Government so recently installed at Westminster, historical discussion for its own sake seems insufficient. How does 'new' Labour view the Party's past record on social policy? Is it likely to be able to do better? To answer these questions the second part of the paper will examine Labour's manifesto commitments in the light of the radically changed social and economic circumstances of the 1980s and 1990s, briefly tracing the development of new thinking about the role of welfare as the Party attempted to respond to the marked policy shifts carried out by successive Conservative Governments. It is always foolhardy to look too far into the future but, in conclusion, it will be important to assess the Blair Government's social policy aspirations in order to see whether the argument that traditional understandings of the role and nature of social welfare have been jettisoned in favour of an emerging conception of the 'post-welfare' society can be justified.

### Creating the welfare state: 1945 and beyond

Credit has rightly been given to the Attlee Governments for their role in developing the welfare state from the 'blueprints' of wartime proposals. In a prevailing context of serious and protracted economic difficulties these Governments created a 'welfare state', operating in a context of full employment, and dedicated to remedying (to paraphrase Beveridge) the great pre-war evils of squalor, idleness, want, ignorance and disease. If the precise detail of Labour's social policy did not necessarily match all the hopes of the architects of the welfare state,[2] the Party's welfare plans mirrored the blueprints produced during the war in important respects. Two clear examples come in the form of the National Insurance system and the National Health Service, where Labour enacted legislation to provide universal social insurance and health care free at the point of need. The third main area, education, differed in that much-needed changes to the system had already been written into the 1944 Butler Education Act, passed under the wartime coalition Government, Labour being left to implement existing legislation.

Despite widespread enthusiasm for these social reforms, it is in the nature of things that new policies contain problems of their own and, in each of these cases, Labour's initial attempts to develop universal social provision led to subsequent debates about the nature and objectives of the welfare state. In this sense the Attlee years created as many problems as they solved. Whether in opposition or in power, the Party was persistently confronted by the need to find a programmatic 'formula' that would successfully combine economic growth with greater social equality.

This the Attlee Governments in many ways had done, if only by default. Bolstered initially by a loan from Washington and later by Marshall Aid,

Labour, elected in July 1945 with an overall majority of 146 seats, was able to establish a new welfare system without having to rely purely on export-led growth to pay for it. Even so, the 1945–50 Government could not afford to be too generous with welfare provision as witnessed in the creation of the National Insurance system. By implementing the main proposals of William Beveridge's path-breaking report,[3] Labour replaced the plethora of schemes for the unemployed, the old and the sick with a single unified scheme (which essentially remains to this day) but, outside pensions, where the Government was more generous than Beveridge had anticipated owing to the potential political costs of phasing contributory pensions in over a period of years, the Act was also less generous than its principal architect had envisaged. The period during which individuals remained eligible for benefits was limited, for instance, while the benefit levels themselves were substantially less than Beveridge had believed necessary – essentially below subsistence level. Such low levels of benefit forced many people to fall back on means-tested National Assistance 'because retirement, unemployment and the other insurance benefits were pitched too low and did not provide separately for housing costs'[4] – a problem that no Government since has satisfactorily resolved.

Future problems were also stored up in health and education. Following difficult negotiations about the potential structure of a national health service with local authorities and the various sections of the medical profession during the war, it fell to Labour's Minister of Health, Aneurin Bevan, to carve a path through what were decidedly entrenched positions.[5] Although Bevan notionally succeeded in creating a national hospital system, defeating critics who wanted the hospital service to be run by local authorities, he experienced a good deal of difficulty in developing an administratively coherent service largely because of the necessity of making concessions to the medical profession in order to secure their support for the political ideal of free medical care. As Rodney Lowe[6] has pointed out, the new NHS was hardly a picture of administrative rationality, and this lack of coherence had knock-on effects on spending. In an effort to placate the doctors, particularly the hospital consultants, Bevan gave the medical profession representation, and thus control over spending, at all important administrative levels of the health service. Allowing the doctors such power without requiring corresponding responsibilities for finding the necessary resources 'impeded the development of a cost-effective...service',[7] as evidenced by spiralling costs in the late 1940s.

Compared with health, education policy initially appeared less fraught but in fact contained particularly intractable problems which surfaced in the late 1940s. The 1944 Education Act made secondary schooling compulsory and raised the school leaving age to 15, and the Government's education ministers, Ellen Wilkinson and her successor George Tomlinson, successfully implemented both reforms against a background of teacher and equipment shortages, as well as a dearth of suitable buildings. They were less successful in responding to demands for a more egalitarian education system, however. The apparently unquestioning acceptance of 'tripartism' – the segregation of children at the age of 11 into grammar, secondary modern or technical schools according to intellectual ability – quickly became the focal point of criticism for those in the Party who believed that education should be about more than a simple meritocratic equality of opportunity. Towards the end of the 1940s, the re-emergence of intra-Party debates about the merits of 'multilateral' schools, which had originally surfaced in the late 1920s and 1930s, quickly became demands for fully 'comprehensive' schooling, a policy adopted by the Party in the early 1950s.[8] What was not fully appreciated at the time was the scale of extra resources needed to make comprehensivisation a reality; 'equality', as Labour was to discover, could be expensive.

Table 1    Parliamentary estimates for the NHS, 1948-52 (£million)

|  |  | Gross totals | Appropriation in aid | Net totals |
|---|---|---|---|---|
| 1948/9 | original | 198.4 | 48.7 | 149.7 |
|  | final | 275.9 | 67.6 | 208.3 |
|  | excess | 77.5 | – | 58.6 |
| 1949/50 | original | 352.3 | 92.6 | 259.7 |
|  | final | 449.2 | 90.7 | 358.5 |
|  | excess | 96.2 | – | 98.8 |
| 1950/51 | original | 464.5 | 71.6 | 392.9 |
|  | final | 465.0 | 72.1 | 392.9 |
| 1951/52 | original | 469.1 | 71.0 | 398.1 |
|  | final | 470.6 | 71.0 | 399.5 |

*Source*: adapted from Rodney Lowe, *The Welfare State in Britain Since 1945*, Macmillan, p.176.

So, in each of these three major areas of social provision, Labour's efforts to lay the foundations of a fully-fledged 'welfare state' raised new issues even as increasing levels of social provision began to ameliorate the long-standing problems of poverty, ill-health and access to education. Such a process is of course inevitable, and it might reasonably be thought that, with its well-earned reputation as the founder of the welfare state, the Party would have continued to exercise a progressive, dynamic hegemony over its creation. In fact this was not the case for two reasons, both of which ensured that Labour's understanding of social policy remained firmly rooted in welfare collectivist ideology. First, and most obviously, the Party was in opposition between 1951 and 1964, losing three successive elections to a rejuvenated Conservative Party, possessing a distinct attitude of its own to welfare and able to capitalise on the 'feelgood factor' associated with the 1950s economic boom. Although Conservative Governments did nothing to destroy the welfare apparatus Labour had bequeathed to them, recent scholarship has made it clear that, even by the end of the 1940s, 'the [Conservative] Party had developed a consistent and firm response to Labour's domestic policy approach, based upon the rejection of the use of the state as a tool to redistribute wealth or to maintain the egalitarian trends introduced during the war years.'[9] Confronted by a Government which held a far less embracing view of welfare, preferring where possible private to public provision and 'welfare selectivism' to Labour's collectivist ethic,[10] the Party was compelled merely to defend what was undoubtedly the principal achievement of the Attlee years in traditional collectivist and egalitarian terms.

Second, severe disagreements throughout the 1950s amongst 'Tribunites', centre left 'planners', Keynesian socialists and ethical socialists[11] about the relative importance of different aspects of democratic socialist strategy, and particularly about the salience of public ownership as a distinctively socialist economic programme, not only prevented the Party from developing an agreed programme, but forced a persistent return to the one common factor shared by each of these positions – the continuing belief in state-sponsored welfare spending in the light of the achievements of the Attlee years. Ultimately, these disputes were eclipsed in the early 1960s as politicians from all sections of the Party began to pursue the modernist theme of 'scientific revolution'. The preoccupation with 'science' gave temporary colour to the possibility that increased welfare spending *and* economic growth could be achieved through 'planning' which was expected to perform the dual role of creating the modern, efficient economy necessary to fund continued social provision and 'equality'. These centre left notions[12] effectively won the 1964 general election for Labour, for the Party could now contrast itself favourably with the Conservatives who, after 13 years in Government, were ravaged by an earlier dose of political exhaustion and sleaze.

But Labour's claims to be 'modern' were very much premissed on the belief that the Party now possessed a new formula for an *economic* strategy; social policy itself continued to be conceived in traditional fashion. As Glennerster has stated, the Government's social policy commitments 'were mostly extensions of the agenda the old 1945 Government had left unfinished'.[13] To put it in these terms is not to imply that Labour's social programme was ungenerous or devoid of principle; in fact the Wilson Governments of the 1960s achieved a good deal in the key areas of income maintenance, health and education. But these achievements were accomplished very much within the old framework of the top-down, state-controlled conferment of social rights and benefits, in which 'experts' prescribed remedies for those deemed unable to fend for themselves – a relationship recently characterised by one commentator as 'welfare tutelage'.[14] Of course, if economic and social priorities pulled in opposite directions – if they could not be reconciled under Labour's modernist rubric of 'efficiency' – there was the perpetual risk of support for the Government being withdrawn as it failed to accommodate competing interests.

### Labour in Power: aspects of social policy 1964-70

There is no space here to provide a blow-by-blow account of the Wilson Governments' social policies between 1964 and 1970, but some exploration of their activities is required, particularly as they were so persistently criticised by erstwhile supporters despite their attempts to maintain social spending in economically adverse circumstances. Indeed, the issue is not so much that Labour Governments *failed* to achieve improvements in significant areas of the welfare state during the 1960s, but that their efforts to do so aroused such animosity. A brief examination of the fortunes of the major areas of social policy in 1964–70 will show whether this level of hostility was warranted.

*Table 2*   Public expenditure, 1961–71 (selected services) (amount and as % of total public spending)

|  | 1961 | | 1966 | | 1971 | |
|---|---|---|---|---|---|---|
|  | £m | % | £m | % | £m | % |
| Social security | 707 | 12.1 | 2577 | 9.1 | 4309 | 17.8 |
| NHS | 930 | 9.0 | 1395 | 9.1 | 2784 | 11.4* |
| Education | 1013 | 9.8 | 1768 | 11.6 | 3023 | 12.4 |

* amalgamated with welfare services

Source: adapted from Rodney Lowe, *The Welfare State in Britain Since 1945*, Macmillan, p.339.

### Health

The Government's abolition of prescription charges immediately on coming into office in October 1964 confirmed the widely held impression that Labour was indeed the 'party of the NHS'. This image was further enhanced by successful negotiations with the GPs over pay and conditions of service, Kenneth Robinson, the new Minister of Health, being forced to confront the parlous position of the GPs whose status and living standards had suffered since 1948 in comparison to those working in the hospital service. Amidst threats of mass resignations, Robinson negotiated an agreement which not only gave the GPs more generous remuneration but, through loans designed to encourage group practices, the purchase of better equipment, better reimbursement for support staff and so on, led to an (expensive) 'renaissance in general practice'.[15]

Elsewhere progress appeared less sure and criticisms mounted towards the end of the 1960s as difficulties associated with hitherto hidden aspects of health care became increasingly visible. While standards continued to improve on most health indicators, improvements were slower than in other advanced societies and it also became plain that parts of the system, particularly those dealing with the mentally ill, had been chronically underfunded, not least because of the way the NHS had originally been structured by Bevan. The exposure of neglect in the less glamorous areas of the service drew attention to the hidden costs of a system that was by this time experiencing the twin effects of what Timmins has called 'democratic pull' and 'technological push'.[16] Demand for greater access to health care appeared infinite while the pace of invention continually pushed up equipment and drugs budgets. Although NHS spending in fact increased at an average rate of over 3 per cent per year under Labour, increases were less than promised and unevenly spread, being in part due to the fulfilment of pre-1964 Conservative spending commitments. Budget cuts imposed in 1968 highlighted Labour's problems with health in symbolic fashion. With the Health Minister's support, prescription charges were reinstated and this intensely political decision, however economically necessary it may have been, was held by critics to breach the hallowed principle on which Bevan's NHS had been founded – free health care for all. So, despite the fact that health spending rose in the Wilson years, the impression was very much one of a health service experiencing strain under a Labour Government. As one contemporary analysis suggested, the Government failed to 'score well' on any of the major criteria of increased spending, better planning, rising standards of care, better pay and conditions for staff and a more democratic, consumer-oriented service.[17]

*Income maintenance*

A similar story of good intentions and some good initiatives being overshadowed by spending constraints can be told in relation to social security. With regard to the former, many of the changes for which the Wilson Governments deserve credit occurred in the first two years of office. In aggregate terms social security spending rose substantially as a percentage of GDP from 7.2 per cent to 9.3 per cent between 1964 and 1970. Flat-rate pensions were increased in March 1965 and short-term earnings related benefits were introduced for widows, the sick and the unemployed.[18] Institutional reforms saw the old Ministry of Pensions and National Insurance reorganised into a new Ministry of Social Security, while a Supplementary Benefits Commission – part of the new Ministry – was created to replace the National Assistance Board. These changes, by creating a more accessible and user-friendly environment for claimants, were regarded as vital if levels of benefit take-up were to be improved.

But criticisms abounded. Writing shortly after the Government's fall, Atkinson argued that the bulk of the increase in social security spending could be attributed to increasing unemployment and the effects of an ageing population rather than to Labour's generosity. He also commented that the

Government had done little for those in low paid work, stating that increases in family allowances had barely kept pace with higher taxes and prices.[19] Significantly, too, Labour was attacked for failing to 'diminish the importance of selectivity'[20] and introducing a range of means-tested benefits such as rent and rate rebates which were held to breach the principle of 'universality' – the payment of benefit to all in specific categories of need. However, the bitterest criticism of Labour's approach to income maintenance was reserved for the issue of child poverty. The Government's failure to take seriously evidence about the 'rediscovery of poverty',[21] particularly child poverty, produced by leading intellectuals in the newly formed Child Poverty Action Group (CPAG) led to a sustained campaign demanding the substitution of 'child endowment' for child tax allowances. A widening of the campaign symbolised by a CPAG memorandum, released to the press in the autumn of 1969, which claimed that 'The Poor Get Poorer Under Labour' caused heated exchanges between Richard Crossman, Labour's Secretary of State for Social Security, and the Group's new Director, Frank Field.[22] Although Field has since stated that the figures used by CPAG were not entirely accurate and that a 'careful reading of the memorandum showed that it did not contain the evidence',[23] it is noteworthy that, even with an election looming, those on the left were quite prepared to castigate the Government for its apparent failure to support the worst off – testimony, perhaps, to a lack of political realism, but above all to the deep sense of frustration about the unfulfilled promise of the early 1960s.

*Education*

This sense of disappointment was also apparent in education which, in view of the amount of resources devoted to it and the Government's success in expanding higher education, creating Educational Priority Areas and so on, may seem paradoxical. But as one commentator has recently put it, 'in the 1960s education was the political talking point'[24] and expectations were high. While the state education system had grown rapidly under the Conservatives during the 1950s, these Governments had remained committed to preserving two key elements of the secondary system as it had developed after the war – an independent sector and the tripartite segregation of state secondary education. They had also failed to find the resources to raise the school leaving age to 16, as provisionally laid down in the Butler Education Act. In each case Labour undertook to do better: the independent sector would be fully integrated into the state system; selection would be abolished in secondary education, all secondary schools being transformed into comprehensives; and the school leaving age would be raised from 15 to 16.

In the event, Labour entirely failed on two counts and, at least in the eyes of Government critics, only partly succeeded on the third. No real headway was made against the private sector,[25] while hopes of raising the school leaving age were dashed in 1968. Tony Crosland, who had recently been moved from education to the Board of Trade, remained convinced of the need to raise the age limit to 16 but his plans fell foul of the spending cuts which followed devaluation. Despite a vitriolic battle in Cabinet between erstwhile Gaitskellite allies, he failed to get the decision reversed.[26]

Comprehensive schooling is a more complex issue, for Labour undoubtedly made headway on its promise to abolish selection. Crosland's famous circular 10/65 'requested' local education authorities to prepare plans for comprehensivisation and this the great majority of them did. Pushed gently from 'behind' by Conference and the newly formed pressure group, the Comprehensive Schools Committee, the Government presided over the creation of in excess of 1,000 comprehensives before it left office in June 1970, thus fundamentally breaching the selective principle. The difficulty, as keen comprehensivisers like Brian Simon and Caroline Benn saw it, lay in the related problems of the lack of resources devoted to the transformation of the secondary sector and the vagueness about what the term 'comprehensive' actually meant. Permitted by the Ministry of Education to choose from a range of possible options, LEAs were often simply forced to adapt existing provision because funding was not made available for new buildings, teachers or equipment. Inevitably a fairly loose interpretation of comprehensivisation emerged.[27] With this prevailing vagueness in mind, Benn and Simon argued that, while there were ostensibly over 1,300 comprehensive schools in Britain by 1970,

> if a very pure definition of comprehensive schools were used ... where all selection at 11 and throughout the secondary stage has been completely abolished, the percentage of the secondary population receiving comprehensive education...would be...not more than 10 per cent.[28]

But the sense of disappointment was not simply about semantics. Labour's promises about education had raised hopes about the more equal society to which, it was fervently believed, greater access to education would contribute. The perceived failure to deliver greater access to educational opportunities informed much of the subsequent criticism of Labour's education policy – a point highlighted at the time by Howard Glennerster. In his contribution to the Fabian collection, *Labour and Inequality*, Glennerster acknowledged that resources had indeed been devoted to education, but argued that 'the expenditure on higher and sixth form education which largely benefited middle class children effectively outweighed the other attempts that were made to spend more on those types of education that primarily benefited the less fortunate.'[29] These findings were subsequently supported by other studies, notably the Oxford Social Mobility Project.[30] However, the nature of the criticism is, for present purposes, more important than the accuracy, or otherwise, of the claim because it implied that Labour's welfare collectivist ideology was insufficiently sensitive to the complex nature of social inequalities and, by extension, to the nuances of social spending.

## Explaining 'failure'

Contemporaries were plainly disillusioned with Labour's social policies during the 1960s and the reasons for their disappointment shed light on the dilemmas of social democracy in the welfare collectivist era. It was very far from the case that one causal factor could explain the disillusionment. Different sections of the labour movement, including the 'semi-detached' pressure groups which burgeoned during the 1960s, were critical of different aspects of Government policy and indeed it was precisely this sense of being attacked for different, and indeed contradictory, reasons that lent the Wilson Governments an air of crisis in the later 1960s. There was, however, one common denominator which provoked this diversity of criticism. The conspicuous failure of the National Plan – the centrepiece of Labour's economic strategy which was expected to yield growth of 25 per cent over five years – placed enormous pressure on other programme commitments.[31] Faced by an unexpectedly large balance of payments deficit and an ensuing financial crisis, Labour's economic strategy was effectively compromised before it had properly got under way. From the outset the Government had to decide whether to devalue sterling and chose not to do so, thereby creating difficulties for industry just at the moment when enhanced export performance was required for the Plan's fulfilment. This choice also strained the voluntary incomes policy agreed with the trade unions before the Government came to power and Labour's fate, particularly after further financial crises in 1966, became closely bound up with the deep-seated struggle between Government and unions over incomes policy.[32]

The result of economic failure was a pragmatic economic programme which, following the eventual decision to devalue in 1967, took the form of an emphasis on exports amidst continued attempts to exercise downward pressure on wage costs and cut public spending – the hallmarks of Roy Jenkins's Chancellorship. Because the attempt to reconcile economic and social priorities favoured the former it is not altogether surprising that the Wilson Governments encountered the kind of hostility alluded to above; the irony is only that social spending nevertheless actually rose during this period, although the rise was less than had been promised.

This brief acknowledgement of the consequences of the demise of the National Plan provides only one possible explanation of the Government's failure to convince supporters of its good intentions. Looking rather more widely, it is clear that the Wilson Governments also fell victim to significant economic and social changes which made a mockery of Labour's claims to be the party of modernity.

*Table 3*   Actual as against planned growth rates in constant prices, 1964/5 to
1969/70 volume terms, % per annum

| Service | Actual | Planned |
|---|---|---|
| Housing | 3.8 | 7.1 |
| Education | 4.9 | 5.7 |
| Health and welfare | 3.4 | 4.8 |
| Social security | 6.5 | 6.6 |

Source: adapted from Howard Glennerster, *British Social Policy Since 1945*, Blackwell, p.95.

While labour market changes, which were increasingly to threaten full employment, were being experienced by the mid-1960s in the form of a decline of manufacturing jobs and a rise in service sector employment, the first socially mobile products of post-war educational expansion were starting to find political voice just at the point when post-war assumptions about economic and social stability were coming to seem complacent. In many advanced industrial democracies, leaders of emerging social movements – the student movement, 'women's liberation', the anti-war protests associated with American involvement in Vietnam, and the nascent movement for workers' control – found themselves confronted by a conservative, hierarchical and male-dominated social world where, in their eyes, established elites wanted to control the nature and direction of social and political change rather than embrace an emergent 'new politics'. Partly by virtue of their increasing numbers and partly because of structural changes in economy and society, the iconoclastic influence of these new movements became an increasingly important political phenomenon in the later 1960s.[33]

The British Labour Party was caught up in these processes. Old orthodoxies and traditional ways of doing things came to be challenged and radically undermined during the 1960s with the result that, by the later years of the decade, much of the Party's programme, and for that matter the very membership of the Government itself, looked dated. Perhaps the most significant issue was that Labour was no longer regarded, as it had once so clearly been, as a potential repository for new thinking. Party 'experts', who since the 1930s had been 'brought in' to fashion, *inter alia*, Labour's social policies, had in the process contributed much to the character of British socialism.[34] But this top-down, elitist process began to be eroded by the explosion of political argument during the 1960s. The precise content of the new ideas is not of direct relevance here, but definitions of key concepts like 'equality' and 'socialism' contrasted sharply with the perceptions of Party intellectuals. Rather than being defined as a status, or set of rights, conferred by a beneficent Government on grateful recipients, equality came to be understood as a condition to be explored and experimented with in a new spirit of participation – a status to be 'taken' rather than 'given'.

Faced by a Government whose notions of state collectivism had so clearly failed to redistribute economic and social goods in their favour, rank and file trade unionists and constituency activists, increasingly influenced by these new ideas, began to demand greater democratic control of Labour's policy-making processes. Significantly, semi-detached pressure groups like the Institute for Workers' Control, as well as internal groups like the Campaign for Labour Party Democracy, had their origins in the late 1960s. Indeed, the latter, which was to spend much of the 1970s attempting to wrest control of policy-making from the leadership, had its first incarnation in the form of the Sheffield-based Socialist Charter group created in the highly symbolic year of 1968.[35]

### Signs of change: Labour's social policy in the 1970s

Labour's (mis)fortunes in the 1970s have to be understood in the singular and dramatic context of increasing internal struggles over Party identity and rapidly accelerating economic decline – effectively the difficulties of the 1960s writ large. In one sense, then, the conditions were atypical, at least in comparison to either the 1960s or the 1990s. For this reason there is little need to provide a blow-by-blow account of Labour's rather courageous efforts to maintain its abiding welfare collectivist ethic in such adverse circumstances. Social provision did not fare too badly in an atmosphere of falling productivity, rising inflation and unemployment, and endemic industrial unrest, all of which had preceded the oil price shock of 1973, but each of which was severely affected by the economic cataclysm that this event produced.

*Table 4*   Social expenditure: annual growth relative to GDP, 1960–77

|  | 1960–70 | 1970–74 | 1974–77 |
| --- | --- | --- | --- |
| Total social spending | 1.40 | 1.50 | 0.98 |
| Social security | 1.42 | 1.17 | 1.25 |
| NHS | 1.21 | 1.43 | 1.05 |
| Education | 1.46 | 1.27 | 0.99 |

Ratio of increase greater than one signifies that expenditure on a given programme was rising faster than GDP

*Source*: adapted from Rodney Lowe, *The Welfare State in Britain Since 1945*, Macmillan, p.341.

Proposed spending levels were certainly cut from 1975 onwards, with severe reductions following the 1976 IMF crisis, but the significant feature of the 1970s, so far as social policy is concerned, is that, even when it came to be recognised that the 'party was over', to paraphrase Crosland's 1975 verdict on local government spending, Labour continued to try to reconcile economic and social priorities. And not entirely without success. In an atmosphere of increasing restraint, Barbara Castle established the Resource Allocation Working Party (RAWP) to produce a formula for the more equal distribution of health service spending. Despite clear problems with the formula, RAWP was broadly judged a success in so far as it achieved a shift of resources northwards, away from London and the south east.[36] Again, Castle's introduction of programme budgets for the NHS successfully secured funding in an increasingly cold climate,[37] but the downside to these achievements came in the form of virtually endemic industrial action as health service employees from ancillary workers to consultants demanded better pay and contracts. Action by the junior doctors, in particular, combined with the protracted dispute over the Government's decision to phase out pay beds, actually resulted in rising numbers of people opting for private health care arrangements in the late 1970s.

Labour's social security record has also been judged positively because the Government succeeded in directing resources towards the most needy groups at a time of spending restrictions. This attempt to maintain a sense of social justice in adverse circumstances met with the kind of approval which had been noticeably lacking in the later 1960s, one observer noting that 'to have achieved a shift to social security at a time when real incomes were static or declining was a major achievement.'[38] Of course, it is important to remember that a good deal of this shift was accounted for by (then) unpredecented levels of unemployment, and other aspects of the income maintenance programme fared rather less well, the Government's record on low pay being an obvious example.[39]

*Table 5*    Change in social security expenditure (by groups of recipients), 1973/4 to 1978/9

|  | £m | % |
|---|---|---|
| Elderly | +1760 | +27 |
| Disabled and long-term sick | +560 | +47 |
| Short-term sick | - 30 | - 4 |
| Unemployed | +630 | +91 |
| Widows and orphans | −10 | −1 |
| One-parent and other benefits | +220 | +30 |
| Total expenditure | +3220 | +30 |

Source: adapted from David Piachaud, 'Social Security' in Bosanquet and Townsend (eds), *Labour and Equality*, Heinemann, p.172.

But, even despite these laudable efforts to maintain social spending, Labour appeared to cling to the ideas and practices of welfare collectivism primarily because it palpably lacked an alternative. The sense of lack of direction was almost tangible after 1975, being most aptly epitomised by Crosland who, shortly before his death in 1977, spelt out a much-reduced vision for social and public policy which effectively prefigured the Conservative years to come. He acknowledged that taxation could not be increased and that public spending could not be allowed to rise, thus puncturing the core assumptions upon which welfare collectivist social policy had been based. To be sure, Crosland saw some hope for greater equality in measures to outlaw racial and sexual discrimination and the ability of Governments to prioritise existing spending to benefit the worst off – but all this was a world away from the hopes and assumptions of the post-war period.[40]

Only in education did there appear – belatedly – to be faint signs of a shift in policy. Traditional concerns with spending as the key to greater equality of access and opportunity were displaced by a growing debate about the nature and purposes of education itself. As Tessa Blackstone noted,

in the first two years of the Labour Government one of its main preoccupations was trying to complete secondary reorganisation. From 1976 on it became more preoccupied with the question of education standards and with how to adapt the content of education to meet the requirements of industrial growth.[41]

If the final flourish of the first phase was encapsulated in Education Secretary Shirley Williams's 1976 Conference speech in which, replying for the platform, she admitted 'that not all comprehensives are truly "comprehensive"',[42] and needed to become so, this homage to welfare collectivism was quickly superseded by Callaghan's 'Ruskin Speech', delivered in the same month. Replying to criticisms – notably from right wing 'Black Paper' writers[43] – about falling standards and the failure of the secondary curriculum to prepare pupils for jobs in industry, the speech marks the point when the logic of the new world of low growth and rising international competition finally began to impinge on Labour's thinking about welfare. As is well known, the Prime Minister drew attention to new 'hard and irreducible economic facts' which demanded a new approach to education which should attempt not merely to equip children for their role in society but 'train' them for their 'economic role' in the world of work.[44] Reflecting the change of approach, the Government also accepted the legitimacy of demands for higher standards by enhancing the powers of the Assessment of Performance Unit – the national agency for monitoring schools' performance while also acting on industry's call for a closer relationship between education and employment. Here Labour's 1977 Green Paper, drawn up by an apparently reincarnated Shirley Williams, emphasised the links between school and the workplace and argued that 'young people need to reach maturity with a basic understanding of the economy and activities, especially manufacturing industry, which are necessary for the creation of…wealth'.[45]

The new stress on 'relevance' was accompanied by spending cuts which saw the education budget reduced by £50 million in real terms. To be sure, this was a small amount, and it was concentrated mainly in the further and higher sectors, but the move was symbolic. Labour had begun to dissociate itself from the welfare collectivist ethic which had exercised such hegemony over the Party's social policy since the Attlee years. Although there was no overt repudiation of traditional methods at this point, welfare provision began to be conceptualised differently, apparently being given less of a privileged claim on scarce economic resources. In this way growth came to be regarded as an issue quite distinct from any commitment to welfare per se. This trend was continued with a vengeance when a Conservative Government committed to containing the scope of the welfare state was elected in 1979.

## Rethinking social justice

If Labour's difficult years in Government during the 1970s brought home lessons that could perhaps have been learned in the 1960s, the result, so far as social policy was concerned, was that Labour began to recognise just how impossible it was to combine economic growth with commitments to ever-increasing social spending. Not surprisingly, in view of the fact that this realisation effectively removed its central raison d'être, the Party imploded as 'left' and 'right' joined battle over the nature of future 'socialist' objectives. But, however inevitable this process of internal struggle actually was, it was very much an internal affair. Looking inwards delayed the realisation that the ultimate demise of welfare collectivism had not been entirely due to the Party's failure somehow to do better, but was partly attributable to broader structural forces which began to have a noticeable impact on society and economy from the mid-60s onwards. A developing understanding of the nature of these forces for change has been an important element in the Party's attempt to redefine 'social democracy' over the past 15 years.

Looking back, it is plain now that the endemic weakness of the British economy, which Labour (and Conservative) Governments had to confront, owed a good deal to changing global conditions with which Britain was not best placed to deal. Deindustrialisation, mass unemployment and changes to both the labour market and labour process, have affected Governments across the industrial world as they try to adapt to the demands of 'globalisation'.[46] In Britain's case 'deindustrialisation' – the trend away from male manufacturing employment – began in the mid-1950s, becoming an absolute decline a decade later.[47] Subsequent increases in service-sector employment have not only failed to soak up sufficient amounts of labour to prevent endemically high unemployment, but have led to a greater proportion of casual and part-time jobs which are lower paid, with lower rates of unionisation.

*Table 6*    Percentages of the British workforce employed by sector, 1951-91

|  | Primary* | Production** | Services |
|---|---|---|---|
| 1951 | 8.9 | 43.6 | 47.4 |
| 1961 | 6.6 | 44.3 | 48.7 |
| 1966 | 5.4 | 44.0 | 50.3 |
| 1971 | 4.3 | 42.9 | 52.8 |
| 1976 | 3.3 | 39.5 | 57.2 |
| 1981 | 3.2 | 35.3 | 61.5 |
| 1986 | 2.6 | 30.6 | 66.8 |
| 1991 | 1.9 | 26.9 | 71.2 |

* Before 1975: agriculture, fishing, forestry, mining, quarrying. After 1975: agriculture, fishing, coal, oil and natural gas extraction and processing
** Manufacturing, gas, water, electricity and construction

*Table 7*    Growth of Part-time Employment in Britain, 1951-91 (employees in employment, all industries, thousands)

|  | Males | | | | Females | | | | All |
|---|---|---|---|---|---|---|---|---|---|
|  | FT | PT | All | %PT | FT | PT | All | %PT |  |
| 1951 | 13,438 | 45 | 13,483 | 0.3 | 5,752 | 754 | 6,506 | 11.6 | 19,989 |
| 1961 | 13,852 | 174 | 14,026 | 1.2 | 5,351 | 1,892 | 7,243 | 26.1 | 21,269 |
| 1971 | 12,840 | 584 | 13,424 | 4.4 | 5,467 | 2,757 | 8,224 | 33.5 | 21,648 |
| 1981 | 11,511 | 718 | 12,164 | 5.9 | 4,321 | 4,141 | 9,462 | 43.8 | 21,105 |
| 1991 | 10,432 | 1,015 | 11,447 | 8.9 | 5,962 | 4,738 | 10,664 | 44.4 | 22,112 |

*Table 8*    Rate of Unemployment in the UK, 1945-93 (annual averages, %)

| 1945-64 | 1.8 | |
|---|---|---|
| 1964-73 | 2.5 | |
| 1973-79 | 3.8 | |
| 1979 | 5.7 | |
| 1980 | 7.4 | all these figures on old basis of calculation |
| 1981 | 11.4 | i.e. counting those registering at job centres |
| 1982 | 9.5 | |
| 1983 | 10.5 | |
| 1984 | 10.7 | |
| 1985 | 10.9 | |
| 1986 | 11.1 | |
| 1987 | 10.0 | |
| 1988 | 8.1 | |
| 1989 | 6.3 | |
| 1990 | 5.8 | |
| 1991 | 8.0 | |
| 1992 | 9.8 | these figures compiled on basis of latest |
| 1993 | 10.4 | definition |

Source (tables 6–8): adapted from Sean Glynn and Alan Booth, *Modern Britain: An Economic and Social History*, Routledge, pp.278-83.

Far from attempting to stem the tide of change, Conservative Governments embraced it. Welfare arrangements were altered in an effort to accommodate moves towards labour market flexibility, the hope being to 'sell' Britain as a low-wage, low cost economic competitor in the world market. In Jessop's phraseology, Britain began the process of moving from a 'Keynesian welfare state' to a 'Schumpeterian workfare state', the jargon tracing a shift from the beneficent paternalism of the welfare collectivist era to a developing sense of 'welfare' as a set of practices designed to foster the new enterprise culture.[48] Simple amounts of expenditure are less significant here than the nature of the reorganisation of welfare provision and delivery in the wake of the state's abandonment of any attempt to balance economic and social needs. Even though spending on many services has generally increased in real terms over the past 18 years, the ways in which these services are organised have been progressively altered, key changes dating from the 1987 Conservative election victory.[49] In a prevailing context of privatisation and 'marketisation', reforms in health and education reflect a preoccupation with the use of internal competition to drive up standards according to quality criteria defined by the central state. 'Purchaser-provider' splits in these areas have taken rather different forms, but both have seen a greater accent on provider accountability to service users[50] even as the central state has set punitive cash limits for service provision. In social security, emphasis has shifted from a welfare collectivist concern for 'relative equality' between claimants and the rest of society to a Schumpeterian preoccupation with the maintenance of downward pressure on benefit levels and ever-tighter eligibility criteria – all in the name of preventing 'welfare dependency'.

Now, while these changes fundamentally challenged Labour's welfare collectivist ethic, it would be wrong to suggest that the Party has simply been a passive onlooker as ideas about the role and nature of social policy have been transformed around it. For one thing, Labour was already beginning to amend its traditional assumptions in the late 1970s, as mentioned, but much clearer instances of new thinking began to emerge from the left-of-centre academic fringe in the early 1980s. Even by the time of the 1983 general election, surely the Party's darkest hour, sympathetic social policy experts were beginning to argue that 'all is not well in the welfare state as we know it – and not just because of Mrs Thatcher's cuts.'[51] By the mid-to-late 1980s, market socialists associated with the Fabian Philosophy Group were advocating a rather different approach to welfare provision based on greater user empowerment.[52] A new emphasis was placed on 'liberty' rather than on the 'equality' of traditional welfare collectivism, the central principle being 'democratic equality', defined as 'a more equal distribution of primary goods to secure a fair value of liberty'.[53] Importantly, the now-common suggestion that citizenship duties should be expected as a condition of the receipt of individual welfare rights and benefits also emerged from market socialist circles.[54]

The Labour Party itself paid little formal attention to these ideas until after the 1987 election defeat. But, stung by the scale of the Conservative victory rather than the fact of defeat itself, the Party embarked upon a two-year policy review during which time it began to accept two important modifications to its traditional welfare collectivist position. First, there was formal acknowledgement that the role of the state should be limited, Neil Kinnock commenting in the review's main published document that 'there is a limit to what the modern state can and should do.'[55] In economic terms Labour had seemingly abandoned its belief that the state should attempt to manipulate economic outcomes. The only form of 'intervention' now considered feasible was 'market management' through medium term supply-side policies, the aim being to promote long-term economic stability. Second, this recognition of 'the efficiency and realism which markets can provide'[56] found an echo in the acceptance of individual liberty, as opposed to social equality, as the primary goal of social policy. *Meet the Challenge, Make the Change* made it clear that citizens 'had to take responsibility for their own lives and fulfil their obligations to others',[57] leading one critic to suggest that social policy now existed purely in the highly constrained context 'of a monetarist rationale for restraining welfare expenditure in order to foster economic growth'.[58]

In fact, this judgement was premature. Despite the rhetoric, the policy review produced some fairly traditional proposals for welfare. Commitments remained to raise spending on an NHS still free at the point of need, to maintain and extend the comprehensive education system and to raise social security benefits to more adequate levels while ensuring that the income maintenance system became more accessible to service users.[59] In reality, then, the 1992 election marked a half-way stage. Labour had only partly abandoned its welfare collectivist ethos, the commitments to increased social spending, accompanied by promises to raise direct taxation indicating that a prospective Labour Government was still some way from fully endorsing Schumpeterian workfarism.

The position changed rapidly after the Conservatives unexpectedly won a fourth term. If Labour under Kinnock's leadership had begun the process of moving towards a 'post-welfare' ideology on broadly Schumpeterian lines, further changes were in store. The Commission on Social Justice (CSJ) appointed by the late John Smith in the wake of the 1992 election defeat, together with the changes in both ideology and Party structure which have followed Tony Blair's election as leader after Smith's untimely death, mark the two most significant stages on the way to what may be called the Party's present 'social Schumpeterian' stance.

## The Commission on Social Justice

In its final report, the Commission on Social Justice (CSJ) made a case for a conception of social justice defined as a hierarchy of four ideas. First, a free society needs to be founded upon the equal worth of all citizens expressed in equality before the law, political and civil liberties and so on. Second, all citizens are entitled to have their basic needs for food, income, shelter and health met by the state. Third, in order to ensure self respect and equal citizenship there must be the widest possible access to opportunities and life chances and fourth, to achieve the first three conditions it is important to recognise that not all inequalities are unjust, but that those that are should 'be reduced and where possible eliminated'.[60]

These four main ideas translate into a number of policy options intended to close the prevailing 'justice gap'. In short, 'fair taxation', the widening of access to wealth, and a 'modern form of full employment' set in an economic framework which encourages 'long term investment in people, ideas and infrastructure' provide the basis for a conception of citizenship grounded in responsibilities as well as rights.[61] This policy framework is set in a context of increasing structural change in society, economy and polity. Looser patterns of employment have to be accepted, for example, not just to match the changing requirements of business but to meet the difficulties posed by a less stable family environment. Employment flexibility will be necessary if childcare and care of the elderly are to be undertaken without having to resort to total dependence on the welfare state. In addition, new pension arrangements and methods of funding them will be needed to accommodate changing attitudes to 'retirement', particularly as the number of older people in the population expands.

The mechanisms for achieving these objectives reflect Schumpeterian arrangements, the emphasis being placed upon matching economic with social 'investment' to 'empower' individuals and communities in the context of an emphasis on economic growth. Economic investment in labour, technology, education and training, child care and community resources to ensure high productivity and full employment, and social investment to secure freedom from poverty, a more equitable distribution of wealth, strong families and flexible welfare provision are expected to create a society based on individual opportunity and strong community.[62] In practical terms, the state's role is to encourage positive attitudes to employment by paying unemployment benefit to part-time workers and facilitating the transition from welfare to work. The state here is enabling rather than paternalistic. Eschewing traditional ideas of the top-down conferment of social rights, the CSJ wanted to equate guaranteed basic rights to education and training, to a guaranteed minimum income, fair taxation and so on with corresponding duties, particularly to work where work is available – this injunction being rather curiously extended to mothers with children over five years of age[63] – but also to employers who should provide good working conditions, fair wages and employee partnership arrangements.

Leaving aside for the moment the question of their feasibility, it is important to note that these ideas signal a further stage in the abandonment of welfare collectivism. Although the CSJ's proposals were labelled as a 'fairly traditional social democratic strategy', this judgement is based on the view that 'the overall ambition remains one of redressing social ills through growth'[64] which on the basis of the analysis here is too broad to be particularly useful. The point, surely, is that the role of the state has been transformed from a guarantor of social rights to relatively passive social actors to one of an enabler and supporter of active individuals, and where necessary a 'coercive' force, reminding individuals of their duties where they choose to remain inactive. In this way, while a flavour of the old formula of economic growth specifically for social welfare remains, the CSJ nevertheless placed a much greater burden of responsibility for redress on individuals themselves.

## Labour under Blair

This social Schumpeterian position has been given an added boost by a new Labour leadership able to capitalise on earlier Party reforms. Blair's successful 'transformation' of the Party would have been unthinkable without the prior initiatives taken by Kinnock and Smith. The new leader built upon Kinnock's reforms of Labour's policy-making apparatus[65] and Smith's successful attempt to reduce the power of the trade union bloc vote at Conference – both leadership-friendly measures – by jettisoning Clause Four of Labour's constitution, thereby ending any ambiguity about Labour's stance on economic ownership. Each of these internal measures is intimately connected to the new ideas which emerged during the Policy Review and the deliberations of the CSJ in so far as they have reduced the sources and strength of 'old' Labour opposition to them.

Relatively unencumbered by historical baggage, then, Labour under Blair has continued to develop the ideas discussed by the CSJ. What has emerged is a dual strategy, one part of which elevates economic stability above all else as 'the essential platform for sustained growth',[66] but the other part of which stresses the potential for the creation of a more 'organic' sense of society and social obligation as meeting the needs of both society and individuals – the spirit of the idea being encapsulated in Blair's phrase 'social advance and individual achievement'.[67] Pride of place is given to greater productivity in the free market, Government's role being conceived in the enabling terms of investing in an educated and skilled workforce, creating opportunities for employment, new businesses and so on. Social spending commitments must if possible enhance, but certainly not inhibit, this overriding goal and for this reason a 'carrot and stick' approach appears to be the hallmark of contemporary social policy. Where individuals act responsibly to make the most of educational opportunities, to find work – to 'get on' – the state will support their efforts through effective social provision and the extension of social rights, enabling them to feel they have a 'stake' in society. Where they are not judged suitably responsible, however, the state can get tough: claimants may be refused benefit, juvenile offenders, the voluntarily homeless and others may find themselves subject to the rigour of 'zero-tolerance'. In short, where individuals make the most of their 'stake' the aim is to draw them in to an extended web of belonging; where they do not, there will be penalties. A brief examination of proposed changes in social security and education policy will illustrate the new 'stakeholder' approach.

Labour's manifesto proposals for social security provision other than old age pensions are contained in terms of 'welfare to work', a phrase redolent of the CSJ's ideas. Accepting that the state has a responsibility to the unemployed, 'to help people into jobs – real jobs' the quid pro quo is that 'the unemployed have a responsibility to take up the opportunity of training places or work' where these are offered.[68] Promising to give 250,000 young people opportunities for work, education and training, the Party makes it clear that they will be expected to make the best of what is proposed because 'rights and responsibilities must go hand in hand, without [the option] of life on full benefit.' A more developed version of this approach is contained in Frank Field's pamphlet, *Stakeholder Welfare*. Beginning with the young unemployed but eventually extending the policy past this group, Field argues that 'every claimant below pensionable age and who is fit for work [should] be expected to plan for what they want to do and achieve during the rest of their working lives', the argument being that 'claimants will have both an opportunity and duty to build their own life rafts from dependency.'[69] In this manner the Income Support system will be transformed in at least two ways: it will change from a passivity- inducing mechanism to a pro-active agency enabling individuals to plan 'the next stage of their lives', and it will also shift the character of social spending away from its historical assocation with the dead weight of 'welfare' to an active, forward looking association with 'investment'.

Of course Field supplements this approach to unemployment and income support with a range of other measures, particularly for pensions, which round out his vision for social security in general. What stand out from each of his proposals, however, are the persistent twin themes of 'rights and duties', and 'individual and social achievement' which comprise the core of the stakeholder approach. This combination can be applied with equal force to education. Recognising that education is 'an economic necessity for the nation',[70] the aim is to produce a better 'product' within existing spending limits. While some reallocation of resources will occur – mainly the abolition of the Assisted Places scheme to fund reduced class sizes – little extra money will be injected into the system. Instead, emphasis is placed on the surveillance of quality and standards in a context of 'partnership' between parents, teachers and local education authorities which stresses the need to make the most of the opportunties on offer. The responsibilities of different actors are to be defined more closely, even to the point of establishing guidelines for minimum periods of homework, while poor performance, whether from pupils or teachers (or for that matter parents), will not be tolerated. To be sure, as funds become available from falling unemployment, so the education system may attract new resources; in the meantime the stress is squarely on individual achievement underscored by a state whose enabling role masks a certain coercive dimension. This, in microcosm, is social Schumpeterianism at work: the traditional welfare element – the top-down attempt to confer equality for its own sake – is underplayed, while 'quality' and 'relevance' are promoted in the name of social and economic efficiency.

## Conclusion

Because it so plainly wants to break away from welfare collectivist understandings of social policy that, in the very different economic conditions of the 1980s and 1990s, have tended to foster dependency, this post-welfare vision is in many ways an attractive one. But it is not problem-free. Much depends, for instance, on the developing nature of 'partnership', for how this evolves in practice will determine the fate of the stakeholding idea. Welfare-to-work policies will depend to a large extent on the willingness of the unemployed to become 'partners', both with the state and with those who provide work, education and training, in taking up the opportunties on offer. Where they prove recalcitrant, 'coercion' will almost certainly follow. In a rather different way, 'partners' in education – LEAs, teachers, parents and pupils – have much in common but their interests can also diverge. If budget allocations can be one source of friction, teaching methods and disciplinary procedures can be others. While it is perfectly possible for a Government to set out guidelines to encourage a 'partnership culture' from the 'top down', it is equally possible that good intentions can be undermined by the inability to overcome the individualism of competing interests which could inhibit the organic development of such a culture from the 'bottom up'. Once again, forms of coercion may be required to ensure that partnership develops according to plan.

This concern about partnership in an embryonic stakeholder society extends some way beyond education and other areas of social policy, where there must at least be a reasonable chance of success in view of the comparatively constrained sets of interests involved. The same may not hold for other rather vaguer forms of 'partnership', say between large corporations and other institutions, and the individuals who either work for them or are affected by their activities. Will Hutton has recently argued that a significant aspect of the stakeholding idea is the notion of a better 'economic and social balance, and with it a culture in which common humanity and the instinct to collaborate are allowed to flower.'[71] In acknowledging the very real difficulties of attaining such a balance he picks out one task in particular on which much else hinges. It is important to get the institutions that lie between the state and the individual – pension funds, business firms, banks, universities, Training and Education Councils (TECs), housing associations, trade unions, even satellite television stations – voluntarily to operate in ways that reflect the costs that individualistic action motivated by self-interest necessarily imposes on the rest of us.[72]

The difficulty, of course, is to secure agreement to this vision and here, ironically, Labour may be faced with the old issue of how to secure 'compliance'. Despite the rather warm images projected by notions of stakeholding and partnership, there seems to be very little in the way of formal mechanisms in the economic sphere to 'encourage' those who decide not to exercise their obligations to society in this way. Nationalisation of the reluctant is no longer, and in many ways never was, an option, and while there might be a range of incentives for corporations, which could encourage positive attitudes towards employment and training, or changes of attitude towards investment practices, the principal method of encouragement seems to be to ask for voluntary co-operation.[73] One early instance of the new partnership culture, as this might apply to the corporate sector, is the windfall tax on privatised utilities. British Telecom is threatening legal action if attempts are made to deprive the company of its profits and directors of the national lottery company, Camelot, at the time of writing, are displaying little desire to forgo hefty bonus payments, so there is clearly still some way to go if progress is to be made towards the spirit of partnership and new-found sense of public service that the Blair Government claims it wants to promote throughout society.

Ultimately, the danger is this. If corporate actors choose not to fulfil their obligations to employees, pensioners, the unemployed and others, in a spirit consistent with the stakeholding idea – if, in other words, they persist in the pursuit of naked self-interest – Labour could find it difficult to gain a sufficient hold on available resources to finance even its limited social ends. Conditioned by an abiding Schumpeterian economic logic, the only 'weapons' the state would have at its disposal would then lie solely in the area of social policy. Here at least Governments can exercise fairly direct influence over the nature and direction of social responsibility either in economically constrained circumstances or, for that matter, in circumstances where the benefits and opportunities afforded by higher productivity are being withheld by corporate producers. In such environments Labour's enabling state may need to become increasingly coercive, individual 'responsibility' being ever more tightly pinned to conformity, to the needs of the economy where older notions of the state's role as 'reconciler' between economic and social priorities are no longer an option. On this reading, although it is clear that welfare collectivism is very much the creature of a bygone era, we could yet rue its passing.

# Notes

1 For sources of pre-war Labour thinking see Elizabeth Durbin, *New Jerusalems: The Labour Party and the Economics of Democratic Socialism*, Routledge and Kegan Paul, 1983; Nicholas Ellison, *Egalitarian Thought and Labour Politics: Retreating Visions* Routledge, 1994. For debates about the nature of wartime reconstruction see Paul Addison, *The Road to 1945*, Quartet Books, 1977; Stephen Brooke, *Labour's War: The Labour Party During the Second World War*, Clarendon Press, 1992. General accounts of the Attlee Governments are provided by K. O. Morgan, *Labour in Power, 1945-1951*, Clarendon Press, 1984; Peter Hennessy, *Never Again: Britain 1945-1951*, Vintage Books, 1993.

2 See Rodney Lowe, *The Welfare State in Britain Since 1945*, Macmillan, 1993.

3 William Beveridge *Social Insurance and Allied Services*, Cmnd 6404, HMSO, 1942.

4 Nicholas Timmins, *The Five Giants: A Biography of the Welfare State*, Harper Collins, 1996, p.136.

5 See Rudolf Klein, *The Politics of the National Health Service*, Longman, 1995; Morgan, 1984.

6 Lowe, p.171.

7 Lowe, p.179.

8 For the internal 'politics' of Labour's education policy see Brian Simon, *Education and the Social Order, 1940-1990*, Lawrence and Wishart, 1991; Nicholas Ellison, 'Labour Then and Now: Equality in Education Policy Since 1945', unpublished paper for ICBH Summer Conference, 1991. The debate leading to Labour's decision to adopt comprehensive schooling as Party policy can be found in the Labour Party, *Annual Conference Report*, Labour Party, 1952.

9 Harriet Jones, 'A Bloodless Counter-Revolution: The Conservative Party and the Defence of Inequality, 1945-51', in Harriet Jones and Michael Kandiah (eds), *The Myth of Consensus: New Views on British History, 1945-64*, Macmillan, 1996, p.13.

10 See Iain Macleod and Enoch Powell, 'Social Services: Needs and Means',

Conservative Political Centre, 1952.

11  Ellison, 1994.

12  See Thomas Balogh, *Planning for Progress: A Strategy for Labour*, Fabian Tract 346, Fabian Society, 1963; Richard Crossman, 'Planning for Freedom' in *Planning for Freedom*, Hamish Hamilton, 1965; Labour Party, *Signposts for the Sixties*, Labour Party, 1961.

13  Howard Glennerster, *British Social Policy Since 1945*, Blackwell, 1995, p.95.

14  Anna Yeatman, *Postmodern Revisionings of the Political*, Routledge, 1994.

15  Timmins, p.223.

16  Timmins, p.260.

17  Nicholas Bosanquet, 'Inequalities in Health', in Peter Townsend and Nicholas Bosanquet (eds), *Labour and Inequality*, Fabian Society, 1972, p.63.

18  Much to Richard Crossman's horror. Crossman had spent a good deal of his time during the 1950s working with the 'Titmuss Group' on a new pensions plan intended to provide greater equality of pensions in old age. He was disappointed when Wilson opted for an immediate rise in flat-rate pensions. The move was expensive and did nothing to bring closer a fairer distribution of income for older people.

19  A. B. Atkinson 'Inequality and Social Security', in Townsend and Bosanquet, p.17.

20  Michael Hill, 'Selectivity and the Poor' in Townsend and Bosanquet, p.241.

21  See Peter Townsend and Brian Abel-Smith, *The Poor and the Poorest*, Bell and Sons, 1965.

22  R. H. S. Crossman, *Diaries of a Cabinet Minister, vol. III, Secretary of State for Social Services, 1968–70*, edited by Janet Morgan, Jonathan Cape and Hamish Hamilton, 1977, p.791. See also Mike McCarthy, *Campaigning for the Poor: CPAG and the Politics of Welfare*, Croom Helm, 1986.

23  Quoted in Timmins, p.278.

24  Glennerster, *British Social Policy Since 1945*, p.133.

25  Although the Government honoured Labour's manifesto promise to appoint a Public Schools Commission to recommend ways of integrating the private sector into the state system, the Commission never really tackled the issue head-on. Its report to the Party Conference in 1968, far from advocating integration in fact recommended the continued existence of private schools with a proviso that they should take half their numbers from the state sector. Not surprisingly, Conference rejected the idea and no further proposals were put forward.

26  R. H. S. Crossman, *Diaries of a Cabinet Minister, vol. II, Lord President of the Council and Leader of the House of Commons, 1966–68*, edited by Janet Morgan, Jonathan Cape and Hamish Hamilton, 1976, pp.642–46.

27  See John Ahier, 'The Politics of Educational Change: The Case of the

Yorkshire Middle Schools', in John Ahier and Michael Flude (eds), *Contemporary Education Policy*, Croom Helm, 1983.

28 Caroline Benn and Brian Simon, *Half-Way There: Report on the British Comprehensive School Reform*, Penguin, 1972, p.57.

29 Howard Glennerster, 'Education and Inequality', in Townsend and Bosanquet, p.97.

30 See A. H. Halsey, A. F. Heath and J. Ridge, *Origins and Destinations*, Clarendon Press, 1980; also see A. H. Halsey, *Change in British Society*, 3rd edition, Oxford University Press, 1986, pp.140–41.

31 See Roger Opie, 'Economic Planning and Growth' in Wilfred Beckerman (ed.), *The Labour Government's Economic Record, 1964–70*, Duckworth, 1972; Alan Budd, *The Politics of Planning*, Fontana, 1978; Jim Tomlinson, *Public Policy and the Economy Since 1900*, Clarendon Press, 1990.

32 Robert Taylor, *The Trade Union Question in British Politics*, Blackwell, 1993.

33 Eric Hobsbawm, *The Age of Extremes: The Short Twentieth Century, 1914-1991*, Michael Joseph, 1994, pp.300–301.

34 The entire 'culture' of Labour's policy-making had revolved around the adoption of expert recommendations. From the Webbs, through Tawney and Cole, the 'New Fabians' of the 1930s and the 'Titmuss Group' of the 1950s, Party policy had been the creature of a tightly knit, self-perpetuating network of academics. As for the orthodox view that the Party Conference somehow controlled policy, it would be more accurate to say that Conference endorsed (and it usually did) the ideas devised by experts.

35 See Lewis Minkin, *The Contentious Alliance: Trade Unions and the Labour Party*, Edinburgh University Press, 1991, p.164.

36 See Nicholas Bosanquet, 'Health' in Nicholas Bosanquet and Peter Townsend (eds), *Labour and Equality*, Heinemann, 1980; Glennerster, *Social Policy Since 1945*.

37 Timmins, pp.342–43.

38 David Piachaud, 'Social Security' in Bosanquet and Townsend, p.173.

39 Chris Pond, 'Low Pay', in Bosanquet and Townsend.

40 Tony Crosland, *Socialist Commentary*, October 1976, p.3.

41 Tessa Blackstone, 'Education', in Bosanquet and Townsend, p.232.

42 *Labour Party Annual Conference Report*, Labour Party, 1976, p.274.

43 See for example, C. B. Cox and A. E. Dyson, *Fight for Education: A Black Paper*, Critical Quarterly Society; Caroline Cox and Rhodes Boyson, *The Fight for Education*, Black Paper 4, Davis-Poynter, 1975.

44 Timmins, p.326.

45 Labour Party, *Education in Schools: A Consultative Document*, Green Paper, Cmnd 6869, HMSO, 1977, p.35.

46 A much used and abused term (see Paul Hirst and Grahame Thompson,

*Globalisation in Question*, Polity Press, 1996). There seems to be little disagreement about the fact of rising economic competition on an international scale as increasing numbers of countries begin to enter the world market. The fact that emerging economies can compete with the older industrial societies on labour costs and labour processes has plainly affected the latter's approach to economic policy-making. That said, the further argument that 'globalisation' is contributing to a decline in the power of the nation-state is a more contentiously fought issue. For contrasting views see Hirst and Thompson, and Susan Strange, *The Retreat of the State*, Cambridge University Press, 1996.

47 See John Allen and Doreen Massey, *The Economy in Question*, Sage, 1988; Sean Glynn and Alan Booth, *Modern Britain: An Economic and Social History*, Routledge, 1996.

48 Bob Jessop, 'The Transition to Post-Fordism and the Schumpeterian Workfare State', in Roger Burrows and Brian Loader (eds), *Towards a post-Fordist Welfare State?*, Routledge, 1994, pp.24–25.

49 See Christopher Pierson, 'Continuity and Discontinuity in the Emergence of the "Post-Fordist" Welfare State' in Burrows and Loader.

50 Although there is a good deal of debate about who constitutes a 'user'. In education, for example, as noted in Peter Taylor-Gooby and Robyn Lawson (eds.), *Markets and managers: new views on the delivery of welfare*, Open University Press, 1993, pupils, parents and/or employers and industry could legitimately be placed in this category, but their interests are likely to be very different.

51 Howard Glennerster quoted in Pete Alcock, 'The Labour Party and the Welfare State', in Martin J. Smith and Joanna Spear (eds), *The Changing Labour Party*, Routledge, 1992, p.143.

52 Typically through 'weighted' voucher systems to provide a redistributionary element to user 'choice' in education and a much more powerful tribunal system for rights enforcement in areas not susceptible to the use of vouchers. See Julian Le Grand and Saul Estrin (eds), *Market Socialism*, Clarendon Press, 1989.

53 Raymond Plant, *Equality, Markets and the State*, Fabian Tract 494, Fabian Society, p.7.

54 See Raymond Plant, 'Social Rights and the Reconstruction of Welfare' in Geoff Andrews (ed), *Citizenship*, Lawrence and Wishart, 1991; Geoff Mulgan, 'Citizens and Responsibilities' in Andrews.

55 Labour Party, *Meet the Challenge, Make the Change*, Labour Party, 1989, p.6.

56 Labour Party, *Looking to the Future*, Labour Party, 1990, p.6.

57 Labour Party, *Meet the Challenge*, p.6.

58 Alcock, p.139.

59 Labour Party, *Meet the Challenge*, p.52.

60 Commission on Social Justice, *Social Justice: Strategies for Renewal*,

Vintage, 1994.
61   Commission on Social Justice, *Social Justice in a Changing World*, IPPR, 1993, pp25–29.
62   Commission on Social Justice, *Social Justice: Strategies for Renewal*, pp102–104.
63   Commission on Social Justice, *Social Justice: Strategies for Renewal*, p.240.
64   Christopher Pierson, 'Doing Social Justice: The Case of the Borrie Commission', in Joni Lovenduski and Jeffrey Stanyer (eds.), *Contemporary Political Studies*, Vol II, PSA, 1995, p.846.
65   See Eric Shaw, *The Labour Party Since 1979: Crisis and Transformation*, Routledge, 1994.
66   Labour Party, *New Labour Because Britain Deserves Better*, Labour Party, 1997, p.11.
67   Tony Blair, *Socialism*, Fabian Tract Fabian Society, 1994, p.7.
68   Labour Party, *New Labour*, p.19.
69   Frank Field, *Stakeholder Welfare*, IEA Choice in Welfare Series, 32, IEA, 1996, p.334.
70   Labour Party, *New Labour*, p7.
71   Will Hutton, *The State to Come*, Vintage, 1997, pp.66–67.
72   Hutton, p.65.
73   Hutton provides some ideas, but they are not included in Labour's manifesto and would anyway require at least the acquiesence if not the positive endorsement of powerful institutions like the pension funds. See Hutton, pp.70–74.

# Commentary

*A. H. Halsey*

The new Labour Government is probably going to have to learn that the important offices of state are now the Home Office, Education and Social Security, rather than the Treasury and the DTI. For so long the Labour Party has asserted – quite understandably given its origins and the period in which it came to prominence – that the overriding determinant of welfare was economic. What it now needs to realise, despite the common wisdom, is that we have entered a new era in which that economic problem is largely – and perhaps more because of technology than public policy – solved. It is a matter of empirical fact that this Government, Tony Blair's Government, is presiding over a country which is three times better off than that which Clem Attlee and his very brave welfare state creators faced in 1945. If you extrapolate the rate of growth that we have had, even though we have moaned about it, over the last 20 years, we are going to be, by the middle of the 21st century, three times better off again. The point is, however, that it is the problem of production which has been solved (or at least is being solved) and not the problem of distribution.

The problem of distribution, then, is still something which is very much on our hands. It takes the form of very high rates of unemployment, and ministerial agonising about how we can produce a highly educated country in order to solve that problem. But it really should be seen by the Blair Government as part of the wider picture of what one might call the new politics of an affluent culture – meaning by culture that there are realms of politics into which the Government is now obliged to penetrate which simply were not recognised as important for much of the post-war period during which Labour was previously in power. Fifty years from now we shall talk about the record of the Blair Government according to whether it successfully penetrated that new politics of an affluent culture in order to deal effectively with the problem of distribution.

Education is a good example of all this, but also an area in which there is cause for optimism. It is typical – if not altogether surprising – that Labour allowed its political opponents to take responsibility for the extraordinary quantitative advance of further and higher education, both in the early

1960s and in the late 1980s, while at the same time failing to realise that, in order to ensure such advances would lead not just to liberation but also to greater equality among individuals, Government had to devote most of its attention (and resources) to the early rather than the later years. Now, at last, the Party seems to have learnt that you have to start at the beginning and not just expand at the top end. If you really want to be egalitarian – or even if all you really want is to have a workforce that is going to mean something in the world – then the effort has to be greatest at the nursery and primary end of education. Nevertheless, the politics of an affluent culture largely remain to be invented – even when it comes to education. We may, for example, have to recognise more fully that it has less to do with schools as such, but much more to do with families, with relations of parents to children – though whether this kind of new politics is best effected by Downing Street issuing diktats and directives about homework etc. is a moot point.

Another area which will require creative thinking is welfare. Society is rich enough, whatever some may say, to provide for its citizens; but the question remains, how should we assess entitlement to such provision? This is something that Mr Blair and his colleagues, if they are still interested in socialist equality or even just liberal equality of opportunity, must face. Ideas like the citizen's or basic income have been around a long time but never adopted, not least because their emphasis on entitlement as both the result and guarantor of participation in society – rather than as a reward for previous or potential economic activity (narrowly defined) – goes against the ethos of 'old' Labour. We have to face the political problem of redistributing increasingly affluent economic output and, at the same time, a growing 'burden' of increased leisure – the modern reversal of conditions which originally gave rise to socialism and the labour movement. Given the higher proportion of people continuing to live on into old age and given renegotiation of the division of labour so that many more women are in employment, things need to be rethought, even revisited. To suggest that, essentially, people must work or they won't eat may be (however much Mr Blair may wish to deny it) firmly in the Labourite tradition, but it is not an adequate answer in this age of socio-economic flux. Better (though controversial) to turn one's attention to other parts of that tradition – to the 'social wage', for example, that could form the basis of a state-guaranteed income that would change (necessarily so) the way people think about all sorts of issues, from occupational flexibility over the life-cycle to the crucial importance of family-based childcare. Whether the new Government is capable of thinking such thoughts remains, of course, to be seen.

# Commentary

*Christopher Price*

Economic and sociological explanations of political phenomena are always necessary but never sufficient. We need to throw a few psychological pebbles into the pool.

First, unity is crucial when it comes to rethinking welfare. In 1945 Labour had deep and real popular backing which sustained the Government. In 1964–70 it had, even with a big parliamentary majority in the late 1960s, very flaky popular support. As a result the 1945 Labour Government sustained a will to succeed; the 1964 one did not. Psychologically (*pace* the Nenni telegram episode) the 1945 Parliament, until just before the end, was united. The 1964 one was still, psychologically, gripped by the Bevanite schism. Indeed, it is difficult, today, to convey the depths of hatred and contempt the right and the left in the PLP had for each other in that period. The schism was so deep that a vocabulary of betrayal and failure inevitably arose out of it.

Second, we need to understand old Labour's addiction to welfare collectivism. Psychologically, it was an addiction born of enlightened capitalism, millennial Marxism and (most of all) Victorian imperialism. Many of Attlee's Cabinet, for all the anti-colonial rhetoric, were Victorians and imperialists at heart. They had no sense of an inclusive democratic collective of women and blacks, the bright and the stupid. It was the duty of the bright and fortunate to minister unto the poor and stupid. Britain had just won a world war through disciplined democratic centralism, as had Stalin; Labour politicians naturally assumed they could win the peace in much the same centralist and collectivist way. This also accounts for Labour's 'little-Englander' mindset. It is undoubtedly true that previous Labour Governments had little sense of global trends and 'broad structural forces'. The British did not notice such things because they were accustomed to imposing their will on the world. It was this blinkered, imperial mindset which prevented Wilson from devaluing; and Enoch Powell was right to characterise the attraction of Europe to the likes of Wilson and Heath as the 'spectre of a surrogate for Empire'.

Finally it is right to point out that Wilson and his colleagues had no concept of strategy. The new language and philosophy of managerialism, as applied to civil society, had not yet taken root. They simply were not psychologically ready for new models of welfare. Wilson well understood what it was to be a good civil servant: he had been one himself. But civil servants, then at any rate, were static, not dynamic folk.

'Liberty' may have been beginning to be linked with issues of creativity, growth and economic success, but 'liberty' has never been high in Labour iconography: the 'liberty' of the 1968 student revolt, for example, terrified the Labour Government which liked society to be plannable and predictable.

The Blair recipe seems to be a psychologically skilled mixture of libertarian and authoritarian ideas. He also seems to understand the long game and the principles of strategy. Above all, he understands the new media imperatives of the age and the need to connect electronically with popular moods. But the devil, in terms of welfare and education, will be in the details. Just how big a private sector in health and education is going to be tolerable? Just how big or small should be the meshes in the safety net and at what level should the net be spread? How will Blair define the essence of the new Labour communitarianism? For five elections the Conservatives read the popular mood well and successfully played the tactics of 'percentage politics' with the electorate. Blair's strategy could look very different, but is still dedicated to achieving – and may achieve – the same sort of success.

# Chapter 4

# The moral agenda

*David Walker*

When Labour was a socialist party, it had a predefined moral agenda centred on rejection of most aspects of the system of production based on private enterprise. As a non-socialist party Labour has no intrinsic moral position. It becomes a sort of political magpie picking up bits and pieces of behavioural judgement or else a ship driven by the winds of attitudinal and electoral change: if New Labour appears, for example, in favour of homosexuality the reason could be as simple as the presence in the ranks of MPs elected in May 1997 of several 'out' gays.

At some point between the creation of Young England by Benjamin Disraeli and friends in 1844 and the creation some 130 years later of the Centre for Policy Studies, the Tory Party established to its own satisfaction – and to that of the millions of voters who endorsed it in the interim – that capitalism and morality were fully compatible but the problem of their relationship was never again to be spoken of. The young, that is to say early middle-aged, Disraeli had his doubts. The Tory intellectuals and policy derring-doers who joined Sir Keith Joseph at the CPS did not care or believed, with Friedrich Hayek,[1] that morality (defined as those extra-market norms of good conduct on which, as Hayek realised, market operations depended) had their doubts too. This, of course, was the true meaning of Lady Thatcher's most famous aphorism about there being no such thing as society: her half-digested Hayek complemented her fear that the moral underpinnings of free market capitalism were fragile and certainly not to be talked about by politicians or rationalist policy advisers.

It is among the great historical triumphs of the British Conservative Party that for nearly a century and a half this critical problem in political philosophy should not only be suppressed internally but largely kept out of public sight too, at least as a source of contradiction or intellectual confusion. The explanation, of course, is the Tory Party's pragmatism about the sticking plaster state. Where there is old age poverty, let there be no repeal of Liberal Party pensions. Where lack of income prevents access to health care, let the vermin toast Aneurin Bevan.

But this chapter is not about the Tory Party. I start this way in order to dramatise my question. Capitalism subverts the moral order, dissolves rules, rewards anarchism: how then are necessary norms of good conduct to be recovered? This was the classic problem of Francis Hutcheson and Adam Smith which they tried to answer by discovering a natural anthropology of moral sentiments or through what Colin Kidd has called sociological whiggism, that is to say the evolution in history of containing and constraining institutions.[2] The Tories, as a capitalist party, tried several tacks. For a century or longer they got away with the deception of landed hierarchy as a collar around capitalist necks – there is a measure of Joseph Chamberlain's failure. Later the invention of welfare state Toryism put the question off again. It was the advent of Thatcherism which made an answer acute, what norms of good conduct, what rules can be specified by the party of free, that is to say unruly, anomic enterprise?

The reinvention of Labour under Tony Blair's leadership as a capitalist party makes the question squarely one for them, too, to answer. Where, if you accept (even if you do not actually celebrate) the advance of global capitalism, are the rules, the restraining bolts of anarcho-individualism, to come from? New Labour in its novelty does not have the historical resources of the Conservatives to call up, that tissue of historical contradictions from which Tory rhetoricians can still glibly draw – namely the candidates for the party's leadership. If New Labour wants to play the moral card – and there is evidence it will carry into office the moral discourse and morality-policies it began in Opposition – it will have profound difficulties and will, sooner or later, fail or, more likely, fall into a slough of market-correcting, ad hoc judgements informed by nothing more substantial than a rather tepid progressivism, an 'ism' which may amount to no more than doing what Labour Governments tend to do, worrying about the progressivity of the tax system, bending certain public policies towards the have nots, striving to be a straight arrow in international affairs and – not least because your Secretary of State for National Heritage is an out gay – doing nothing markedly illiberal on the sexual orientation front.

We could argue about when in the twentieth century the Labour Party became socialist, whether at a Party Conference moment, i.e. 1918, or by the more gradual diffusion of a set of ideas. But it is fair to say that the party led by Ramsay MacDonald into Government in 1924 was socialist – for the purposes of my argument (by which I intend socialism to be a solution to the morality problem outlined above). Socialism, John Dunn explained,[3] was a child of Platonism: there will be another time, another place in which the Good will be manifest; you might look for signs of the Good in the really existing practice of socialist parties or even the regimes established by those parties but even if you did not find it in either, it would still be there, as it were a rising sun invisible over the horizon, casting the existing (capitalist) world into shadow.

Labour never needed to worry about the lack of rules in capitalism because, lightly, hesitantly, distantly, rhetorically it believed in capitalism's replacement by a moral order, that is to say by *the* moral order. As we all know, the exact content of the moral order of socialism was never spelled out, perhaps never could be spelled out. In 1931 it was deferred. In 1946 it looked like state control of some at least of the means of production. In 1965 its harbinger was George Brown's National Plan. In 1974 it resembled the Meriden Motorcycle Co-operative. The point is it always in some ways looked different from the existing capitalist set-up and moreover could draw on wells of sentiment and motives to act that were believed to be intrinsically different. Socialism was morality, fraternity, equality, community. Its problem was not extramarket values, principles for distribution and redistribution but the market itself, or rather how to organise production either effectively or without slavery.

We could trace the various broad streams, through Tawney and the Christian socialists, but even in the writings of the revisionists the same conceit holds – there is that classic passage in Tony Crosland's *The Future of Socialism*[4] where he scolds colleagues for not celebrating with him the hedonism of the workers as, prospering under planning, they head off for their Continental holidays – for Crosland, as for Marx, in nirvana production and consumption join in perfect harmony. David Marquand calls Crosland a 'passive hedonist', a binary opposite to his gallery of moralist activists, starting with Gladstone and finishing, question mark, with Tony Blair.[5]

With Crosland comes the question: was 1960s liberalism, in which he partook even while remaining a collectivist, the Trojan Horse in socialism's decomposition as evidenced two decades on by the incoherence of, say, Ken Livingstone, who at one and the same time would dragoon people out of unfair market relationships but never dream of touching on their gender relationships? To be say, gay, was a celebration of rainbow pluralism but to be a capitalist proscribed.

Roy Jenkins has recalled how he had set out the programme for his great legislative changes enacted during the 1964-70 Wilson Government in a 1959 Penguin Special, how three to five of the first Wilson Cabinet were resolutely opposed to his reforms while most of the rest just hoped they would somehow go away.[6] There is confirmation of this. Jenkins picked up a note in Alec Cairncross's latest diary for 1965 of a remark attributed to the Chancellor of the Exchequer Jim Callaghan on Jenkins' move to the Home Office: 'we'll have to watch him. He's too kind to these buggers.'[7]

If by the 1960s we want to believe in some chord linking Mick Jagger and Harold Wilson, Lord Jenkins on a Lambretta, a mind, a moment, we are in the realm of fantasy. Politics and culture went their own ways, in the sense that popular song and Cabinet paper were just not connected. This is true not just in the technical sense that you can scour Richard Crossman's contemporaneous diary in vain for a reference to the Troggs but in the figurative sense that political and cultural operations had anything in common, especially some identifiable common cause.[8] But what identifiably did happen in the 1960s was the meeting and matching of two strains of thought. One was a kind of rationalisation which said the private enterprise (capitalist) economy even in its market attenuated or Wilsonian form depended critically upon greater individual freedoms: the freedom of the economic actor necessarily implied his freedom to fuck or more pertinently still, her freedom to leave behind a failed marriage. That rationalisation had of course been incipient for decades, if not centuries: consciousness dawned on or about 1 October 1968.

The second was an uncorking of the romantic belief that we are all creators and custodians of our own happiness – an idea with strong American antecedents which themselves drew heavily on Scottish Enlightenment thought. This became, at least for some, a belief corrosive of the stoicism of women confronted with inequality, or younger people facing the stolidity of their elders and betters or everyone facing restraint on consumption, literal and figurative. A key example of a man of the 1960s is the Prince of Wales: for all his preaching, in his own life personal fulfilment is all.

Measuring and tracking changes in people's core beliefs is difficult – no data series exists for the 1960s, or 1970s for that matter. But insofar as these strains of thought and public sensibility did coalesce in the real time 1960s they procreated and gave birth to big things including the women's movement or, more accurately in the British case, the growing discontent of individual women in their domestic and occupational circumstances with obvious inequalities and discriminations offending the capitalist code of individual autonomy and thwarting their bid to realise themselves in approved romantic mode. This is what Alain Touraine calls 'subjectivation' – the creation, even the celebration, of inner states which in turn can work against the forces of rationalisation and modernity, for example in drug cultures, the flowering of anti-rational belief systems.

The 1960s were honest, in the sense of holding the system up to its own ideals of freedom and equality and finding it wanting. But what followed was a kind of prevalent individualism – the politics of me – which in the 1970s took shape as collective selfishness in trade union anarchism and in the 1980s undergirded greed-is-good Thatcherism.

The paradox of the 1960s was how individualism was unsheathed within a social democratic context in which government itself was valued. A central problem of politics at the millennium is recapturing an idea of government or at least of a sphere of public activity when the politics of the personal, the grail of self fulfilment especially through sex, is so popular. The problem for New Labour as a capitalist party is to face down or rescind those values and reflexes we are here labelling '1960s' which seem so

essential to capitalism's expansion and material prosperity. David
Marquand has categorised Margaret Thatcher as a moralist individualist,
meaning she wanted to bring on stage a body of values to somehow keep
anarcho-individualism on the straight and narrow in a way that once,
perhaps, Protestant religion had done. But isn't the problem the same for
New Labour?

Whatever the evolution of Tony Blair's private beliefs, his public use of
'moral talk' dates from his spell as shadow Home Secretary during John
Smith's leadership. In a speech he made when the Bulger murder hit the
headlines early in 1993, he talked about the need for a 'rediscovery of a sense
of direction as a country'. We needed to stop being afraid

> to start talking again about the values and principles we believe in and
> what they mean for us not just as individuals but as a community. We
> cannot exist in a moral vacuum. If we do not learn and then teach the
> value of what is right and what is wrong, the result is simply moral chaos
> which engulfs us all.

On the face of it, neither the style nor the content of that is new. The words
could have come from Jim Callaghan, addressing the Police Federation –
for which he was, of course, a Parliamentary Adviser – circa 1969. But Jim
Callaghan – I am labouring the argument – was a socialist, however
attenuated, for whom 'community' and rectitude, however unspecified,
were rooted in a fundamental critique of the economic system. Labour's
penal thinking never developed much, it is true; the abolition of capital
punishment was nodded through on Labour's watch but did not come from
the party's bowels. Why should it, since retributive justice is perfectly
compatible with the pursuit of social justice through income redistribution
and changes in the structure of property ownership? Jack Straw's harder
line stance, for which he is so excoriated among metropolitan liberals, is of
a piece with older Labour reflexes; the trouble is Jack Straw is a partisan of
the project to do away with older Labour, its personnel and its ideological
baggage.

Writing in *The Times*, on 17 April 1997, Tony Blair contrasted his core
beliefs in family and community, as a clear alternative to Tory obsessions
with self interest. 'It is our right, and I would say our duty, to put politics
in a moral and ethical context', he said in an election speech in Southampton.
That 'was not preaching to people about their personal lives but a recognition
that politics is not just about efficiency or competence. It is also about
making choices not only because they are prudent and sensible but because
they are just.' You cannot, you might say, hang a man on the evidence of
his election rhetoric but these passages shape my question: just what is New
Labour's moral and ethical context? There are two answers.

One is that it is merely the common or garden public morality, that is to
say the broad structure of public evaluations of conduct that you can infer

or construct out of the British Social Attitudes surveys or, like the Department for Education and Employment, by convening a 150-strong panel of teachers, ministers of religion, good people and true, and asking them to draw up a document of agreed values. But the resulting products are unlikely to be terribly specific or necessarily consistent. Estelle Morris, the Schools Minister, says the spiritual, moral, social and cultural development of our children is just as important as academic knowledge but, asked to prescribe content that goes beyond platitudes, she is struck dumb. Do such platitudes constitute the 'clear and specific moral vision' that Raymond Plant asked for as a prophylactic against social democracy's tumbling into 'the type of politics that has to do with the power of strong coalitions and interest groups, as in the 1970s'?[9]

The second answer is that New Labour, and particularly its leader, have come to power committed to an identifiable set of ethical propositions and/or norms of good conduct. Thus Mr Blair attends worship in Roman Catholic churches and expresses his personal antipathy to abortion; he identifies John MacMurray and Peter Thompson among his spiritual influences, which point towards a gospel of social activism but not socialism. The difficulty here is trying to discern a set of precepts, both for individual conduct and collective policy. Thus Mr Blair is personally against abortion but also believes, as a matter of policy, in the woman's right to choose, at least in consultation with two doctors as specified in the 1967 abortion reform. Mr Blair personally, we infer, believes in the permanence of marriage and by extension the sinfulness of divorcees; as a matter of policy he has no intention of rescinding recent divorce legislation nor by extension using Government powers to enforce the marriage contract.

This is the charge brought by crusading newspaper columnists such as Melanie Phillips of *The Observer* who has argued that New Labour should bring to the radical promotion of marriage the same degree of crusading zeal as David Blunkett brings to reversing the cultural slide or alleged decline in educational standards. But Ms Phillips, without ever quite having the courage or intellectual tenacity to spell her position out, is an authoritarian and absolutist. What is moral is what she, in consultation doubtless with her God, says is moral.

New Labour, by contrast, show very little sign of taking the authoritarian path down which lies the end of the messy live and let live pluralism, also known as moral chaos, in which we live on the basis, still, of Lord Jenkins' 1960s liberalism. With Jack Straw and curfews for ten-year-olds it is not morality that is at issue but a kind of social functionalism – whether or not it is right for children to be at home tucked up in bed looked after by a mother and a father, it is functional, in a crime prevention sense, for them to be at home and and Jack Straw, to his credit, has avoided jumping on the 'two parents are necessarily better than one' bandwagon.

New Labour's flirtation with communitarianism needs to be understood in these terms. It is not that Amitai Etzioni and friends have produced a doctrine.[10] But even if they had, what New Labour seems to have been after are solutions to pressing problems of public policy, like rising crime rates. Meanwhile Robin Cook has promised a more moral foreign policy, a headline manifestation of which is a refusal to sell arms to despots and dictators and human rights abusers. At its weakest this might just mean a ban on the sale of land mines – a moral stance sufficiently eclectic to secure the endorsement of Princess Diana. At its strongest, it could be socialism: that is to say, the bringing to bear of judgements of utility or worth on the products of markets and altering production schedules accordingly – nothing very New Labour about that. I am struggling for a sense of what 'morality' means as in this Blairism:

> The health of the family and the strength of the nation ultimately reflects the quality of honest, decent, truthful government, government which has a moral dimension and which always makes sure that justice has a high place at the Cabinet table.[11]

## What might 'a moral dimension' mean?

First, if morality means – as it does for the *Daily Mail* and related police officers of appropriate conduct – sexual continence, a moral Government might consist of a Cabinet from which, like Arthur's round table, were excluded adulterers, wife-beaters, seducers and the like. Transparency is a characteristic of modern British society: doing what I say, not what I do, is unacceptable. At the moment Tony Blair's Cabinet is not self-evidently more uxorious than its predecessor. Time will tell whether the penchant of Labour for sexual dalliance is less. Perhaps they will just be more careful. On one level to question the private conduct of ministers is utterly trivial because – on the analogy of Palmerston – it does not seem especially relevant to their conduct of policy. Yet on another, a Government that identified with promoting virtue – conduct officially labelled good – would nowadays have to be exemplary. It and its servants would have to be virtuous. The scarcity of saints in public implies this Government would be taking a big risk if it played the moral card.

Second, a moral dimension might mean leading with your chin on touchstone issues: surrogacy, gay marriage, in-vitro fertilisation, women in combat. The indications are, per Tessa Jowell, Health Minister, that this Government like its predecessor is going to shelter behind reviews and committees and an effort to rest policy on commonly held beliefs. The party that contains, at least on its back benches, the victor of Enfield Southgate, seems unlikely to be anything other than friendly to gay enterprise. Is that to have an immoral dimension? Only, presumably, if you allow your morality to be dictated by the Chief Rabbi or the Ayatollah. But the point here surely is that New Labour has no intrinsic position on say, the contention that sex between a 20-year-old man and a 11-year-old boy is immoral. Insofar as it supported the passage of the law that makes the act illegal it condemns the act, but not because it has a generalised or generalisable view of homosexual sex. A test case is whether New Labour moves to repeal section 28 of the Local Government Act 1988 which, exceptionally, expressed Leviticus as official morality.

But that is to get caught by the ayatollahs and define morality as what two people do to each other in bed, as opposed to conduct on the shop floor, in the boardroom or City dealing room. To conclude I return to my starting question: does New Labour as a party of free market capitalism have a solution to the problem of where the freedoms necessary for the market to function should be curtailed? Or, rather, a principled solution, a consistent story about itself that would allow us to anticipate New Labour's position on any emergent issue, particularly those to do with individual freedom defined 1960s-style or the great moral issues as defined by rabbis. The answer is no. Labour will strive to palliate the interest groups which make it up and so will do nothing to alter the abortion settlement. But as for that 'clear and specific moral vision' requested by Lord Plant, New Labour has not got it, but that is because – socialism abandoned – it cannot.

# Notes

1 See for example F. A. Hayek, *Studies in Philosophy, Politics and Economics*, Chicago University Press, 1967.
2 Colin Kidd, *Subverting Scotland's Past*, Cambridge University Press, 1993.
3 John Dunn, *The Politics of Socialism*, Cambridge University Press, 1983.
4 C. A. R. Crosland, *The Future of Socialism*, Jonathan Cape, 1956, p.521.
5 David Marquand, 'Moralists and Hedonists' in David Marquand and Anthony Seldon (eds), *The Ideas that Shaped Post-war Britain*, Harper Collins, 1996.
6 Roy Jenkins, *A Life at the Centre*, Macmillan, 1991.
7 Alec Cairncross, *The Wilson Years: A Treasury Diary. 1964–66*, The Historians' Press, 1997, pp.104–105.
8 R. H. S. Crossman, *The Diaries of a Cabinet Minister*, Hamish Hamilton and Jonathan Cape, 1976.
9 Raymond Plant, 'Social Democracy', in Marquand and Seldon (eds), op. cit.
10 Amitai Etzioni, *The New Golden Rule*, Profile Books, 1991.
11 For more of the same see Tony Blair, *Britain*, Fourth Estate, 1996.

# Commentary

*Joe Bailey*

When I was a little boy I used to make faces, and my mother used to say 'Be careful, the wind will change and you'll get stuck like that.' In a way, that is what has happened to the current Labour Government: it has got caught making faces and striking attitudes, for very good reasons, and its face has got stuck. There are two aspects to this: the first is the idea that somehow the world in which the Labour Government operates is the same as the one in which it – and indeed the Conservatives – used to operate and, therefore, that it can use the resources that were then used to build a new morality; the second is the question of what this new morality could consist of, given the shift in the relationship over the years between the private and the public, the personal and the public.

By and large historians and political scientists love continuity: history is about drawing parallels. This may have been comforting, but, in some respects, it is no longer possible to do. One does not have to subscribe fully to the rococo rhetoric of post-modernism to believe that the current juncture is different in certain very interesting ways from what has gone before, both morally and politically. The most obvious feature of this newness is the collapse of the old moralities. It doesn't matter what you want to call them, or how you want to link those moralities to ideologies, be they liberal, socialist, Christian or new-rightist. What is clear is that none of these ideologies and moralities – which in various ways make up the new Labour Government's inheritance – are really quite up to the job.

The characteristics of this changed world are myriad, but I would like to point to three aspects – they are by no means exhaustive or exclusive – which the Labour Government will be listening to and reading. The first is exemplified in the recent work of Anthony Giddens, who gives quite a good description of why the world (which he would call a 'reflexive' world, a late modern world) is not as it was but is instead needing to be preoccupied by the issues which those a generation or two below us are actually interested in, within tunnels under the ground, within clubs, on the streets, the kinds of things that might just be engaging them – issues which largely bypass contemporary political scientists and historians but which

Governments simply will not be able to ignore. The second focuses on the fact that the world seems newly 'risky' in all sorts of ways – the food you eat, the air you breathe, the sex you have – all of which are affected (at least potentially) by Governments. And the third reason why the world is not as it was in 1945 or 1964 or even 1974, is that we are aware in a new way of the importance of what we might refer to as 'difference' or 'otherness' and aware of how the way we differ from one another as subjects (individual or collective) has dramatic implications for social change, not least in terms of how conflicts can be resolved and co-operation can take place.

Given all this, one way of looking at the moral agenda is to look at it through the lens of the distinction between private and public conduct or morality, both of which Governments almost inevitably affect. It seems to me that the Labour Government takes over in an era when the shift from the public to the private has been very dramatic, not just economically but also in terms of what one might call the soul – the concern with the self and with personal happiness and all the institutions and organisations that surround that, from what people say to their GPs, to the kind of self help books that they buy, to the anxieties that they have about whether they are good, moral, healthy people and what their capacities and potentials are. But it has also, paradoxically, been an era when the personal has become political and the political – that is to say the public – has penetrated into the private, for example in the family and in relationships, particularly relationships between genders.

This opposition indicates that while there may have been a shift away from the certainties of the public moralities of socialism and liberalism, any resulting vacuum could not simply be filled by the sort of morality posited by new right individualism. But neither is there much indication that it can be filled by anything emanating from New Labour. What you see in its morality, in so far as it is visible in various areas, is simply the inherited and now lightweight baggage that has been taken from the old public philosophies, with nothing – whether we choose to look at the populist rhetoric of Jack Straw's penal policy or the traditional ethical concerns of Robin Cook's foreign policy – truly coherent to replace them. The challenge facing the new Government, of course, may not be just that it must find and promote some new morality, but that it may have to operate in a world where no such thing is even possible any more.

# Commentary

*Michael Phelan*

It is all too easy – especially when looking at previous Labour Governments and in the context of what seems like years of Conservative 'sleaze' – to fall into the trap that morality essentially boils down to sex. There is more to it than that. In the run up to the 1997 election, the Catholic Bishops in this country issued *The Common Good* which clearly set out a set of moral principles for communicants to look at when trying to decide on how to vote: social morality was just as high up the list as sexual continence. But this is not to say that there is no room for disagreement on what that morality is or how – or even whether – it can be facilitated, as the hostility (not least among people in their own party) both Jack Straw and (less frequently) Tony Blair have generated by some of their ideas in this area demonstrates.

Much of that hostility, of course, is a proxy for a wider distrust of the new Prime Minister within his own ranks – a distrust that has its roots, firstly, in the idea that Labour leaders betray the Party's supposedly socialist principles and, secondly, in a more particular suspicion that this Labour leader is not even socialist to start with. Those who believe the latter may have a point, but it is rather more complex than they imagine and has perhaps not a little to do with Mr Blair's association with Christian socialism, with his avowed belief that socialism is about ethical values rather than particular forms or methods of government – with ends, if you like, rather than means. As a Christian, he believes in the two Judeo-Christian commandments of loving God and loving thy neighbour as thyself and it is the latter that results in political activity. But this leaves considerable room for both manoeuvre and debate within the Party and the Government. This debate, though, will have to be conducted in an atmosphere of tolerance: just as some simplistic authoritarian populism is undesirable, those liberals who sneer at any arguments which can be made to smack of it need to remember a few home truths.

Unsurprisingly, given the fact that there is more contact crime on a per capita basis in this country than there is in the United States, law and order is at the top of the moral agenda for the ordinary people whom Labour can, after its overwhelming victory at the 1997 election, claim once again to represent. Now representation is about leadership, but it is also about reflecting popular concerns. Jack Straw's concerns about street crime, especially involving young people – like Tony Blair's concerns about single-parent families – stem from genuine concerns within society. They are not simply responses to media-hype. Supporters of the Labour Government need to remember that, in reflecting such concerns, their leaders are not necessarily being morally judgmental, but morally – and above all socially – aware.

# Chapter 5

# Managing the state and the state as manager

*Gerard Alexander*

## Introduction

In post-war Britain, as in all other industrialised countries, the role and management of the state has been central to political debates, and control of state structures – expected to be achieved by winning elections – has been the basis of competition between political parties and the interests, ideologies, and leaders which inspire and mobilise them. This debate and competition has primarily revolved around two themes: the role which political parties and leaders believe the state should play in terms of enforcing outcomes, regulating behaviour, or delivering services in political, economic, social, or cultural affairs; and administrative efficacy – whether political leaders and parties perceive existing state structures as a politically or technically efficient aid or obstacle to the goals they pursue through state structures. While 'the issue of the proper sphere of government' and 'the efficiency of the machinery intended to achieve the aims it sets itself'[1] are conceptually distinct, they are also interrelated: the capacities and efficacy of state structures help shape what roles the state is believed capable of playing, and the roles which specific parties and agendas assign to the state can in turn result in important modifications of state structures.

The central argument of this paper concerns the fact that throughout the post-war period, Labour Governments have seen state power as a privileged instrument or means in their attempts to achieve their domestic goals, which should be understood centrally as greater (though far from complete) social and economic equality and an improved quality of life for all citizens, especially the neediest. Unfortunately for Labour, many of the Party's post-war internal conflicts over politics and policy were not elevated debates between groups who conceived of Labour's objectives differently but rather became polarised disputes between those who believed that state-based means to the Party's ends were contingent and flexible versus those who argued that such means were permanent, indeed that in some sense specific means were ends themselves. This was 'unfortunate' because Labour's electoral performance – and hence its ability to serve the cause of British social democracy – would have been better served had its long-running debates over the role of state planning, whether or not industries should be state-owned and how state-owned industries should be structured, and the division of labour between central and municipal state authorities, been more productively posed in terms of the changing efficacy and efficiency of these various means. As a result, at crucial points it fell to the Conservatives to reorient state roles and manage the state machinery to serve those purposes, even when the objectives being pursued had originally been established by Labour.

The Party's deepening programmatic commitment to state-based solutions, moreover, often shielded from view the fact that Labour in power resorted to specific means and instruments based on highly contingent historical, ideological, and political factors. Available choices for the pursuit of its goals had always ranged from purely voluntary collective action (such as co-operatives) to a variety of state measures, including enforced regulations to municipal services, and – at its most extensive and intensive – national state ownership and service delivery. Choices regarding specific uses of the state were never systematic: even the Attlee Governments which relied on the state as industrial owner and manager and deliverer of social services eschewed those roles in cultural matters, and the Wilson Governments used practically the full range of state roles to address different problems. Contingency and flexibility characterised Labour in power if not Labour in principle.

Eventually, it would be electoral constraints which helped generate political debate within the Party concerning state roles and machinery at the programmatic level as well. Differences of opinion regarding these questions emerged in internal Party debates in the 1950s and early 1960s and became urgent once again in the 1980s and early 1990s. In particular, since 1979, the Labour Party had found it difficult to maintain electoral popularity while retaining Labour's traditional menu of preferred state instruments aimed at achieving the goals socialists have pursued. Surprisingly, in retrospect, it proved nearly as difficult for Labour to agree to alter its preferred means – the types of state involvement which the Party favoured – as it might have been to alter its stated ends. As a result, just as the Tories were punished electorally at the end of the Second World War for their reluctance to expand the state's role, so Labour was punished electorally after 1979 for being reluctant to pursue goals by new and different means.

In a short-term sense, much of this cost generated by a reluctance to concede traditional means may have been unnecessary. In particular, the electoral constraints which eventually forced Labour programmes and candidates to cede ground on the roles it traditionally assigned to the state at the same time permitted Labour to maintain commitments to a number of key historic Party goals including the quality of life delivered by social services and made possible by income distribution. In that sense, much of the dispute concerning means and ends occurred because many in Labour confused the two, believing for example that means such as state ownership were coterminous with socialist goals and values such as full employment and a more equal distribution of income. Over their protests, the means politically available to Labour, both in office and out, have proved highly adaptable: the state as owner, as aggregate demand manager, as indicative planner and catalyst for developmental modernisation, and as 'contractor out' for social and even cultural services have all been relied upon, and the British state machinery has been repeatedly reformed to reflect and facilitate these changes.

This paper reviews these changes in support of an argument that Labour's confusing of means and ends has for much of the post-war period significantly contributed to its losing elections and hence being marginalised from power. It also reviews a possible counter-argument advanced by neo-liberal policy-makers and social democratic political scientists, which suggests that the interaction between politics and state management may produce a type of 'feedback', in which the manner in which Governments manage the state can affect political competition, which in turn influences how Governments are able to manage and use the state in the future. Even if these theories are correct, however, the specific changes which have been made both in policy and state structures since 1951 would not appear to threaten Labour's core objectives. Indeed, it is striking that despite decades of debilitating internal conflict over the types of state roles to utilise as means and the state machinery needed to fulfil those roles, Labour now returns to power with the basis of social democratic governance – popular support for an extensive welfare state and the notable income redistribution that requires – largely intact (relative, for example, to public support for nationalised industries).

### Historically contingent post-war choices regarding the role of the British state (1945–1956)

Throughout the inter-war and early post-war period, Labour maintained a number of core objectives concerning economic and social outcomes, including lessening economic and social inequalities, ensuring stable growth and employment, and an improved quality of life especially for poorer members of British society. But the Party's election programmes and eventually its legislative record demonstrated important variations in the means selected to achieve them, with commensurate shifts in the role which Labour meant the state to play and how state agencies were to be structured and organised. While Labour's objectives were not limited to economic and social ones, such economic issues as macroeconomic management, ownership of industry and land, planning, industrial policy, the welfare state, and job creation played increasingly prominent roles in political debates within and between all parties in Britain's troubled economic context from 1918 onwards. The changing role which Party manifestos and leaders assigned to state structures reflected the impact of a series of influences: the Party's trust in, and assessment of the efficacy of, the state, including the civil service with whom a Labour Government would work directly; the perceived credibility of various solutions to enduring and new challenges; and, throughout the inter-war period, electoral constraints, including voters' own assessments of both the efficacy and the efficiency of the state in pursuing common goals through particular means.

A range of options were available for achieving Labour goals through social and political action:

- voluntary collective action (such as co-operatives);
- state enforcement of outcomes through regulative power (regulations of standards of behaviour, 'hard' economic planning);
- state distribution of resources (subsidies, transfers of income, indicative planning, payment for services);
- management by state entities (direct operation and delivery of services);
- ownership by the state (municipal or national public enterprises).

Only some of these options assigned the state a central role in achieving goals, and – most important for the trend in British politics over the next half century – even when the state was considered as the preferred means of pursuing goals, debate could and did exist over the appropriate level of state involvement (e.g., municipal, regional, or national) and extent of state involvement (ranging from 'mere' legal regulation through payment for services to ownership and direct service delivery).

Prior to the Second World War, debates were held within the broader Labour movement concerning which of these means would best achieve socialist ends, although precise prescriptions were often unnecessary given the long road to power which was assumed. Nonetheless, programmatic commitments to, for example, state ownership vs. other forms of social ownership (such as that represented by the Co-operative Movement) fluctuated, and limited debate occurred regarding how industries which might be state-owned should be run. A substantial role was assigned to municipalities in Labour thinking regarding a number of policy areas, and numerous hospitals and utilities were under municipal control even before the war. Syndicalist views championing workers' control were prevalent through the first two decades of the century (for example in the postal workers' union) and Clause IV of the Labour constitution left open the question how socialised property would be managed. Dahl has argued that the Labour movement continued debates over the management of socialised industries – workers' control vs. central state control – until nearly the end of the war.[2]

The experience of the Second World War substantially restructured all these prior debates. The exigencies of war triggered a vast expansion of central state capacities in economic management and planning of a range of economic and social functions, including wartime production, welfare, construction, and education. This expansion helped generate a corresponding increase in leaders' and the public's estimation of the efficacy of the national state machinery; important also was the fact that the wartime Labour leadership were generally disabused of any potential scepticism they may have had regarding the loyalty of British civil servants to implementing a Labour programme.[3] This increased credibility and trust helped inform the dramatic post-war expansion of the central state's role as a solution to economic and social problems, the forms of which included nationalisations, the direct state provision of a wide range of social services associated with the modern welfare state, and what turned out to be a temporary continuation of wartime planning tools including rationing and controls on imports, prices, foreign exchange, and building. There were, of course, important variations in the extent of the expansion of state functions and size in different policy areas, but the overall story is one in which long-standing debates over the range of means of pursuing Labour's core economic and social goals were consistently resolved in favour not only of the state but of the central state as the preferred instrument and moreover the central state as owner, manager, and direct provider of services.

In the case of ownership of major industries, of all the possible alternatives – co-operatives, workers' management, municipal control – debates over the nature of socialisation were resolved with the very specific result of central state ownership. Not only would workers not manage, but it was the national level of state structures which was consistently favoured: to Herbert Morrison's occasional regret, municipal authorities were shorn of a number of functions including electricity, water, and health services. The National Health Service, for example, was the product of simultaneous 'nationalisation' along two dimensions: both privately owned and municipal hospitals were subordinated to central state ownership and control.[4] The roles assigned to the central state during the defining years of 1945–51 ran the available gamut: the state as owner and manager, as direct provider of services, as aide in economic development and modernisation, as distributor of income and resources, and as enforcer of outcomes through regulation. The only two significant limitations on expanding state intervention in economic life were the eventual slowdown in nationalisations and abandonment of the bid for permanent planning controls. In this sense, planning (indicative or otherwise) was one of the few uses of state structures and prerogatives which the Attlee Government left idle as a tool, to be picked up in the 1960s.[5]

The early post-war trend towards central state ownership, management, and direct service delivery was based on identifiable assumptions concerning the central state's comparative advantage over alternatives – including individuals and other levels of government – when it came to the ability to achieve economies of scale, to raise the levels of capital needed for modernisation of industry, to rationalise and plan complex and inter-related operations, and to achieve harmonious labour relations. Crucial as well was the assumption that *competition* between autonomous units of production or service delivery was not critical to efficacy or efficiency, even over the long term, and that the *profit motive* was an unnecessary and even suspect motivation in certain arenas of activity. And last was a generalised (though usually left unstated) sense that when it came to such technical matters as education and health care, for example, '[t]he gentleman in Whitehall really does know better what is good for people than the people know themselves'.[6] Obviously, each one of these assumptions was later to come into question, from within and without the Labour movement.

Initially, however, these assumptions were broadly credible; Herbert Morrison was not the only 'fervent champion of the British administrative class' and Labour was not alone in calling for an expansion of the role of the state in social and economic matters.[7] Insofar as there was a 'political consensus' in post-war Britain, this was due to cross-party convergence concerning both social and economic ends and central-state instruments as a means of achieving them. Agreement was not complete. In a number of instances after 1945, Tories disagreed with Labour concerning means: Conservatives strongly opposed planning and permanent controls, proposed to decentralise the new public corporations and called for a greater role in the housing programme both for home ownership and for private builders (like those who had built many of the 'Wheatley houses' begun by the minority Labour Government in 1924). But in many other areas the Conservatives largely accepted both Labour objectives – the Tories campaigned in 1950 and 1951 on commitments to full employment and the welfare state – and in fact to a substantial extent Labour's means of achieving those goals – the Tories opposed further nationalisations and promised to privatise steel and road haulage but in the end left the vast bulk of the nationalised sector intact. Nor was this acceptance entirely new: Ian Gilmour emphasises that it was pre-war Liberal and Unionist Governments which first created public corporations and which nationalised royalties from coal mining in 1938, and such Conservatives as Harold Macmillan had identified areas of common ground with Labour throughout the inter-war period.[8] Most post-war Conservatives joined Labour in placing greatly expanded state structures at the centre of economic and social life. The end result was not only that the state assumed ownership of a range of industries, but in addition the central state directly staffed and managed greatly expanded hospitals, health clinics, housing projects, pensioners' programmes, and the myriad other operations composing the post-war state system.

This post-war consensus over social and economic objectives and reliance on central state means was not limited to the leadership of Britain's two main parties. The efforts of the leading proponents of this consensus were powerfully buttressed politically by the fact that electoral pressures also militated in favour of state-based solutions and at least permitted and perhaps encouraged the use of state structures for direct management and service delivery. The Tory defeat in 1945 and the subsequent reorientation of the Conservative economic and social programme are typically interpreted as the products of insistent messages concerning public support for extensive state intervention aimed at achieving full employment, a substantial nationalised sector (for instance in coal mining), accessible healthcare, adequate nutrition and housing, and other welfare state benefits. Even those many Conservatives who did not champion an expanded state role out of sincere conviction certainly accepted it from 1950 onwards nonetheless, out of electoral expediency.

The reasons for this electoral pressure are not hard to discern: just as Party leaders were influenced by wartime administrative experience, so the British public was influenced by changing understandings of what instruments were considered credible solutions to common problems. So long as these perceptions and understandings favoured not only Labour's ends but also the means it had selected, electoral pressure constrained mainly the Tories, including their historic shift towards a nationalised sector and the Keynesian welfare state. This contextual factor, however, could and would cut both ways: as public perceptions regarding efficacy and efficiency altered over time, so, too, would the constraints placed on those parties who would use the state for their purposes.

But this record of events demonstrates the degree to which the selection of the means of addressing Labour's social and economic objectives was the result not of structural or functional inevitability but of political contingencies, including changing ideologies and personnel, administrative experiences, and electoral pressures. The contingent nature of these choices is demonstrated by two other post-war developments. First, the British state 'model' was not imitated everywhere in western Europe. Elsewhere in the region, publics and parties were generally agreed on objectives comparable to those in Britain, including full employment, stable growth, industrial modernisation, and improved qualities of life. But the means by which those goals were pursued varied greatly. Extensive nationalised sectors, for example, emerged only in Britain, France, and Italy.[9] In contrast, Sweden – later perceived as the epicentre of European social democracy – generally shunned nationalisations in favour of alternative forms of state-enforced outcomes aimed at full employment and improved welfare (especially demand management and labour market policies). The Federal Republic of Germany also did not develop a substantial nationalised sector and instead both Christian Democratic and Social Democratic Governments preferred to pursue social goals through extensive welfare programmes and co-determination, which established a junior role for trade unions in the management of private enterprises.[10] These varied approaches even within European social democracy demonstrate that state structures could be used in very different ways to pursue similar ends.

And second, perhaps most revealing of the contingent nature of the British choice to use state structures and direct management as a means of pursuing economic and social ends was the fact that the British 'model' was not the preferred approach in all arenas of social life even in Great Britain itself. Housing, for example, was swiftly devolved to the municipal level. And more sweepingly, the same period which witnessed the vast expansion of central state involvement in economic affairs also witnessed consensus over a highly qualified role for the state in cultural and moral matters. The component of the 'post-war consensus' which is commonly discussed concerns widespread agreement on an extensive but strictly non-revolutionary role for the state in the economy. But theoretically equally important, if usually only implicit, was a post-war consensus concerning the role of the state in the making and shaping of values and culture, a role which was minimal. In isolated cases in western Europe, the post-war period continued to witness extensive political conflict over the role of religion and 'official' values in enforcing public mores and behaviour, but in most countries, these disputes – which had stood at the heart of as much political conflict as class tensions – were resolved in favour of a specific cultural consensus alongside the economic one. The key difference was that the former crucially involved a minimal state role in sharp contrast to the extensive role accorded to the state in the latter.[11] Despite the existence of an official religion in Britain, no large state structures were created in the post-war period systematically to enforce standards, behaviour, or outcomes in cultural and moral matters comparable to those designed to enforce or achieve economic and social outcomes. Even in those cases in which the state was used to promote specific cultural activities and forms, the state was not owner and direct deliverer of the 'products' themselves. We need pick only a few examples: the BBC remained an autonomous agency rather than one under direct Government management. The Workers' Educational Association (WEA) received grants from the state, but was voluntarily staffed and self-governing, and turned actual teaching over to the extra-mural departments of participating universities. The Arts Council of Great Britain began as an *ad hoc* wartime agency which initially directly organised and managed theatre groups and was converted to a permanent institution by the outgoing Tory Government in 1945 which instead typically gave grants to artistic groups rather than staffing them directly. In a sense, the WEA and Arts Council were foreshadowings in cultural matters of the 'contracting out' of social services in the 1980s, and the Attlee Governments happily promoted them.[12]

## Labour's conflicts over the role and the management of the state (1956–83)

After 1951, Labour's reliance on the state as owner and manager proved increasingly complicated for a variety of ideological, experiential, and electoral reasons. To describe this situation as a series of ongoing 'crises' may be an exaggeration, but the electoral defeats of the 1950s made debates on the subject take on an urgency. The Conservative campaign in 1951 was boosted by Labour's continuing use of wartime controls, and in particular the two subsequent successive electoral defeats of the 1950s provoked leading figures within Labour ranks to criticise the Party's stated commitment to socialise the means of 'production, distribution and exchange' as a major culprit in Tory victories. For our purposes, the long-term crisis in Labour's relationship with the state as an instrument and machinery took two forms. The first, and ultimately more important politically, concerned elite and public perceptions of the state's ability to perform effectively and efficiently newly assigned functions, deliver its many services, and adopt new functions as well, in particular the project of industrial modernisation and 'planning' attempted under Wilson after 1964.

Above all, a number of events from the 1950s to the 1970s undermined support for the state as owner and direct manager of industry. Wartime assumptions concerning the relative advantages of state ownership proved problematic: the state proved not always able to achieve harmonious industrial relations with trade unions; the fiscal crisis of the state left private financial markets the only arenas capable of raising the large amounts of capital needed for ongoing modernisation of either private or nationalised industries; economies of scale were acknowledged to be not so much exaggerated (though they were at times) as accompanied by diseconomies of scale, such as lack of agility in swiftly changing markets and ossification of centralised bureaucracies. Gentlemen from Whitehall occasionally made mistakes. And perhaps most important of all, competition and monetary incentives – profits – were increasingly perceived to play vital roles in ensuring long-term efficiency and competitiveness in a wide range of complex activities.

The most immediate criticisms concerned the role the central state played as owner of industry. The Conservative Governments after 1951 reversed few of the nationalisations, but of course did not propose new ones, and in the mid- and late 1950s, a number of 'right-wing' Labour leaders began openly to criticise a continued emphasis on state ownership. This critique was advanced by numerous figures, but received elaborate discussion in 1956, when Anthony Crosland joined an argument which had been advanced by Douglas Jay and other early Keynesians 20 years earlier, concerning 'the growing irrelevance of the ownership of the means of production'.[13] Crosland argued, first, that the state was inadequate as an owner and manager: bureaucrats made mistakes, resources were allotted for reasons of politics rather than efficiency, and planning in the state sector tended simply to replicate past economic behaviour. Second, he argued that the state was also unnecessary as an owner and manager because Labour's traditional objectives of full employment, rising wages, education, and quality of life could be effectively achieved through the state's fiscal powers of taxation and spending. In 1962, Jay himself returned to this theme, insisting that '[p]rogressive direct taxation is ... more effective and immediate in its redistributive power than the spread of public ownership'.[14]

Crosland advanced an important distinction: not between a role for the state and no role, but rather between those roles which Crosland believed were unnecessary and inferior – the state as owner and manager – and those roles which Crosland believed were preferable – the state as taxer, spender, and direct deliverer of welfare services and education. This was hardly an isolated view, even at the time: the 1950 pamphlet *Keeping Left* (which bore the signatures of Barbara Castle, Ian Mikardo, and Richard Crossman among others) and Nye Bevan's *In Place of Fear* expressed disappointment with what nationalised industries had achieved up to that point; the former remarked that '[i]n the last few years we have learned to distinguish the means of socialisation from its ends'.

The revisionist appeal for reinterpreting the proper role for the state found inspiration and reinforcement in electoral constraints. Throughout the 1950s, a growing number of Labour leaders believed that the Party's reliance on the state as owner and manager was becoming a political handicap in a Britain in which public assessments regarding alternative possible solutions to problems were changing. Analyses of the 1950s defeats addressed factors from changing ideological times to shifts in Britain's class structure, but broadly converged on the problematic nature of emphasising ownership as a primary function of the central state. Indeed, opinion polls had shown that as early as during the Attlee Governments, public support for further nationalisations had sharply ebbed, and the implication that Labour intended to nationalise more and more industries appeared to be an overly valuable tool in the Tory campaign arsenal throughout the 1950s. The 1959 defeat made the issue urgent: in its aftermath, Jay voiced the concerns of many (initially too prudent to state it openly) when he famously wrote that '[t]he myth that we intended to "nationalise" anything and everything was very powerful in this election...We must destroy this myth decisively; otherwise we may never win again'. He went on to propose non-central state forms of social ownership, such as co-operatives and municipal enterprise, and specifically emphasised that a choice of an alternative means 'would not damage the real basic aim of the Movement'.[15]

The intra-party conflict sparked by the traumatising defeat of 1959 was bitter and hard-fought, and resulted in Hugh Gaitskell's famous defeat in his attempt to amend Clause IV of the Party constitution.[16] The dispute might have been made easier by the fact that Labour's use of central state ownership had been a politically contingent choice made at the end of the war, and by the revisionists' insistence that the debate did not concern Labour's ends themselves. Neither would prove to be of much value. Reformers had recognised that change would be politically difficult: Crosland had identified a 'psychological resistance to revisionism', and argued that champions of state ownership blurred the difference between commitments to broad ends and those to specific means, a habit he detested:

> the worst sort of confusion is the tendency to use the word [socialism] to describe, not a certain kind of society, or certain values which might be attributes of a society, but particular policies which are, or are thought to be, means of attaining this kind of society, or realising these attributes.[17]

But altering the menu of the preferred means by which a well-established party pursued its objectives proved complicated and traumatic. Many in Labour did find it extraordinarily difficult to abandon the means which had come to be seen either as ends in themselves or at least as symbols of progress towards Labour's objectives of equality, social justice, and dignity in work. Revisionists suggested that the opponents of reform lacked the pragmatic flexibility concerning means which a Tory dissident, Ian Gilmour, believes is required in all successful politics; they were instead, in Gilmour's words, 'indissolubly wedded to nationalisation in a state of unholy deadlock'.[18] The deadlock ensured that after Gaitskell's defeat over Clause IV, the issue of Labour's policy towards socialisation would be sidestepped indefinitely. With a few exceptions, Labour essentially adopted the policy of 'ni...ni' that the French Socialists adopted after 1947 until the Common Programme of the left in the 1970s and again after Mitterrand's U-turn in 1983: *neither* more nationalisations *nor* privatisations.

The revisionists' attitudes towards different forms of state action was not mere window-dressing for wholesale 'rollback', for the revisionists believed that markets continued to be inefficient as well as unjust. As a result, criticising the state as owner did not mean denigrating the state as deliverer of services, distributor of income and resources, or enforcer of outcomes by any other number of means. Labour leaders and thinkers continued to be united around a substantial confidence in the ability of the state effectively to staff, operate, and manage complex and extensive programmes of quality service delivery, including education and those associated with the welfare state (health care, job training, etc.); indeed it was in such activities that Crosland wished Labour to concentrate its efforts. He, Gaitskell, and the other modernisers of the period possessed a profound faith in the remaining potentialities of aggregate demand management and the largely untapped ones of indicative planning, in the service of an economic growth which they believed could by itself nearly make possible many of Labour's long-term social goals.

What would fill the gap of the state as owner would hardly be monotonic: the types of state action implemented in 1964–70 were striking in their diversity, and the Wilson years continued to demonstrate the extra-ordinarily politically contingent nature of the choices made regarding the role of the state in shaping economic, social, and even cultural life. When it came to the steel industry (and, had Labour won in 1970, probably Britain's ports as well), the role preferred was the state as owner and manager. When it came to cultural matters, state power was considered undesirable in some areas (pornography began being liberalised in 1959, gambling in 1960, homosexuality and abortion in 1967, theatre censorship in 1968, and divorce in 1969, and the death penalty was abolished in 1965), and where the state was used to shape culture – as with the significant expansion of funding to the Arts Council under Jennie Lee's authority – the actual production of art and now the construction of arts facilities were both 'contracted out'. In terms of construction, for example, not only were municipal authorities such as the Greater London Council deemed appropriate agents, but so were private developers. The aggregate demand management assicated with this era could even be construed as relying on contracting out: state structures were used to regulate the overall level of money supply and state spending, but the countless decisions constituting patterns of British wage settlements, consumption, and savings were left to millions of individual citizens.

Labour's continuing confidence in certain types of state action – and a corresponding ambition to retool the state machinery to further those types of action – was perhaps best demonstrated by the efforts of the Wilson Governments (1964–70) to reorient state action towards microeconomic intervention. While Wilson had opposed the scrapping of Clause IV ('You don't have to be a fundamentalist to say that Genesis is a part of the Bible'), he did not sponsor substantial further ventures of the state as owner and direct manager, but did mount a major effort based on the assumption that state structures could aid in development and modernisation: the state as adviser, shareholder, distributor of targeted resources. Indeed he believed that a state role of this kind was vital, and launched a corresponding and ambitious effort of departmental reorganisation and reform of the machinery of government in order to perform these functions effectively. Although Crosland had written that highly detailed state economic planning had been effectively undermined by a generalised 'disillusion-ment with the whole notion of trying to control short-term production decisions from Whitehall', he served as a junior Minister at the Department of Economic Affairs (DEA), which was meant to be, in Peter Hennessy's words, 'Labour's secret weapon' against the traditionalist orthodoxy of the Treasury.[19]

This overall agenda belied a desire to borrow what was perceived as the best of France's post-war developmental state, which was understood in terms of both objectives (technological and industrial modernisation) and means (targeted state aid and imitation of certain features of the French state machinery). The results included:

- the 1965 strategic 'National Plan' drawn up by the DEA;
- the Wilson Governments' numerous efforts to aid private industry in research and development, applications of technological innovations, and export competitiveness;
- the Ministry of Technology's effort to buy into industry in order to produce a network of interlocking relationships suitable for the transmission of the 'indications' inherent in indicative planning;
- and, after 1974, the various efforts at planning agreements and industrial policy made through the National Enterprise Board (NEB).

This ambitious attempt to use state structures in new ways proved disappointing, both before 1970 and after 1974, being in many ways eclipsed by wage issues and especially macroeconomic concerns such as the balance of payments and inflation. The other experiments of 1974–79 reflected a rapidly spreading uncertainty as to how the state should intervene in economic and social life, and ultimately a collapse in the intellectual credibility of several schools of thought. Labour's broad 1974 programmatic proposal to renew the nationalisation agenda seemed to indicate an enduring faith in the state as owner, but the tendency (begun under Heath) for the state to bail out failed industries suggested the state as last-resort and caretaker of decline. Inflation was attacked through tripartite bargaining and wage policies which removed bargaining from collective private hands, but these approaches only worsened Labour's relationship with its own union base. By 1979, Labour was in trouble, and not just electorally; its understanding of what the state should and could do was in crisis.[20]

It was largely within the context of this reformulated and uncertain agenda that the second aspect of Labour's troubled relationship with the state took shape, internal to Labour's relationship with state structures and Labour plans for them. First, the relationship between Whitehall and at least some portions of Labour became more sceptical and tense. While members of the Attlee Governments had converged in agreement on the civil service's loyalty and efficacy in implementing their programme, Labour Ministers' views on the subject of Whitehall's willingness to attempt to execute a Labour programme in good faith became increasingly polarised during the Wilson and Callaghan Governments (1964–70 and 1974–79). Criticisms from 1964–70 would only sharpen after Callaghan, with especially intense complaints coming from the Party's left, as Barbara Castle, Tony Benn, and others portrayed at least the senior civil service as a notable obstacle to the socialist agenda.[21] But more specifically, arguments were advanced that Whitehall had proved willing and able to implement nationalisation but would need to be made considerably less 'amateur' and more efficient if it was to implement more complex socialist next steps, particularly indicative planning of developmentalist modernisation. It was in this spirit that a Labour in opposition in the early 1960s analysed Whitehall and that a Labour in power after 1964 embarked on a significant round of departmental reorganisations.

In part these efforts aimed simply at improving overall Whitehall efficacy, for instance in the endorsement of the Fulton report's call for more uniform civil service grading and the creation of a Civil Service College to facilitate the emergence of a more specialised and highly trained administrative cadre. In addition, much of the attention paid early on under Wilson to the machinery of state was harnessed to new functions of planning and microeconomic intervention, to be accomplished through the new DEA and the Ministry of Technology overseeing the Industrial Reorganisation Corporation (IRC). The proposed Civil Service College stood to mirror the French *Ecole Nationale d'Administration* and contribute to a developmentalist state on the French model.

This envy of the French state role and the machinery that appeared to all observers to make that role possible, extended to Edward Heath as well.[22] As opposition leader and Prime Minister, Heath would question first principles of both the role of the state and the machinery needed to achieve that. The October 1970 White Paper on *The Reorganisation of Central Government* and the establishment of both the Central Policy Review Staff (CPRS) and Programme Analysis Review (PAR) were in some sense extensions of the ambitious focus on machinery which Wilson initially displayed (although both the CPRS and PAR were limited by the subsequent Labour Governments before being abolished after 1979). After 1974, the Labour Government promoted planning agreements through the Department of Industry, but in terms of significant retooling of Whitehall in the service of changing state functions, the 'era of large-scale departmental reorganisations was over'.[23]

### Abandoning state ownership and management as means but not Labour ends (1983–97)

Since 1979, Labour has faced several new crises regarding both the roles it had crafted for state structures since 1945 and the machinery of the state that it had contributed to and cultivated. Labour's implicit compromise regarding the state as owner proved untenable; the roles for the state as aggregate demand manager and especially as indicative planner were largely abandoned; and, most unexpected of all, the notion of the state as direct administrator and deliverer of services came under attack and began to erode sharply. Many Labourites continued in their pattern of interpreting such challenges (which concerned the specific ways in which Labour used the state in pursuit of its goals) to constitute challenges to Labour's overall social and economic goals themselves, and fought them tenaciously as a result. Time and again, Tory challenges to Labour legacies were permitted if not propelled by electoral support, as public views of the perceived efficacy and efficiency of state-based solutions to social problems continued a gradual process of change. As a result, the battles over means almost always resulted in eventual surrender anyway, and in the process not only took an enormous toll on Labour's short- and medium-term popularity but have also distracted attention from the striking fact that many of Labour's core objectives – especially the quality of life delivered by social services and the income distribution which made that possible – survived 18 years of Tory rule largely intact.

The 1980s and 1990s have posed a series of profound challenges to Labour's traditional agenda for the state, and presented more sharply than ever distinctions between the ends to which Labour continued to be devoted and the means politically available to it. The first challenge concerned ownership. By 1979, the notion of the state as owner had already been brought into question, and the Party had seen the notion of the state as owner and direct manager of industry indicted from within its ranks and without, and after 1979 these indictments were translated into one of Margaret Thatcher's most successful challenges of traditional Labour uses of the state. The Conservative privatisation project, which continued well into the 1990s, met with considerable if ineffective resistance both from those forces within the Labour movement which considered nationalised enterprises a socialist goal in themselves and from those who might under other circumstances have been latter-day revisionists but who greeted most Thatcherite initiatives with reflexive opposition.

However, it was not only most Conservative leaders who were no longer enamoured of the state as industrial owner. Many voters were not either, an orientation only reinforced as some of them also became shareholders in privatised industries. The electoral constraints which after 1983 were generally acknowledged to exist regarding state ownership forced renewed discussion of ends vs. means, and generated many of the same lines of argument as had surfaced in the wrenching and inconclusive debate over Clause IV. The terms of that debate, however, were not simply repeated but were, rather, posed in more profound terms. If the debate of 1959–60 revolved around the question 'can we win if we propose further nationalisations?' the debate after the 1983 defeat asked 'can we win if we oppose extensive denationalisation?'. 'Ni…ni' was no longer sustainable as a compromise. Ultimately, it was neither debate nor the policy review but events which resolved the discussion, as surveys and elections demonstrated that proposals for renationalisation would contribute significantly to maintaining Labour at the margins of British politics. Just as the Conservatives were forced after 1945 to accept a role for the state which many preferred not to implement, so Labour was impelled – on the state as owner more than on any other issue – to accept policies which its Governments would certainly never have implemented themselves. But the fact that for much of the decade Labour attempted a last-ditch defence of the state as owner – conceding privatisation in area after area only after they were accomplished facts – did more than reflect divisive politics internal to the Party: it associated Labour in the minds of many voters with an array of state roles which by the 1980s simply lacked credibility or desirability, and almost certainly helped do as much damage to the Party's image as had the Winter of Discontent (in the wake of which, after all, Labour had still won 37 per cent of the vote, compared to 28 per cent in 1983 and 31 per cent in 1987).

But several other roles which Labour had come to assign to state structures also came under assault after 1979. Among these was the state as catalyst of developmental modernisation. That Conservatives altered the role of the state in this area came as little surprise: Conservatives had – at least in principle – been condemning systematic intervention in industry since the late 1960s, and by 1979, Tory (and public) confidence was low that state structures were effective or efficient means of directing capital to either promising or failing industries, planning investment patterns, or encouraging development of poorer regions (subsidies continued to flow in politically problematic Northern Ireland). But even many in Labour met this shift in the state's posture with relative indifference. Many in the Party had harboured suspicions about the ability of Government to plan a complex economy any better than private companies seemed able (or unable) to do, and specific planning projects had often disappointed; few believed by the 1990s that state intervention was the key to improved international competitiveness, for example. Other factors may also have contributed to the relative political ease with which the state's role as indicative planner was abandoned: the Party's commitment to planning had always been vague; it was one of the state roles not associated with the essence of the Labour heyday embodied in Attlee's Governments; and it had been revived under Wilson with far fewer years of debate from below and far further from the Party's formative period than was the case with nationalisations.

In this sense, the most unexpected assault on the specific roles which the post-war consensus had assigned to state structures concerned its role as direct administrator and deliverer of welfare and health services. The Thatcher and Major Governments began to implement one component of the global neo-liberal revolution that has become of increasing importance: the notion that even when the state budget pays for services associated with the welfare state, it should contract out actual delivery of those services. In the UK, this trend was not part of a systematic policy of cutting overall levels of support for the welfare state (levels which have not fluctuated significantly), but was an attack on what had been an almost unquestioned cross-party consensus. Traditionally, state personnel had acted not only as staffers of the armed forces and tax collectors but also as educators of children, jailers of inmates, trainers of the unemployed, caretakers for the elderly and disabled, builders and then managers of housing estates, and doctors, nurses, and hospital administrators. With increasing momentum after 1979, neo-liberals proposed that actual delivery of these services be contracted out to non-state providers.

Even initial steps in these directions in Britain have been condemned by some as particularly pernicious and inappropriate forms of 'privatisation', but contracting out social services is in reality very different from the privatisation of nationalised enterprises. In the case of the latter, the state abandoned nearly all responsibility for and participation in those entities, whereas in the former, the state continues to pay for services, selects the providers, sets minimum standards they must meet, and oversees their results; in sum, it makes possible and enforces the outcome of service delivery. As with state ownership of industry, this challenge does not immediately concern the degree to which Labour's traditional social and economic objectives are being fulfilled, only the means by which they are. Perhaps nowhere is this challenge to traditional state roles more advanced than in the United States, where, beginning from inconsequential levels in the early 1980s, today perhaps half of the American states pay for but contract out management of jails, child care, drug and alcohol abuse therapy, adoption services, programmes for the elderly, hospital operations and administration, mental health and mental retardation programmes, community health services, job training and collection of child support payments. The result is what has been termed a 'mixed economy of welfare', in which Governments pay for services but private organisations deliver them. For example, the federal and state Government provide the vouchers for America's basic nutrition programme ('food stamps') and recipients use them to acquire food from private grocery stores.[24]

A number of common arguments mounted against this reorientation of the state's functions are misdirected. There is no reason why services should decline in quality simply because they are contracted out: state-delivered services were often unsatisfactory anyway, and a contracting-out state can concentrate its efforts on monitoring social service providers as carefully as it wishes; for that matter, recipients with vouchers can and do 'vote with their feet' for the providers they prefer. In the case of social and health service provisioning, concern that profit should not be a motive – however debatable that concern might be even in principle – can be rendered irrelevant: much American contracting out goes to not-for-profit groups and organisations. Perhaps just as important for politicians, political parties, and the people who study them, contracting out not only does not mean the end of state standards and oversight, but it also does not mean the end of a compelling need for legislative skills, debate, and disagreement. At least one major failure of contracting out in the Thatcher years was the residential care programme for the elderly, begun in 1981 but eventually abandoned in 1993 after design flaws accidentally provided incentives for mushrooming costs. The only necessary losers from contracting out are state bureaucracies and the concept of public sector employment, and surely they are not what the Labour Party's historical mission has been all about.

Moreover, it is untrue even to suggest that retooling state roles and state structures away from the state as owner and manager and direct deliverer of services is a complete rupture with Labour's past choice of means. Those older state roles were not part of Labour's original heritage, not even of Labour's 1918 constitution, but rather the result of choices made by Labour, contingent on the perceived wisdoms and exigencies of particular historical circumstances. Moreover, the state as owner and manager or as direct deliverer of services was never the norm in matters of culture and the arts or, under Wilson, in terms of aggregate demand management or indicative planning. Rather, Labour has itself utilised the range of possible state roles in the pursuit of its overall social, economic and even cultural objectives.

In other words, through the 1980s and 1990s, Labour could have remained committed to its core social ends or objectives even while tolerating changes in the contingent, state-based means by which it had historically pursued those ends – the state as owner and even as administrator and provider. Not only would this not necessarily mean a relaxation of ends, but it would not even mean the abandonment of all uses of the state as means to those ends: the state stands to remain crucial to the post-administrative welfare state as enforcer of outcomes (e.g., making possible and monitoring delivery of social services). For this reason alone, neo-revisionism is not Thatcherism, as Martin Smith emphasises: the Labour policy review of the 1980s left intact a positive role for the state in helping individuals 'gain greater freedom, choice and welfare', as well as helping ensure stable economic growth, research and development, and other broad economic goals. Among the ways the policy review's conclusions resembled Crosland's 'revisionism' is precisely in arguing that different means – including different means of state intervention – can be utilised to pursue the same ends.[25]

Given these changes in the roles the state plays, the past 18 years of Conservative governance have also logically witnessed important alterations in the management of the machinery of the state itself. The abandonment of the state as owner of industry entailed dismantling the administrative and regulatory machinery erected to control and direct the nationalised sector, while the abandonment of indicative planning meant dismantling much of Wilson's and then Heath's industrial policy-related reorganisation and staffing. Even more striking conceptually are the changes enacted with the contracting out of certain social services, with obvious declines in personnel and the development of mechanisms for contracting, monitoring, and standard-setting. A central goal of the Next Steps studies was precisely the separation of policy-making functions from service delivery. In all of these changes the tension between the dispersal and the concentration of power for which the Thatcher years were famous was visible. No better example could be given of the profound gap which may separate the ends a movement pursues from the means by which it does so: it is in terms of the means/ends disaggregation that we can best understand the often commented upon irony of the Conservatives seeking to disperse power from the central state by first concentrating it in executive and national state hands to accomplish that – overriding not only Parliament but also local government in the process.

This was joined by the additional irony of Conservative Governments adopting some of the Labour Party's own proposals for the reform of the state machinery. It had been the Conservatives in opposition in the late 1960s who called for bureaucratic (especially departmental) amalgamation and simplification in Whitehall, and Fabians (beginning in 1973) who responded with a contrasting call for greater diversification and the use of semi-autonomous agencies to enhance state efficacy, efficiency, transparency, and even accountability.[26] In the end, it would be Thatcher who moved to begin reorganising state structures along those lines, in the Next Steps programme aimed at expanding decision-making autonomy and stricter accountability regarding both inputs (costs) and results.[27] Some in Labour have welcomed the impulse behind these changes even while criticising specific forms, while others have argued that agencies not under strict Cabinet control are susceptible to greater political partisanship in civil service staffing.[28]

Since the early 1980s, in other words, Labour has not been fighting the last war – a term which might describe a rearguard action fought in defence of ideological first principles – so much as disputing tactics while fighting against an enemy who was effectively focused on strategy. It is testimony to the power of the moral discourse of post-war western European societies that even a Labour Party distracted by battles over the specific means by which its objectives would be pursued and the machinery of state needed for that, and one marginalised by repeated electoral defeats, could nonetheless return to power in 1997 with certain portions of its preferred political landscape intact. Above all, public support for a relevant welfare state, and the distributive fiscality that requires, proved in its essential features impervious to the Thatcherite emphasis on individual self-reliance.

One can only imagine how different Labour's margin for manoeuvre might have been in 1997 – indeed, how different the new Labour Party might have been – had the Party spent the past 18 years cultivating the basis of social democratic policy-making embodied in support for the welfare state instead of confusing that with a state-owned aircraft industry and instead of promoting outmoded state structures, promoting efficient delivery by proposing innovative answers to such questions as:

- how to design incentives in out-sourcing contracts so that private providers have an interest in delivering quality welfare services;
- how to measure private providers' perfomance with meaningful indicators as opposed to easily quantifiable but misleading ones;
- how to minimise risks of fraud by contractors;
- how to make monitoring of delivery less expensive, perhaps through competing private providers and then letting citizens choose the providers they find more satisfying.

## A new danger for New Labour?

The analysis above argues that Labour has made a series of politically contingent choices regarding the means by which it has chosen to pursue its social and economic ends; that those means involved extensive and intensive roles for the central state; that erosion of public support for those means should not have been confused with Labour's overall objectives; and therefore that received means can be sacrificed without sacrificing ends. This argument is based on the key assumption that the means by which an end is pursued do not in turn affect the end itself, and so it is of concern that a number of political scientists and policy-makers have advanced the notion that the means by which policies are pursued do influence ends, specifically by affecting the support which those ends are likely to attract.

In particular, both social democratic political scientists and neo-liberal policy-makers have suggested that welfare state policies can be designed so that they either reinforce or erode sectoral and class support for distribution of income and the welfare state as a whole. Is it possible that changing the way the British state serves as a means to fulfilling Labour's objectives appears harmless at first, but might be very gradually eroding the public support for income distribution and welfare state which withstood the Thatcher years?[29]

The first version of the notion that means (policy design) can affect ends themselves (support for policy objectives) has been advanced not so much in written theorising as in real-world behaviour by neo-liberal policy-makers, who in a number of cases have designed the way in which welfare state programmes are paid for in the hope of eroding long-term support for the programmes themselves. This approach has most often taken the form of separating taxation for different social programmes from the general tax pool of the state. Neo-liberal policy-makers in different countries in the 1980s, for example, made support for pensions, unemployment assistance, and health services distinguishable from general tax payments so as to make clear to ratepayers their costliness, which they believed was hidden through pooling all tax funds. Evidence regarding the efficacy of this strategy has yet to be generated.

Secondly, political scientists Gosta Esping-Andersen and Bo Rothstein have separately advanced analyses which suggest that the design not of the inputs of social programs but of their outputs can crucially influence public – above all cross-class – support for the welfare state with which European social democracy is associated. Esping-Andersen argues that the fundamental social democratic challenge is political: achieving middle-class support for distributive welfare state policies, that is, a cross-class alliance including both workers and significant portions of the middle class. His study of divergent socialist experiences in Scandinavia concludes that welfare state policies have been designed either in ways which tended to reinforce such cross-class alliances or in ways which tended to erode them. In other words, configurations of policy, rather than mere epiphenomenal means by which ends are pursued, in fact help to determine what political alliances were likely to form over the long term and hence which ends are politically viable at all. Specifically, where welfare state benefits are reserved only for the poorest or where different levels of benefits accrue to groups based on their income, the interests of different income groups are pitted against each other, and cross-class solidarity becomes less likely:

> It is of paramount importance that entitlements and services be universal, generous, and attractive; otherwise, there will be incentives for the better-off to seek private market solutions…[and] exit opportunities destroy the basis for broad solidarity. Social democratic class formation depends on the eradication of differential entitlements, means-tested and targeted benefits, individualistic insurance schemes, and 'self-help' principles. Reforms must avoid situations in which collective services breed discontent between those who pay and those who receive.[30]

Rothstein derives a comparable conclusion from a somewhat different theoretical approach, arguing that individuals can develop a 'contingent consensus' on welfare state policies when the policies themselves are designed with certain specific characteristics. He presents survey evidence that the support which different welfare state policies attract from the middle class sometimes vary substantially within a single country consistent with those design features, and that middle-class ratepayers are notably more likely to support welfare state policies which they perceive (a) to have objectives they believe just; (b) are supported financially by more or less all citizens at least in terms of a limited contribution; and (c) are run efficiently rather than wastefully. Rothstein's prescription is similar to that of Esping-Andersen: with the added caveat that social services must be efficient to attract support, Rothstein also emphasises the importance of the universality of social benefits.[31] The powerful and enduring cross- class support for the National Health Service which benefits all – and the lack of support for nationalised industries which only benefited some – both conform closely to this analysis.

However, even if Esping-Andersen and Rothstein (and strategic-thinking neo-liberal policy-makers) are right to conclude that the means which a political movement chooses can end up affecting the ends which it pursues, their interpretations do not suggest that the changes which have been made in state roles and state machinery in Britain since 1945 would threaten cross-class support for the welfare state. First, social and health benefits can remain universal, even if actual delivery of them is contracted out to non-state providers; the danger for social democracy would be the expanded means-testing which some Tories began calling for soon after 1945, not contracting out universal benefits. Second, generally pooled tax payments for the aggregation of welfare state programmes can be retained (against alternatives such as *The Economist*'s recent suggestion that the NHS should be paid for through a dedicated fee). Moreover, Rothstein's analysis suggests that certain recent reforms may actually strengthen support for the welfare state: if private (including not-for-profit) providers of social services are perceived to be more efficient than state agencies, then contracting out may actually augment middle-class willingness to pay the taxes needed to support the programmes in question. Esping-Andersen and Rothstein's warnings about the long-term political dangers of poor short-term policy design speak to the creation of 'residual' welfare state policies in the US, not recent reforms in the UK.

Certainly, ending or at least sharply curtailing the role of the state as direct provider of social and health services has not yet been associated with any apparent significant erosion of support for the funding necessary for those services. Using 1979 as a benchmark, public support has clearly declined for nationalisation of industries, but often overlooked by defenders of the state's old roles is the striking fact that support for income distribution and the provision of welfare services, especially to the needy, has remained remarkably stable.[32] In the United States, the 1990s have brought the end of income support as an entitlement, an event which the liberal US Senator Daniel Patrick Moynihan described as 'the day the New Deal died'. But nowhere in Britain or in western Europe has such a significant shift regarding ends themselves occurred.

Recent political experiences, however, do suggest that one circumstance can erode support for Labour, for its goals, and especially its ability to pursue them from office, and that is not a change in means and state roles, but rather obstinate refusals to modify old state-based forms whose credibility and popularity have themselves eroded. It seems an unlikely coincidence that the two western European socialist parties which suffered the greatest declines in support for ideological reasons in the 1980s and early 1990s were Labour and the French Socialists: parties in the countries with among the largest state-owned industrial sectors in Europe and which were tightly bound – by history, union ties, and the profound power of inertia – to state ownership and management as ends in themselves.[33] Altering the menu of available means runs the risk that support for social democracy might erode; refusing to alter that menu ensures that it does.

## New state opportunities for New Labour

The new Labour Government faces many of the same constraints which faced the Party in 18 years of opposition in the sense that public support remains low for many traditional roles assigned to the state in pursuit of its objectives. However, the new Labour Government has two great advantages: first, it has apparently been freed of the disputes over means that have dogged it for decades, and it is also greeted by a number of historical opportunities for reformulating the means by which it pursues its most enduring goals. First, the role of the state has by no means been thoroughly discredited: income distribution and efficient delivery of social and health services remain popular, and municipal and especially regional governments may provide avenues for policy-making which is granted greater popular legitimacy by the public than is the central state. In fact, Labour's evolving views on regional government should serve as a model for the Party of the value of programmatic flexibility concerning means to enduring ends.[34] Second, the reforms begun under the rubric Next Steps constitute at least in intent a dramatic break with traditional forms of organising state structures, and Labour now has the opportunity to continue or modify this programme in ways that reinforce efficacy and efficiency. And third, because the Party appears to have buried four decades of internal disputes over whether means to its ends are adaptable or permanent, Labour has an opportunity not only to help retool the state to better pursue its historic goals of quality of life and income distribution, but also to elevate to the level of principle the idea that its means are contingent, an idea that characterised Labour in power and practice but eluded its programme and stated teachings. To a surprising extent, it is Labour and not the Tories who have won the more important post-war debate – over ends and not means – and Labour now has the opportunity to focus its attention and energies where it counts.

# Notes

1 G.K. Fry, *The Administrative 'Revolution' in Whitehall: A Study of the Politics of Administrative Change in British Central Government Since the 1950s*, Croom Helm, 1981, p.46.

2 Robert A. Dahl, 'Workers' Control of Industry and the British Labour Party', *American Political Science Review*, No 41, 1947, pp.875–900.

3 Kevin Theakston, *The Labour Party and Whitehall*, Routledge, 1992, chapters 1–3.

4 For the debate over how the NHS was to be structured, see John E. Pater, *The Making of the National Health Service*, King Edward's Hospital Fund for London, 1981, chapter 5.

5 Regarding the potentially sweeping proposed legislation for controls, see Neil Rollings, ' "The Reichstag Method of Governing"? The Attlee Governments and Permanent Economic Controls', in Helen Mercer, Neil Rollings and Jim D. Tomlinson, eds., *Labour Governments and Private Industry: The Experience of 1945–1951*, Edinburgh University Press, 1992, pp.15–26.

6 Douglas Jay, *The Socialist Case*, Faber and Faber, 1937, p.317.

7 Bernard Donoughue and G.W. Jones, *Herbert Morrison: Portrait of a Politician*, Weidenfeld and Nicolson, 1973, p.153.

8 Ian Gilmour, *Dancing with Dogma*, Simon and Schuster, 1992, p.93.

9 In the last of these, the nationalised sector was largely the product of prewar events, and continued to be organised within Mussolini's IRI.

10 Co-determination was initiated in core heavy industries by the Adenauer Governments, but substantially expanded in 1976 by a Social Democratic-dominated coalition. Douglas Jay considered this approach worth experimenting with in the UK. See Jay, *Socialism in the New Society*, Longman, 1962, pp.331–33.

11 Perhaps the leading case in which a 'post-war cultural consensus' did not emerge was France, where substantial political battles over the role of the state in religious education continued into the 1980s.

12 Keynes had been critical of the wartime Council for Encouragement of Music and the Arts' initial policy and became chairman of CEMA in

1942. For a discussion of CEMA's evolution, see Robert Hewison, *Culture and Consensus; England, Art and Politics since 1940*, Methuen, 1995, pp.29–44.

13  Antony Crosland, *The Future of Socialism*, Jonathan Cape, rev. ed. 1963, chapters 2 and 4. Crosland nonetheless endorsed Labour proposals to 'municipalise' (at least sub-standard) private rental property. For a general overview of the revisionist debates, see Stephen Haseler, *The Gaitskellites: Revisionism in the British Labour Party, 1951–64*, Macmillan, 1969.

14  Jay, *Socialism in the New Society*, p.180.

15  The *Forward* article is reprinted in Douglas Jay, *Change and Fortune: A Political Record*, Hutchinson, 1980, pp.273–75.

16  Brian Brivati offers a recent and important discussion of this dispute in *Hugh Gaitskell*, Richard Cohen Books, 1996, chapter 14.

17  Crosland, *The Future of Socialism*, pp.61–64, 65.

18  Gilmour, *Dancing with Dogma*, p.93.

19  Crosland, *Future of Socialism*, p. 343; Peter Hennessy, *Whitehall*, Secker and Warburg, 1989, p.182.

20  Summaries of the two periods in power can be found respectively in Richard Coopey, 'Industrial Policy in the White Heat of the Scientific Revolution', in Richard Coopey, Steven Fielding and Nick Tiratsoo, (eds), *The Wilson Governments: 1964–1970*, Pinter Publishers, 1993, pp.102–22; and David Coates, *Labour in Power? A Study of the Labour Government, 1974–1979*, Longman, 1980, chapter 3.

21  Regarding this shift in assessments over time, see Theakston, *The Labour Party and Whitehall*, chapter 2.

22  Hennessy, *Whitehall*, p.238.

23  Theakston, *The Labour Party and Whitehall*, p.137.

24  Only the state of Mississippi provides foodstuffs directly to food stamp programme recipients. For an overview of the contracting out of federal, state, and local American welfare and health services, see *Social and Health Service Privatization* and *Health and Social Services in the Post-Welfare State*, reports published by the Privatization Center of the Reason Foundation. These trends in social services have been matched by other developments which defy easy state/non-state categorisation, including enforcement of collective standards of conduct in such mixed public/private settings as the 'homeowner-associated' neighborhoods and commerical malls in which many Americans spend an increasing amount of their lives. See for example Evan McKenzie, *Privatopia: Homeowner Associations and the Rise of Residential Private Government*, Yale University Press, 1994.

25  Martin J. Smith, 'A Return to Revisionism? The Labour Party's Policy Review', in Smith and Joanna Spear, (eds), *The Changing Labour Party*, Routledge, 1992, pp.24–26. For a statement of this kind from within

Labour, see Giles Radice, *Labour's Path to Power: The New Revisionism*, Macmillan, 1989.

26  Kevin Theakston, 'The Heath Government, Whitehall and the Civil Service', in Stuart Ball and Anthony Seldon, (eds), *The Heath Government, 1970–74: A Reappraisal*, Longman, 1996, p.78; Theakston, *The Labour Party and Whitehall*, pp.134–35, 199.

27  E.g., Patricia Greer, *Transforming Central Government: The Next Steps Initiative*, Open University Press, 1994; somewhat exaggerated claims about Next Steps' accomplishments are making their way into international debates over 'reinventing government': David Osborne and Peter Plastrik, *Banishing Bureaucracy: The Five Strategies for Reinventing Government*, Addison-Wesley, 1997. A more critical discussion appears in Grant Jordan, *The British Administrative System: Principles versus Practice*, Routledge, 1994, especially chapter 5.

28  Giles Radice has been among the leading Labour figures backing the principles behind Next Steps, while Tony Wright, *Beyond the Patronage State*, Fabian Pamphlet 569, Fabian Society, 1995 is among the recent critiques addressing partisan appointments.

29  This analysis assumes that the objective which Labour wishes to preserve at this point from neo-liberal challenges is a mildly distributive welfare state and not the goal of true social and economic equality which privatisation was said to undermine. The focus here is not on the latter because it was lost to Labour decades ago and not as the result of any recent changes: to say that the Labour Party 'had acknowledged covertly since 1945' that at most it would 'manage capitalism' (as Brivati does in *Gaitskell*, p.441) is ultimately the same as saying that in 1945 Labour, like many of its continental European counterparts, abandoned any short – or even medium-term prospect of fundamentally revising capitalist property relations and the existence of distinct social classes. Privatisations and contracting out cannot be blamed for the loss of what has been lost for some time.

30  Gosta Esping-Andersen, *Politics Against Markets: The Social Democratic Road to Power*, Princeton University Press, 1985, p33.

31  Bo Rothstein, 'Administration and Legitimation: A Comparative Perspective', paper delivered at the American Political Science Association annual conference, 29 August–1 September 1996.

32  See for instance the data in Peter Taylor-Gooby, *Public Opinion, Ideology and State Welfare*, Routledge, 1985.

33  Labour lost over a quarter of its share of the vote between 1979 and 1983, while the French Socialists lost nearly half of their first-round parliamentary ballots between 1981 and 1993. The Italian Socialist Party (PSI) has undergone a steeper percentage decline in support, but primarily for non-ideological reasons. The contrasting socialist experiences of the 1980s are the theme of Herbert Kitschelt, *The*

*Transformation of European Social Democracy*, Cambridge University Press, 1994.

34 See for example, David Marquand, 'Halfway to Citizenship? The Labour Party and Constitutional Reform', in Smith and Spear (eds), *Changing Labour Party*, pp.44–58.

# Commentary

*William Plowden*

It is important to recognise that, whatever the superficial battles, there was a fairly high degree of bipartisan consensus on the role of the state during the post-war era, particularly on industrial policy generally and, say, policy towards the regions and even the nationalised industries more specifically. It is also important to recognise that such policies were not necessarily the failures they were made out to be by the Thatcher Government. Even that Government, where it moved away from those policies, often did so in an unplanned and opportunistic manner. State intervention in certain areas is not necessarily an economic or a political liability and, in spite of Labour's desire to distance itself from the past, should not be seen as such by the new Government.

On the other hand, it is undeniable that certain elements of the Conservative legacy as regards the state are extremely and explicitly valuable to the Blair administration. For one thing, constraints on trade union power mean that the public is much less likely to expect that the advent of a Labour Government threatens a repetition of the 'Winter of Discontent'. Other developments, though less immediately apparent, are just as important. For instance, there is the stress on evaluation and assessment which now pervades the public sector culture: things are no longer done just because that's the way they've always been done, and people – and the units they work in – are judged in terms of results delivered against sets of criteria based on objectives. The new Government can use these and other techniques to get more out of a civil service (though one rather demoralised by the Conservatives) than they've ever been able to before – particularly if they capitalise on their evident desire to ensure political managerial control of the centre of the machine, for example, via a newly empowered Cabinet Office.

Another element of the Conservative legacy that should be built on is the changing relationship between the providers and the consumers of state services, a changing relationship symbolised until now by the Citizens' Charter, but which is also reflected in the ideas promoted by left-leaning think-tanks like the Institute for Public Policy Research. The new Labour

Government needs to realise that the issue here – just as it is with constitutional changes affecting the relationship between the central and the local state and also freedom of information – is not so much the diminution of the state as the sharing of state power with those whom the power ultimately exists to benefit.

# Commentary

*Martin Smith*

Although it is all too easy to caricature states as either weak or strong, it is clear that Labour did not develop the sorts of interventionist or corporatist mechanisms which were common in other countries. Labour Governments did very little to use their position to expand state power: indeed in a range of policy areas they reduced it. The 1945 Labour Government basically gave up wartime planning controls, and when it created the NHS, although it was intended to be a national service, it was actually one that gave a tremendous amount of power to the doctors and was essentially locally run. Similarly, industrial relations, particularly in that immediate post-war period, was left to voluntary arrangements between trade unions and business.

It is, then, quite difficult to sustain the argument that Labour had a strong state tradition. Labour Governments, like Conservative Governments, relied on a whole range of different forms of organisations for delivering services. With the exception of social security, it has always been rare for the British state to be the executor of policy; it nearly always relies on local government, quangos, non-departmental bodies, public corporations and other organisations to deliver services. As many have argued, the Labour Party does not really have a theory of the state. It has tended to accept the tradition going back to Laski that the state is neutral. Labour's position on the state is contingent: its Governments have tended to accept the state that they inherit, without much of an idea of how they were going to change it to deliver their policy goals. Even when it came to, say, industrial policy, when the machinery existed, Labour did not really extend the role of the state much further than the Conservatives: though in the 1960s Labour may have tried to build on the Tories' move in the direction of planning, in the 1970s the National Enterprise Board was really limited to rescuing lame ducks and only one planning agreement – which was broken – was signed.

But if Labour's theory of the state, or the state under Labour, is contingent, to what extent it is true to say the nature of the state itself is contingent? To a large extent it is a reflection of the historical, economic and political conditions of Britain: the nature of the state was shaped by economic pressures, by what Governments were trying to do and by the sorts of coalitions which were necessary to win elections. Whether Labour actually had much choice over what sort of state it had in the post-war period and what sort of state it has in the post-Thatcher period is an open question. If you look at the way the state has changed in the post-Thatcher period, the changes really have been quite fundamental and ideological. They have been driven by Thatcherism, but also by wider economic forces, by the fact that people have been less prepared to accept higher taxation and redistribution, while believing that there is less the state can do about the economy and other social problems. In short, the changing nature of the state in the 1980s and 1990s is a structural, rather than just a contingent, change.

In addition, the state that Labour took over in 1997 is fundamentally different from the state in 1979, not least in terms of how it is organised – one of the areas where Thatcherism really did have a major impact. True, this creates opportunities for Labour, but there is a fundamental problem in that the Party has not really thought about what this new type of state means and about the constraints it imposes. The thing about contracts and agencies, regulatory bodies and privatised industries is that the direct line of command is broken. As the controversy over the national lottery organisers, Camelot, illustrated, once a contract is signed, the relationship between the purchaser and the provider has been set for five years and so it becomes more difficult to change policy: the Government can persuade but not command, and that makes governing more difficult and less predictable. If you look at industrial policy – the way the Department of Trade and Industry has changed, the way in which the Treasury seems to be driving large elements of economic policy – even if Labour wanted to develop a much more interventionist industrial policy, it would now be very difficult to implement it without making tremendous changes in terms of the nature of the state. The amount of effort to do that, and the cost and time involved, will probably make it untenable.

Attempts to create a stronger No. 10 and better co-ordinate policy miss the point: how is the centre actually going to control all these new regulatory bodies, these new contracts, these new agencies? The British state has become differentiated and this limits the impact of central control. Regulation and hands-off control may be suitable for issues like water pollution or reducing leaks, but would it, for example, allow a Government to reduce inequality or promote social justice? It seems unlikely that any Government will reassert direct controls: after you get past one or two contracts or agencies and it becomes hundreds, how do you control them? Under the traditional model of the state and the old civil service, despite its problems, its boundaries for behaviour were very tight: there were, in terms of social security for example, very strict sets of rules about who should get what benefit and how. If you can spread power out to different bodies but you want to achieve egalitarian goals it is very difficult unless you have some way of controlling those bodies and ensuring that they are treating people equally, or at least achieve equity.

Interestingly, of course, Labour seems set to fragment state power even further through devolution, through the independence of the Bank of England, and via greater integration into Europe. Such a change may be good in the context of a shift away from a parliamentary system where power was concentrated in the 'elective dictatorship' of the executive; but at least under the parliamentary state there were clear lines of accountability, direction and control. Nowadays there are really only two ways to increase control and to improve accountability. One is to strengthen the regulatory framework – and there are some signs that the new Government will be prepared to make some changes. Secondly, there are ways of making these organisations more directly accountable to their stakeholders by allowing greater participation and in some areas introducing an electoral element. Labour needs to think about democratising different elements of the new state by introducing bottom-up accountability rather than maintaining the fiction that it occurs through the ministers: ministerial accountability maintains the ethos of hierarchical control without the ability to achieve it. To move away from this form of accountability, though, would be an important break from the parliamentary tradition that has to date dominated Labour's thinking on the state. Whether it can or will happen, of course, remains to be seen.

# Chapter 6

# Labour and the constitution
## Part I: the record

*Vernon Bogdanor*

The 1997 general election was a triumph not only for Tony Blair but also for Margaret Thatcher. It was her final triumph in that it ensured that Thatcherism would survive a change of Government. Indeed, Labour was seen as safe to entrust with power only after it had fully accepted the broad outlines of Thatcherism: the priority of the attack on inflation, the importance of the market, the need for the trade unions to be regulated by law, and privatisation – Labour, in short, had to become New Labour if it was to win a general election. 'The Conservatives', Douglas Hurd has said, 'lost the 1997 election, having won the fundamental arguments.'[1] Indeed, the 1997 general election was the first since that of 1918 in which nationalisation, the balance between public and private ownership was not at issue.

One consequence of New Labour's acceptance of the Thatcherite dispensation was the growth of a new consensus on social and economic policy. The main differences between the parties in the 1997 general election lay not in their answers to the question – how should the economy be managed? – but in their answers to a quite different question – did the British constitution need radical reform? For Labour was offering the most widespread programme of constitutional change offered by any major political party at any general election this century. The Party was proposing referendums on devolution to Scotland and Wales and a referendum on a strategic authority for London with an elected mayor; it was proposing reform of the House of Lords, depriving hereditary peers of their right to speak and vote; it was proposing incorporation of the European Convention on Human Rights into British law, thus in effect giving Britain a Bill of Rights; it was proposing a Freedom of Information Act; and, most important of all perhaps, it was committed to a referendum on the voting system to be used for elections to the House of Commons.

Lack of consensus on the constitution is a new phenomenon in British politics. During the 1950s and 1960s, the period of the supposed post-war consensus, there were in fact quite striking differences between Labour and the Conservatives on social and economic questions, but they agreed wholeheartedly on the virtues of the Westminster Model. Admiration for the British constitution was widespread, as strong on the left as on the right. 'In 1953', the sociologist, Edward Shils has written,

> I heard an eminent man of the left say, in utter seriousness, at a university dinner, that the British Constitution was 'as nearly perfect as any human institution could be', and no one even thought it amusing.[2]

In the 1990s, by contrast, it would be hard to find someone on the left with a good word to say for the Westminster Model. Yet Labour's conversion to constitutional reform is highly paradoxical. For Labour has, historically, been a constitutionally conservative party, not a radical one. Moreover, constitutional reform has in the past proved a deeply divisive issue for the Party. In the 1960s, House of Lords reform was defeated by backbench Labour MPs, while the 1979 devolution referendums had been imposed on the Government by hostile Labour Members of Parliament. Both defeats were due as much to hostility from within the Labour Party as to opposition from its Conservative opponents.

Traditionally, the British left has sought to capture the state, not to reform it. Indeed, the 1920s, when Labour came to occupy its place as one of the two great parties in the state, saw the end of a long period of constitutional reform in Britain. Labour's philosophy was the Fabian one, best expressed by Sidney Webb, of the inevitability of gradualness. Socialism was in accordance with the trends of the times. Labour would thus inherit the powers of the British state. There was no need to alter its workings. The first two Labour Governments, under Ramsay MacDonald, were deeply conservative constitutionally. So was the great reforming administration of Clement Attlee which gained power in 1945.

Thus, for most of its history, Labour has been at least as constitutionally conservative as its political opponents, and often more so. Part of the explanation for this is that, while on the Continent, socialist parties faced considerable hostility from their capitalist opponents, in Britain, Labour was able to make its way within the existing constitutional structure, with the active assistance indeed of one of the 'capitalist' parties. For Labour first gained its foothold in the British political system with the aid of the Liberals in the Gladstone/MacDonald pact of 1903, a pact which was accepted by socialists such as Keir Hardie as much as by moderates such as MacDonald and Henderson. It was indeed the Progressive Alliance which enabled Labour to hold its own within the existing electoral system, and it was partly for this reason that Ramsay MacDonald was so opposed to proportional representation. For proportional representation meant that political opinion in the constituencies would 'be divided into watertight compartments – Socialists should vote for Socialists, Labour Party electors for Labour Party candidates, Liberals for Liberals and so on'. 'Nothing', MacDonald concluded, 'has hampered our Movement in the country more than this false idea of independence, that only Labour or Socialist votes should be given to Labour or Socialist candidates. It is humbug.'[3] Moreover, Labour saw itself as a potential majority party, not as a mere appendage to the Liberals. Therefore, Labour could itself eventually benefit from the first past the post system as the 'capitalist' parties had done. 'Speaking quite personally', George Lansbury told the 1926 Labour Conference, replying to a debate on proportional representation, 'he thought that the majority of the decisions under the present system had worked for the other people; but if they were wise, they could now make it work for themselves.'[4]

Thus, while the Conservatives in opposition have on occasion flirted with proportional representation – between 1929 and 1931, in 1950 and 1951 and in the mid-1970s – Labour has been almost the only social democratic party in Europe to remain hostile to electoral reform. During the period of the 1974 Labour Government, Roy Jenkins tried to persuade his Cabinet colleagues to consider 'the matter of the single transferable vote', since otherwise, it would look as if Labour 'were the only party not interested in electoral reform'. But Willie Ross, the Scottish Secretary, pointed out that 'If we were not careful we could see the end of any possibility of a Labour Government.' Barbara Castle noted in her diaries that the Cabinet decided that 'it was obviously best to let this sleeping dog lie as long as possible. So we sent Roy away with a flea in his coalition ear.' Jenkins tried again in Cabinet in November 1975, but was attacked by Denis Healey and by Barbara Castle who reflected that 'these rightists will go on beavering away – until they have finally destroyed the Labour Party's independence and power to govern single-handedly.'[5] 'Proportional representation', Ron Hayward, the General Secretary of the Party, warned in 1976, 'means coalition government at Westminster, on the lines of our European partners, and it is goodbye then to any dreams or aspirations for a democratic socialist Britain.'[6]

Labour now proposes to allow the people to decide on proportional representation through referendum. It also proposes to validate devolution through referendum, and it is committed to a referendum before joining the single currency. Yet, traditionally, Labour has been deeply hostile to the referendum and to other methods of direct democracy. Labour's hostility to the referendum has been shared by other European social democratic parties, who have distrusted it as an instrument of unenlightened demagogy. 'It is obvious', Sweden's Social Democrat premier, Tage Erlander, declared in 1948,

> that referendums are a strongly conservative force. It becomes much harder to pursue an effective reform policy if reactionaries are offered the opportunity to appeal to people's natural Conservatism and natural resistance to change…The referendum system…provides an instrument for blocking a radical progressive policy.[7]

When, in May 1945, Winston Churchill suggested that a referendum be held to determine whether the wartime coalition should be continued and 'the life of this Parliament should be further prolonged' until the end of the Japanese war, Attlee replied that he

> could not consent to the introduction into our national life of a device so alien to all our traditions as the referendum, which has only too often been the instrument of Nazism and Fascism. Hitler's practices in the field of referenda and plebiscites can hardly have endeared these expedients to the British heart.[8]

Admittedly, it was under a Labour Government that Britain's only national referendum was held – in 1975. But the commitment to the referendum came about for reasons of internal Labour politics, not from any principled commitment. Moreover, the European Community referendum was held to be unique and unrepeatable. The White Paper on the *Referendum on UK Membership of the European Community* declared that 'The referendum is to be held because of the *unique* nature of the issue', while a junior minister in the Labour Government, Gerry Fowler, insisted that

> the constitutional significance of our membership of the EEC is of a quite different order from any other issue. It is not just that it is more important; it is of a different order. There is, and there can be, no issue that is on all fours with it. That is why we say that this issue is the sole exception, and there can be no other exception to the principle that we normally operate through parliamentary democracy.[9]

The referendums on devolution were forced on the 1974–79 Labour Government by backbench opponents of the policy. The Welsh Labour Party, echoing the Government's view, had declared that the referendum was incompatible with the ethos of social democracy:

> The question of a referendum involves issues much wider than devolution. The introduction of Government by referendum would be a complete reversal of our whole system of Government. Once this principle was accepted, then any party could call at any time for a referendum on any controversial proposal. Those who advocate a referendum must accept the full implications of this change, and must be aware that any radical changes proposed by a Labour Government – whether extensions of public ownership or abolition of the 11-plus – would have to overcome this new hurdle before being carried out. In effect, Clause IV of the Party Constitution would have to be rewritten 'To secure for the workers by hand or brain the full fruits of their industry' etc. – SUBJECT TO REFERENDUM.[10]

Such an objection, no doubt, has rather less force at a time when Labour has abandoned Clause IV together with many other of its radical aims.

Traditionally, Labour has been just as hostile to other constitutional reforms. The Party has been suspicious of a Bill of Rights since this would mean more power accruing to the judges, seen as reactionary, obscurantist and particularly hostile, in the light of Taff Vale and other judicial decisions, to the rights of the trade unions. For Labour, judges were class enemies, and the Party's hostility was heightened in the 1970s when judges were called on to administer the Heath Government's ill-fated Industrial Relations Act of 1971 which broke down on the rock of trade union resistance. 'If the freedom of the people of this country', Michael Foot declared in 1977, 'and especially the rights of trade unionists – if these precious things of the past had been left to the good sense and fair mindedness of the judges we would have few freedoms in this country at all.'[11]

On reform of the Lords and devolution, Labour's record is rather more mixed. Indeed, Labour Governments have sought reform only to be thwarted by opposition from their own backbenchers. In 1969, a complex scheme for reform of the House of Lords had to be withdrawn when it became clear that Labour MPs would not support it; while in the 1970s, devolution was crippled by the insistence of Labour backbenchers, first, that it be preceded by a referendum, and second, that, for devolution to proceed, 40 per cent of the electorate, as well as a majority of those voting, would have to vote 'Yes' in the referendum. It was this second provision which killed Scottish devolution for, in the referendum of 1979, it was supported by only 33 per cent of the Scottish electorate.

Labour has treated both Lords reform and devolution rather gingerly, and with good reason. The 1911 Parliament Act contains a preamble declaring that 'it is intended to substitute for the House of Lords as it at present exists a Second Chamber constituted on a popular instead of hereditary basis'. It is not difficult to understand why Labour has never sought to transform this aspiration into action. For a second chamber 'constituted on a popular instead of hereditary basis' could prove a far more effective barrier to a Government of the left than the present House of Lords. Indeed any attempt to provide the Lords with democratic legitimacy would encourage it to use its powers to the full, and perhaps even lead to a demand for the extension of these powers.

Until the 1970s Labour was as suspicious of devolution as it was of reform of the Lords. Admittedly, the Scottish Labour Party, founded in 1888, had inherited the Liberal commitment to Scottish Home Rule. With the onset of mass unemployment in the 1930s, however, Labour came to believe that only centralised economic planning could secure an improvement in economic conditions. Tom Johnston, a future Scottish Secretary, warned that a Scottish parliament might have nothing to administer but 'an emigration system, a glorified Poor Law and a graveyard'.[12]

After the Second World War, the Attlee Government nationalised the major public services, such as gas and electricity, taking them away from municipal control. The National Health Service in effect nationalised the hospitals. Aneurin Bevan set his face, as Lloyd George had done, against a separate Welsh or Scottish health service. For social democracy decreed that the benefits one received should be dependent upon need, not upon where one lived. Thus, a deprived child in Liverpool was entitled to the same benefits as a deprived child in Swansea. The establishment of a separate Welsh health service or a Welsh parliament, by increasing the political clout which Wales could bring to bear upon Westminster, would make this aim more difficult to achieve. Michael Foot, when introducing the devolution Bills into Parliament in the 1970s, claimed to be the true heir of Bevan; but, in reality, it was his left-wing critics such as Eric Heffer and Neil Kinnock who were Bevan's children. For they argued, as he would have done, that the problems of the Welsh working class and the problems of the Scottish working class were no different from those of the English working class. They were to be resolved, not by the establishment of parliaments in Edinburgh and Cardiff, but by the coming to power of a Government of the left at Westminster which alone could implement socialist policies.

Constitutional reform, then, is a new platform for a Labour Government to adopt. Why has it done so? A happy man, Bagehot once wrote, is not forever worrying about improvements to his house. By analogy, one might add that a happy political party does not normally concern itself with the constitution. The Liberals certainly did not do so during their years of power. Indeed, they did not come out officially in support of proportional representation until the general election of 1922 by which time they had already been displaced as one of the two major parties in the state. In the years before 1918, by contrast, the leading opponents of proportional representation had been Gladstone, Bright, Asquith and Lloyd George.

If one joins a political organisation, one expects it to be concerned primarily with substantive aims, not with procedural matters. The Royal Society for the Protection of Birds apparently now has more members than all three of the major parties put together. This Society presumably concerns itself primarily with matters of ornithology. Were it to begin concerning itself instead with its constitution and with how its executive committee should be chosen, we should begin to suspect that something had gone seriously wrong with the Society's conception of itself, that it had perhaps lost confidence in its substantive aims. So also perhaps with Labour. When a political party comes to lose confidence in what it has so long stood for, then it will begin to concern itself with procedures. Thus, Labour's concentration on constitutional reform may be a sign less of the Party's continuing vitality, than its lack of confidence in the value of social democracy. Constitutional reform thus becomes not a precondition of social democracy but a substitute for it. The central theme of the twentieth century, American commentator Irving Kristol has declared, is the death of socialism. Labour's conversion to constitutional reform does nothing to disprove this thesis.

## The Blair Government's proposals

Labour's proposals on constitutional reform are riddled with ambiguity. For the House of Lords, Labour is proposing a two-stage reform. The first stage involves removing the right of hereditary peers to sit and vote in the Lords; the second stage, which will come about after some form of inquiry, would be a second chamber constituted on a more popular basis. This is somewhat reminiscent of the Liberals' commitment in 1911. The first stage was the Parliament Act. The second stage would fulfil the promise made in the preamble. It is hardly surprising, however, that the second stage was never reached. For the Liberals realised, as Labour has done, that a second chamber elected on a popular basis would cause a Liberal Government even more trouble than the pre-1911 House of Lords had done. It may not be unduly cynical to suggest that the Labour Government will come to a similar conclusion, so that Labour will not reach the second stage either. If that happens, the House of Lords will be composed entirely of nominated members, and it will become an even richer seam of patronage for the Prime Minister than it is today. The Lords will become simply the largest quango in the land.

On devolution, Labour is faced with a deep-seated dilemma which strikes at the root of its social democratic philosophy. For devolution will create new loci of political power in Scotland and Wales. The Scottish Parliament and the Welsh Senedd will be elected bodies representing the people of Scotland and Wales. They will claim to represent Scottish and Welsh opinion at least as effectively as Scottish and Welsh MPs. Devolution thus places a powerful political weapon in the hands of the Scots and the Welsh; and, just as one cannot be sure that a weapon will be used only for the specified purposes for which it is given, so also one cannot predict the use which the Scots and Welsh will make of devolution.

The more that power is devolved, the greater the possibility of diversity. Indeed, there is no point in devolving power unless one is prepared to admit diversity. It would be pointless to legislate for a Parliament in Scotland and a Senedd in Wales if those bodies were simply to replicate the policies laid down by Westminster for Scotland and Wales. But diversity entails that the Scottish Parliament and the Welsh Senedd may do things that a Labour Government at Westminster finds distasteful. Suppose, for example, that the Scottish Parliament, under a non-Labour majority, were to declare that it wished to reintroduce selection in education; or that it wished to raise revenue for the Scottish health service by charging patients for occupying hospital beds. To forbid the Scottish Parliament to do so would be impracticable, if the Parliament was following the declared wishes of the Scottish people, and it would in any case make a mockery of the idea of devolution.

Labour has chosen as the electoral system for the Scottish Parliament, the German system of proportional representation. Under this system, each elector will have two votes: the first for a constituency member, elected by first past the post; the second for a list of additional members, seven of whom will be elected from each of the eight Euro-constituencies in Scotland. These seats will then be allocated so that the total number – first past the post plus list – for each area will correspond as closely as possible to the share of the vote cast for each party in the area, as measured by its list vote. The list, however, will be a closed one and voters will have no control over the order of candidates on it.

Such a system gives far too much power to the party machine. The elector has no choice over the candidates imposed on him or her through the party list. Candidates who may not have presented themselves to the electorate at all in constituencies could nevertheless be imposed by the party machine. Under first past the post, admittedly, many seats are safe, but it is possible for voters to get rid of Michael Portillo, for example, if the will to do so is strong enough. Under a closed list system of proportional representation, by contrast, Michael Portillo would reappear on the party list. It was the defects of a system of proportional representation of this kind that apparently made Tony Benn tell Neil Kinnock at a meeting of the National Executive that he, Benn, feared that, under proportional representation, Tony Benn would be number 599 on the list and Dennis Skinner would be number 600. Kinnock's reply apparently was 'Would you like that in writing?'

For national elections, Labour is proposing that an electoral commission be established with the task of putting forward a system of proportional representation which will compete with first past the post in a referendum. It will be interesting to see whether a system such as the German is recommended, giving greater power to the party machine; or whether, by contrast, some system such as the single transferable vote, which combines a primary election with a general election, is selected instead. The outcome will tell us much about Labour's intentions on constitutional reform.

The Labour Party is divided on the merits of proportional representation for national elections. Tony Blair has declared himself 'not persuaded' of its merits, while Jack Straw, the Home Secretary, remains a bitter opponent. Having unexpectedly won a landslide victory under the first past the post system on just 44 per cent of the vote, it is perfectly understandable that many Labour MPs no longer wish to tinker with a system that at last seems to have served them well. However, were Labour to retain first past the post, while turning the House of Lords into a quango, it would be tightening the grip of what Lord Hailsham has christened 'the elective dictatorship' even more strongly than Margaret Thatcher succeeded in doing during her long premiership.

## Conclusion

Constitutional reform seeks to redistribute power. The Labour Government's proposals could redistribute power merely from one group of professional politicians to another, away from the House of Commons to members of the Scottish Parliament and Welsh Senedd, and to nominated peers in the House of Lords. Such wider powers as accrue to voters will derive primarily from their ability to choose between a wider range of political professionals. Yet these professionals are, almost by definition, unrepresentative of the people. This is because, for most of those engaged in it today, politics is a full-time activity, a career rather than a public duty. The trouble with socialism, Oscar Wilde once said, was that it took up too many evenings.

But there is a dual dynamic to constitutional reform. For its consequences need not be confined to the redistribution of power between political professionals. Constitutional reform could also point the way towards a much more important redistribution of power, away from the politicians and in the direction of more direct popular involvement in decision-making. Whether this occurs depends primarily upon whether Labour is committed to new forms of popular participation such as the referendum and the initiative, and whether the Party commits itself to a system of proportional representation which opens up the party system to popular scrutiny, rather than keeping it at arm's length from the voters.

Constitutional reform is unpredictable in its consequences. It initiates a process whose results may be very different from those imagined by its supporters. It is perhaps for this reason that Labour has been so wary of constitutional reform in the past. Ernest Bevin once remarked, faced with a difficult foreign policy problem, that within that particular Pandora's box lay a host of Trojan horses. The same may be true of constitutional reform.

# Notes

1 Douglas Hurd, 'His Major Achievements', *Daily Telegraph*, 30 June 1997, p.18.
2 Edward Shils, 'British Intellectuals in the Mid-Twentieth Century', *Encounter*, April 1955, reprinted in *The Intellectuals and the Powers*, University of Chicago Press, 1972, p.135.
3 J. R. MacDonald, 'The Case Against Proportional Representation', in *Labour Party, Proportional Representation and the Alternative Vote*, Labour Party, 1913, pp.27, 28. Quoted in Vernon Bogdanor, *The People and the Party System: The Referendum and Electoral Reform in British Politics*, Cambridge University Press, 1981, p.124.
4 *Labour Party Conference Reports*, Labour Party, 1926, p.273.
5 Barbara Castle, *The Castle Diaries 1974–1976*, Weidenfeld and Nicolson, 1980, pp.69–70, 554.
6 Quoted in Bogdanor, *The People and the Party System*, 1981, p.155.
7 Leif Lewin, *Ideology and Strategy: A Century of Swedish Politics*, Cambridge University Press, 1988, p.235.
8 Quoted in Bogdanor, *The People and the Party System*, p.35.
9 Cmnd. 5925, 1975, p.2, italics added; House of Commons Debates, vol. 881, cols. 1742–3, 22 November 1974.
10 *Why Devolution?*, Labour Party, Wales, September 1976, p.4; quoted in Bogdanor, *The People and the Party System*, p.49.
11 Quoted in Vernon Bogdanor, *Politics and the Constitution: Essays on British Government*, Dartmouth Press, 1996, p.189.
12 Tom Johnston, *Memories*, Collins, 1952, p.69.

# Labour and the constitution
## Part II: the Blair agenda

*Edward Pearce*

Constitutional reform stands placed to occupy centre stage of a Blair Government. It has all the charm of a wadi in the middle of the sub-Sahara. It is after all an idea. And the governing principle of New Labour has been that ideas are like legs to mid-Victorians, necessary but dubious. And those that do exist for the new Government, ideas that is, have a peculiarly metaphysical quality about them. Alec Salmond of the Scottish Nationalists put it best: 'Tony Blair says "Education, education, education" and Gordon Brown says "No money, no money, no money!".' So if Labour want to do anything and maybe get into the history books in addition to being talked about and photographed getting on and off aeroplanes, they had better do something cheap. Which brings us to constitutional reform.

The trouble with constitutional reform is that normally it is associated with theoreticians, academics, naturally high-minded people, Liberal Democrats! Now there are intelligent and thought-out reasons for wanting to make dramatic advances in constitutional change, though whether they have any place in a discussion of Mr Blair's intentions is arguable. I sense a slight resistance in that camp to what Governor George Wallace used to call 'pointy-headed intellectuals'.

### A federal United Kingdom?

Listening to the Tories on the horrors of federalism you really would think from a casual reading of Mr Murdoch's newspapers, that federalism is the nethermost circle of hell administered by Belgians with pitchforks, a sort of assembly line for the deflowering of British virgins overseen by men in armbands. As anybody knows who knows anything about it, the federalism practised in the Federal Republic (as its friends call it), is a system of sophisticated democracy allowing articulation of local and regional concerns with a degree of answerability and financial responsibility for Stuttgart, Kiel, Dresden in ways to make Bristol, Newcastle and Norwich cringe. I do not know whether an all-European federalism would work as well, but assuredly, it deserves intelligent thinking through and not the treatment coming from most of the unspeakable proprietor-instructed

British press. But intra-British federalism, our own arrangement to give the West Midlands powers in the West Midlands, has immediate and pressing appeal. I would suggest to Birmingham people, heirs of Joe Chamberlain, awful but phenomenal Joe, that they should take a long hard look at Munich, and Bavaria behind it. I think that bloody minded Brum and Millionendorf Ltd have more in common than is readily acknowledged, though Munich is prettier.

Doing a lecture tour, I was in Munich at the time of that great power struggle inside the CSU between Theo Waigel and Edmund Stoiber. And as a Munich wag put it, 'They're fighting to see who gets the job that really matters and who has to settle for being Federal Finance Minister'. Stoiber won and Stoiber is Minister-President of Bavaria.

The contrast with our own intensifying centralisation could hardly be more savage. We always were a centralised country and Margaret Thatcher, while mouthing slogans about less government, had as one of her many manias, a perfect determination to usurp the local government she hated. Compare and contrast Stoiber running Bavaria, also Kurt Biedenkopf in Saxony – transferring the old West German model in the East and enjoying great success doing so – with Mrs Thatcher killing off the Greater London Council. Ken Livingstone was/is a cheeky chappy and his internal putsch was an excess, as they used to say of Stalin. But effectively, the GLC was ended because he pulled the leg of the Government, and because under our unconstitutional constitution, a Government with a majority in Westminster can do anything.

Privatise as much as you like, assert that capitalism equals freedom, talk about the little man – just talk, but the central fact about Britain remains this, we have central command politics. Westminster has powers, Westminster knows that no one else appreciates powers as well or uses them as justly as Westminster. Westminster wants to keep power and where possible acquire more. To push the psychiatric metaphor out only a little, we have an anal-retentive system of central government.

## The reform of the House of Lords

The irony is, of course, as we look to reform of the House of Lords as the constitutional change most likely actually to happen, that it was the unreformed, part-hereditary, preponderantly Tory, House of Lords which threw out Mrs Thatcher's vengeful little strike at an elected local authority. Just as it was this dreadful anomaly of a House which recently wrecked one of Mr Howard's bits of early Tudor legislation...after New Labour had signalled cringing assent. It was by another, deeper, irony that powers rightly taken from the upper chamber by Asquith when a quite different bunch of hereditarians was playing silly buggers over the budget (and

Ireland), were invoked in 1986 for Mrs Thatcher to exercise a reflexive act of frankly despotic power. I am not damning the Parliament Act, only pointing out that one year's obvious reform can become the loophole for autocracy in another set of circumstances. And given the concentration of power onto the Prime Minister within that central echelon, we are to an astonishing, and astonishingly little remarked, degree subject to the personality of a single individual. Mrs Thatcher was an authoritarian personality. Her reaction to power was that, to paraphrase Colonel Sanders, it was finger-clickin' good.

Let's run through our heads of Government, shall we, stability-wise: Attlee, normal; Churchill, genially grandiose; Eden, mentally disturbed; Macmillan, neurotic and twitchy; Harold Wilson, twitchy and neurotic, also paranoid; Ted Heath, a permafrost with musical accompaniment; Jim Callaghan, normal; Margaret Thatcher, an egomaniacal anthology of hang-ups, delusions and hatreds; John Major, normal; and now, Tony Blair...Tony Blair admires Margaret Thatcher.

The argument for constitutional reform waxes and wanes with the excesses and restraints of the chap currently in charge of the bank of buttons and what all this surely teaches us is that concentrating on institutions without thought for human nature and the quirks of individuals is not good enough. We can devise all the model constitutions we like. We can rid ourselves of hereditary peers and extend powers to regional authorities, but that is all paper, and high-minded paper at that. The central belief which a reformer should carry with him is a deep prejudice against Prime Ministers.

I am not a great admirer of the American way – rarely was a lower common denominator excavated deeper than in recent American choice of executive manpower. As for the mood of voters, seldom have public tantrums been so lightly gratified. The country which balances Rush Limbaugh and Bill Clinton can't be entirely serious. Nevertheless the impulse of the American founding fathers that the next President-but-three might not be George Washington, so the institution should be fireproofed against executive ambitions, has very great charm. Actually they didn't trust George Washington either and reckoned that he wanted to make himself King. The clever thing about the Americans is that they don't leave paranoia to their leaders, they do their own. But that's all right: anyone who has been governed by Margaret Thatcher can see the point of paranoia.

In perfect earnest, the constitutional reforms worth having are ones which diffuse power and diminish great politicians. The need for such change is also a cool guide to what your average hyped-up, power-hugging, Prime Minister won't be giving us. Yes, of course we shall see changes to the House of Lords. This reform has been talked about timidly enough in the run-up to the election if only because everything was talked about timidly during the run-up to the election. Mr Blair's watered-down manifesto has done him no harm. But on constitutional reform generally, we may expect more rather than less. As I said, such reform is cheap.

So for that matter is the word 'radical'. Radicals in the 1830s were people you did not invite to dinner: Cobbett, Place, Cochrane – shocking people. But ever since Jo Grimond resuscitated it in about 1955, every tentatively ameliorative politician has made promiscuous use of the word. Rockribbed reactionaries have made almost as free. If 'radical' was a girl she would have no reputation at all. But you can see how a Labour Government which may be freezing benefits in an attempt to meet taxation norms laid down by the Tories, will represent the expulsion of a few hundred D'Ascoynes and Mauleverers from the exercise of a legislative dabble in the Whitefish Number Two bill, as radical innovation, at any rate with the light behind it.

Don't mistake me. The House of Lords which rejected a budget to take the edge off destitution six years after the first Rowntree report, the House of Lords which sniggeringly killed Gladstone's Home Rule Bill, fought bitterly against Asquith's and so helped achieve Easter 1916, deserved all and more than it got. If some wellwisher had swept their Lordships out of existence in 1910 or 1945, so much the better for our democratic health; so much, I would add, for our republican virtues. Get rid of the whole boiling of nobility, Kings and Queens and perhaps we could make an honest woman of the word 'radical'.

But now is now and this House of Lords, a gentlemen's club admitting ladies and combining all the qualities of the Athenaeum with all those of the cavalry with a useful access from the county councils, one which can function like a quango but on the odd exalted occasion talks like an agora, one moreover which lately whacked Michael Howard on the head, is largely opposed for reasons of text book democratic theory. It is of course an anomaly, but then in the catalogue of government evil, there are so many worse things to be. My money says that Mr Blair will do the radical thing – in the easy-lay sense of the word. Having deprived hereditary members of the vote as promised, he will move round to some form of mixed franchise. Nomination works pretty sweetly for Governments at present, so why would this Government want to alter it? As for election, well perhaps a slate of elected seats might be staged, but more for show and perfunctory prayer meetings at the altars of reform. It is amazing what credit you can get by moving pieces around – credit for having moved them forward. But more about their Lordships a little later. A completely elected upper house is at any rate logical. But never mind logic, do the victors of a stupendous electoral triumph want to push their luck indefinitely with yet more elections, some of which they might lose?

## The timing of local elections and by-elections

This is the age of the therapeutic by-election, not to mention local government elections and European elections. The pleasure of these, starting with Orpington in 1962, has been to give the Government of the day, whatever its virtues, a rotten time. Ask any Prime Minister since Macmillan. I don't see Mr Blair getting any advice in his earpiece to create yet another occasion for explaining horrible numbers to the Grand Hereditary Dimbleby sometime after midnight. If we can distinguish, as we should, between what ought to happen and what will happen, between good government wisely amended into better government and what people in power think they can get away with, we will expect something else.

If I read Mr Blair aright, he will do to political institutions nothing which does not sustain and hopefully enhance the command power of Mr Blair – New Labour, New Britain, New Quangos. The Labour Party, of course, has denounced quangos and in 1978–79, Mrs Thatcher denounced quangos. She subsequently proved to be into them the way King John was into lampreys. Mr Blair will remove hereditary voting, possibly the inheritors themselves, but will have either a sub-parliament of party nominees and harmless people of distinction or, if he does go for an element of election, he will be drawn to two things which suit party leaders: Fewer elections and more nominations.

We have all noticed that the Tories during an awful general election actually did rather respectably in the local contests, county councils and so on, because exceptionally, they were held at the same time as the general election, thus getting the vote out. One of the few threads of power which centralising Westminster has not drawn together, is that relating to the various election dates. Scotland, Wales, Greater London can all be kept in their place, but people are allowed to cheeck the Government at by-elections, council elections, county borough, London borough and unitary authority elections, and these are scattered like wedding rice over the timetable. As somebody will be murmuring, 'Get a grip'.

If you want to imagine the sort of constitutional reform which will come naturally to New Labour, its leader and his advisors, consider ending the anomaly of local elections affronting a Government in an off year, diminishing its confidence, sapping its morale and generally lowering the tone of strong decisive leadership. In the interest of ending anomalies, it would be credible to shuffle lengths of terms to bring many more local contests together on the date of a general election. Cliché being beloved of politicians, much will be made of the ability of the Americans to choose President and dogcatcher on the same occasion. Arguments of streamlined, up-to-date, high-tech zippishness will be advanced. But ask the old question, the one put in ponderous editorials in provincial newspapers a hundred years ago. *Cui bono*?

Doing badly in lots of small-time council elections is bad for a Government. This is all the argument necessary against it in the real world of naked power which the present admirers of Margaret Thatcher inhabit. A radical reform, as it will be called, of the scheduling of elections makes sense according to the self-interest of the Government. As much is true of by-elections, eruptions of impertinence by voters, an indulgence in flippancy which leaves Peter Snow at 1.45 on a Friday morning in the third year of a Parliament hypothesising a majority of 367. When Orpington happened, coming as it did out of a blue sky and an assumption of 2 per cent swings, it distressed the Macmillan Govern- ment. It helped induce the general panic which, in turn, led to Mr Macmillan's attempt to do Stalin without bullets.

But of course since then, through all the Meridans, Walthamstows, Ashfields, Ryedales and Eastbournes, the Government has put on a brave face and done the insouciance bit. Rotten by- elections are par for the course, a chap gets used to them, they have been around since before Germaine Greer learned to swear, musn't get excited. Though, come to think of it, they got excited about Eastbourne all right: got so excited that they threw Mrs Thatcher over the side on a democratic vote. There is a lot to be said for by-elections. Best of all, Governments hate them and the lesson of the last three years has been of a Government weakened by bad result after bad result. Given a small majority and divided party, cardiac failure can be nearly as regrettable for a ministry as for the corpse. The successive results from Mansfield, Dumfries and St Ives can, like steadily less distant artillery, give a General a hard time.

Is it really beyond the ingenuity of the people who got rid of the rewards of 'the workers by hand and by brain' to find a good modern, gleaming-bright, 'radical', not to say 'new', way of replacing the parliamentary dead – one which doesn't kick the executive in the ear? It won't be easy. The Tories will play merry hell. They had been looking forward to their sessions with Peter Snow and the 31 per cent swing to the Conservatives in Leeds South. It will also be a constitutional outrage which the *Observer* as much as the *Sunday Telegraph* will thunder against. There's tragedy for you. More to the point, Labour has lots and lots of seats and will not be debilitated in the Commons on account of by-election reversals. But then what better time is there for providing against a small majority than when you have a large majority?

Then again there is an instrument to hand perfectly attuned. The dilettanti of electoral reform enjoy the moral arguments which swarm around the list system. It is mathematical and exact. Like the guillotine, it is scientific. But even the purists are put off by the fact that lists are drawn up by party committees not uncommonly influenced by party leaders. We have watched Mr Blair's people disposing of leftwingers like Liz Davies, seen Cabinet shadows being warned by Mr Charlie Whelan against expectation of being in the real thing. In return for small tokens of esteem like peerages, sitting members have been shifted out to make way for terracotta warriors in good standing. If we are going to get rid of a corrupt system, we should make use of it while we can. From the heart of New Labour the refrain of the Emperor Franz Josef rings out 'Is he a patriot for me?'

What was it Mr Blair said in Scotland 'Sovereignty will reside in me'? As John Major would say 'Oh yes'! The idea of drawing up a list of deserving persons who, one by one, in proper order, would replace Smiggs and Briggs when called to their reward has, for any Party Leader, the appeal of cucumber sandwiches on a Deanery lawn in July. But if this looked too Bismarckian, the list might follow in order of nearness to victory in the general election. Jones, pipped by 83 in Wolverhampton waits, trying not to give offence, for the first sad event, hoping that his automatic seat brings a prospective large majority for the next actual contest which will, of course, be the general election. Am I kidding? Not altogether. What has shone out of this Labour leadership has been a preoccupation with holding all the cards of power and using them without compunction if also to no very clear purpose. Power is what is understood, and any constitution reform which is not done for show or public credit will relate to power and the leadership's hold on it.

By-elections (and council elections) at the very least, embarrass the Government. Latterly they have discernibly weakened it. To use one of the ugliest words in the vocabulary, a merger of elections which diminishes that injury and allows everything to be played for at the time when a Government can most easily arrange favourable prospects, would have irresistible charm. Frankly, it does good to talk about it. Most despotic moves succeed by being sudden and live to be applauded for being bold. Nothing could do more good than to talk out loud about the possibility of such a development.

## Electoral reform

As a corollary, I would not expect the Blair Government ever to favour fixed Parliaments. Choice of dates can, as in 1964 and 1992, especially help the incumbent; failure to exercise it, as in 1950 and 1951, is injurious. No way will these people exchange weapons for purer government. 'Mr Mandelson and ethical priorities' is one of those research topics like 'Australian courtly love', which reward only the very diligent.

So how will New Labour play proportional representation? They may, of course, be influenced by their success in playing the old system which incidentally, is changing under our eyes. The Tories, up to and including 1987, had a huge advantage from first past the post. Mrs Thatcher never got above 42 per cent, but on one occasion, it rewarded her with 58 per cent of seats. But if you contrast 1987 and 1992, you see Mr Major keeping all but 0.3 per cent of Mrs Thatcher's vote in 1987 which after all the deranged things Mrs Thatcher did from early 1988 on, is astonishing. But it cost him 39 seats, more than 10 per cent of this holding. The Tories then made an awful botch of the boundary commission. And today they have 31 per cent of the vote, hideous enough a figure in itself, but amounting in terms of seats to 25 per cent. But Labour will almost certainly ask the question, 'What happens when we don't have a huge majority?' At present they don't need the Liberal Democrats. They have an army which, like Milton's servants of God, 'will speed and post o'er land and ocean without rest'. But there is no getting round general elections and unpopularity comes to all of us.

Proportional representation does two wonderful things, it facilitates coalitions (makes them respectable as well) and it facilitates divorce. One cannot speak that word without a melancholy glance at the Conservative and Unionist Party. The Tories have spent the last few years destroying themselves. The power of the right through the memory of Mrs Thatcher, the influence of half a dozen newspapers and especially Rupert Murdoch, has imposed upon a reasonably good Government quite calamitous politics. And obsession out of all proportions with forms of financial integration in Europe has done for the Tory party what transubstantiation did for Church unity. The Tories have a wonderful relationship, they hate each other.

If they carry on in opposition, the way they did before defeat which is pretty much the way Labour carried on after 1979, somebody is going to talk about 'breaking the mould', 'enjoying their politics', 'an idea whose time has come', 'the gang of four', all the old songs. Now under PR, the SDP would have stuck even with Dr Owen about. Under PR, the Conservative Party could give new meaning to the phrase 'natural break'. I don't say it will happen, but academic books never give enough thought to really bad, low motives. And really bad, low motives are what politics is about. And then again, the shock-horror quality of what happened on May Day which, do you remember, the Tories thought they had abolished, will change attitudes out of all recognition. 'All changed, changed utterly', as W. B. Yeats wrote. Though the next line, the one which says that 'a terrible beauty is born' should not be pushed. Getting an election result like that does make a difference. I was generally thought a sensationalist for reckoning that the Tories would suffer a reverse 1983. But it was Professor John Ramsden who took the radical plunge. If there is a Soviet-type award – Hero of Conservative Pessimism perhaps – Professor Ramsden with his 'Tories under 200' should get it.

What matters is that with a thumping majority you think differently. For that matter, after being dragged backwards by the hair through an electoral hedge you think differently. Conservatives for proportional representation!

My guess is that, like sex before marriage, you've got no idea how quickly it will catch on. It is simply unfair that in Scotland the Conservative and Unionist Party should have 17 per cent of the vote and no seats at all. Under PR they would have 11.9 MPs and I think we could stretch a point to 12. Of course they should have them. One of the best of all arguments for PR used to be that there are far more Labour voters in Sussex and Tory voters in Co. Durham than decades of zero representation suggested. People of one persuasion should not feel dispossessed by reason of being in a mere minority. They should have a sympathetic focus and voices speaking for them.

Well now, Labour is doing fine in Sussex, the eternally denied Lib Dems are spreading out, not to mention taking over south-west London, but the Tories are not just missing, feared dead in Scotland and Wales, they don't have a single seat in a single industrial city, the length of Britain. Sheffield, Birmingham, Leeds, Newcastle, Bradford, Swansea, Liverpool, Glasgow, Cardiff, Edinburgh, Leicester, Manchester, Nottingham: *rien ne marche plus*. I haven't done the numbers, but they must have in most of those places better proportions of the vote cast than they do in Scotland. Now we don't really expect that on account of Conservative under-representation in Sheffield, old lag PR phobes like Roy Hattersley will be seized with a St Paul experience. Hat stricken blind on the road to the Gavroche and saying 'PR is right. Give them back Hallam.' But if we think an idea right, we can't stop thinking it, even if that idea removes the burnt stick with which an enemy has just been poked in the eye. Or, putting it more genteelly, we must have equity even if equity means 204 Conservative seats to Labour's 280. If, on the other hand, you want a spot of low-mindedness, the true PR representation of the Lib Dems would be 111 giving the inevitable Lib-Lab coalition 391 seats out of 660, smaller but stabler, a majority which meets the Vicar of Wakefield's definition of a suitable wife. 'I looked', he said, 'for those qualities which would last.'

Will we get it at last – PR? There will be ill-natured people to make the point that the Conservatives are dangerously close to Catch-28, that point, in and around 28 per cent of the vote, at which a party going up sprouts wings and gets scores of new seats and where the party going down finds the parachute not opening, plummets to the pavement and makes double figures and strawberry jam. I think we do get round to PR. We do it, of course, by way of Scotland and Wales. It would be unthinkable not to have PR in the elections for Scottish and Welsh assemblies. In spite of its having been promised in the manifesto, I think we can rely on its happening. After which, quite seriously, the fact of the Tories not being nonsensically annihilated, but putting up a decent tranche of representation in Cardiff and Edinburgh, will make the point.

I am rather a believer in invisible lines. The Suburban Line is the one beyond which house prices come down 20 per cent. There will be another line which, once crossed, leaves PR no longer open to argument. Give the assemblies two years to be set up under that system. Give a little time for the obvious equity all round to give satisfaction, for life to be breathed into the Scottish and Welsh oppositions and we shall be talking Mr Benn's old favourite, 'an irreversible transfer', not of power but of opinion. The English like to follow the mainstream; being a bit of a mainstream themselves, that follows. So create circumstances in which by leakage and irrigation, PR comes to be the mainstream and, just as the Tories will abandon their dead-in-a-ditch unionism-without-Scots, so they, and small 'c' conservative opinion, will come along. The nuisance is the interim, the catching of the mood of cautious Mr Blair, then the tedium of a referendum. PR once ratified by such a vote, let us not have any more of them. For if there is one constitutional change I do not want, it is widespread use of the referendum.

### The use of the referendum, money and monopolies

Parliament, having been fairly elected, should make laws, should lead, should assume a burden of thinking and resolving. Anything else is populism, snapshot opinion taking. It is the means by which in Switzerland, women were kept away from the vote for 60 years after parliamentary Britain granted it. Above all, the referendum is power to rich men. We have to alert ourselves to the whimsical clickers of fingers, the signers of cheques, the slightly crazed O'Gradys talking democracy out of a bottomless contempt for the public. We have to alert ourselves to that undesirable alien, Rupert Murdoch, and his ability with 40 per cent of the press to slew opinion sideways. Referendums are endlessly manipulable.

I am European ten kilometres east of Hamburg, but let's face it, the 1975 referendum went as heavily as it did because the press, bar the *Express*, was overwhelmingly pro-Europe. Change two or three proprietors and you have a press 70-80 per cent anti-Europe. But then I think that the great smouldering unachieved cause for Lib Dem and Labour alike should be the combating of monopoly – monopoly in everything, newspapers and TV stations, monopoly through financial takeovers and the power of multinationals. 'Malefactors of great Wealth', Teddy Roosevelt called the monopolists and their trusts. It's a phrase to savour. But in purely political terms, let's take Henry Paul Sykes as a warning. Money did only a limited amount of harm this time, though the taking of his money – what French tarts used to call *le petit cadeau* – by a fly-past of prideless Tory back-benchers oiling up to a contributor, was a genuinely offensive sight. We have to fear American-style money politics: Ross Perot, the Ronald Reagan committee and yes, certainly, Joe Kennedy's money. My reactions here are old-fashioned puritan socialist. Money has to be chained and fettered.

As a simple pre-condition whether or not Europe puts through anti-monopolistic directives, we should on our own account limit the ownership of the media. And for my money (if you will forgive the expression) 15 per cent of national print outlets and another 15 per cent of provincial papers is enough for anyone, coupled with no holder of so much being permitted over about 5 per cent of radio or TV (itself limited to a 15 per cent ownership ceiling). This is a set of rules consonant with political diversity and directed against the purchase of power. Historically, we have been complacent about newspaper power because in the past it was always seen off. We all wrote essays at university with neat little snippets about Baldwin and the prerogative of the harlot. We all know Lord Beaverbrook for a many-splendoured onlooker, not exactly beautiful, nor yet an angel, but satisfyingly ineffective. Well, now you have seen Rupert. Dennis Potter called his cancer 'Rupert' and I think it is either chemotherapy or cutting out. It won't happen yet. Do not underestimate the power of argument to carry the day even with as minimalist a Government as I expect this one to be. Argument is what we are here for. But PR is a ripe argument, opposition to press monopoly a green one. So stick it in the sun, breathe on it.

But as far as money and Parliament are concerned, we may be more advanced. In the history of ever cleaner government, I suspect that Mostyn Neil Hamilton will be an honoured name. The sort of thing which was chuntered about in obscure books by the other Stephen Dorrill – Dorrill with an 'i' – and moaned about unreadably in the *Observer*, has suddenly become lurid 80 point news. The implacable amorality of Mostyn Neil Hamilton, the disposition of an ethically knackered Tory Party to rally round young Freeby like a wing three-quarter who has lost his shorts was wonderful cinema and, more important, it has forced corruption down market and made it demotic. It has turned 'want of perfect fastidiousness' into 'sleaze'. From words of one syllable there is no hiding place. So let us strike while the sleaze is squishy.

## A modest proposal

We should place a limit on all contributions to politics – with politics being first defined as 'Any political party, individual member of that party, any parallel office such as research department, think tank, associated consultancy or constituency organisation, any group in fact serving the political and electoral ends of the given party'. The ceiling should thus be applied to aggregate givings to all and any of these over any Parliament. To compensate for all consequent shortfall (and whether Gordon Brown likes it or not), Short Money should be joined by Long Money. The state would give measured necessary funds from general revenue to political parties above the aggregate of legal individual contributions, up to one-third of the money spent over the last five years by the Conservative and Unionist Party. Qualification would be based on seats contested with a substantial bonus for seats contested in a second general election. It would be money well spent. It would shrivel the influence of cash purchase politics. It would diminish the say of consultancies and advertising agencies which, as they have increased and are increasing, is a logical progress. State money means less money, means taming the festival of poster paint mendacity which marked the last twelve months – to not an atom of advantage of the party spending it. The bacchanale held by PR men and advertising consultants gathered at the unscrutinised party teat would be curtailed. Such restraint would get the weeping lion and the demon eyes and their Labour equivalents off the hoardings. The coupling of seats contested with reward for second (and perhaps third) contests would work against fly-by-night speculators, persons also restrained by the contributions limits. It would mean a politics, austere, Crippsian, worthy of 1945 and the better for it.

A final thought about the House of Lords. Any fool can get rid of hereditary voting. It is a nonsense that a whip can summon some inert Cinncinatus from the silage and, by way of the 2.20 from Moreton-in-the-Marsh, have him in the Lobby at 5.30 to sustain an elected Government in a hole. But Labour has not given a thought to the positive steps. An elected chamber means more power for the Lords. A nominated chamber means more patronage for the Prime Minister. So the choice is clear. But the self-interest is a bit crass and obvious. Again with a majority of 181, there is a great surplus of heads over work. A Commons committee of legislative revision could actually do the job and the Lords go altogether – much too radical for Mr Blair. For myself, I don't feel strongly here. The House of Lords is a sort of padded shrine, a holy place with comfortable chairs, a club which does thinking. And having genuinely interesting people, historians, biochemists, even a writer of rather baroque detective stories, P.D. James, all assembled isn't a constitutional atrocity, just a sprawl of opinion and a bit of fun for the Prime Minister of the day. The instinct will be to say, 'Let nomination thrive'.

I know all the options, the transferred and full salaried working MPs we made Lords against the great day, about 2009, of an elected upper house. I do not think that this lot will do it and I suspect their conservatism may be well founded for once. An end to the inherited vote finishes the one intellectually indefensible aspect of the Lords. Peerages should, however, have criteria for being awarded. But perhaps membership should lapse for defective attendance and/or contribution. And if it comes to that, what is the need for actual titles? A nominated untitled house, with nomination subject to criteria and perhaps a scrutiny committee, might meet most requirements. One last thought – the cleaning of politics is more important than making it more efficient. God save us from the people with thick glasses who want Parliament transferred into an IBM block, probably a stretch of Victoria Street, with no Gothic-revival archways, just lots of office space and room for creches, with MPs efficiently housed and kept at work, discouraged from drink, adultery and the nonsense of debate. MPs today live in the architectural equivalent of a novel by Walter Scott; I do not want them translated into a Web site for advanced administration. Politics should be honest and its participants chosen by non-rip-off methods; those 12 Scottish Tories are symbolically important. But contrary to widespread fallacy, 'honest' is not coterminous with 'boring'. Given a foundation of equity, we don't want our MPs to be zomboid good citizens abstaining from things and buzzing quietly in well-conducted cubicles. Politics, for all the reform we throw at it, should be enjoyable and have at least a working relationship to chaos theory.

# Commentary

*Austin Mitchell, MP*

New Labour's constitutional plans are the legacy of an approach to power based on a deep inferiority complex about the party and about the policies we have traditionally advocated in the past. New Labour won in 1997 not because of any real programme or manifesto but because the electorate hated the Conservative Government and wanted them out. As a result Labour has a majority too big to govern with and nothing very much for it to do – particularly in the economic sphere where we have abandoned any pretence of redistribution or even of stimulating growth by demand management. Indeed, not content with taking the politics out of politics, we are taking the governing out of government, handing power to the Bank of England, to commissions of enquiry, and perhaps also to those who can be bothered to take part in referendums. As a result the Government – and the serried ranks of Labour backbenchers – have little to do apart from getting on with the business of constitutional reform.

This is not to say that the issue is unimportant, and it is certainly convenient. In the election this issue had a middle-class appeal, and they were the section of the electorate we were hoping to win over. It made us look radical, when we were in fact presenting ourselves as a deeply conservative party of the status quo. It capitalised on the grievances developed under the Thatcher Government, which had used strong executive power and abandoned most forms of consultation. The answer was to listen to the people, to go into constitutional reform, to free up the system. People in the Thatcher years tasted power, exercised choice and made their voice heard in economic matters as consumers. However, they did not gain the same influence and the same capacity in constitutional matters – in their role as citizens, either of the UK or (more specifically and more urgently) its component parts, especially Scotland. This is why devolution is vital.

But, perhaps more by accident than by design, devolution is likely to be the beginning rather than the end of a wider process. The desire to be heard, to have a say and to get government closer to the people is potentially a widespread one. Clearly Scotland needs to have priority because that is where the immediate grievances, problems and pressures are. But it may be that there is as much resentment, as much a feeling of impotence, as much remoteness from central government in, for example, Yorkshire as exists in Scotland. In any case the pressures generated by devolution for Scotland will build up pressure within other areas, not least because they are all in competition with each other for development funding – a competition in which Scotland may well be advantaged because of its new-found autonomy. One thing may well lead to another, and we will move towards regional assemblies all round.

Just as importantly the setting up of devolved parliaments and assemblies in Scotland and Wales will have all sorts of other knock-on effects constitutionally. If the Scots Parliament, for example, is elected for a fixed term – a good thing if one is in favour of limiting the power of the executive in any legislature – then it is hard to see how fixed terms can be avoided at a national level. Without constitutionally synchronising elections how else, given the fact that mid-term elections almost always see the Westminster incumbent defeated, are we to avoid the inevitability of the devolved Parliament being run by parties opposed to those in control in London – a situation which may well lead to calls for full independence?

The same is true of PR. People have more confidence in a Parliament which actually represents their wishes, as expressed in their votes. Again, of course, a lot depends on timing. The New Zealand referendum was won because by the time it was held the people hated both parties so much that they wanted PR just to teach them a lesson. If the Labour Government becomes unpopular in the next two years there is a better chance of PR being carried in a referendum than if there is a popular Labour Government recommending first past the post. But it is also true to say that the case for PR may spread as people look to Scotland and Wales and see how much fairer the system is.

Yet in concentrating on major reform we have to be careful not to forget the need to make superficially more minor, but nonetheless important, changes, particularly to the legislature itself. Reform of the House of Lords is perhaps the least of these, but it will still be useful – particularly if it is chosen by nomination and thereby avoids being packed with career politicians in the same way as the Commons. Reform of the processes of the latter, though, is vital. It should, then, be a central issue, and include at the very least the strengthening of the committee system and the facilitation of pre-legislative scrutiny. Fortunately there is every likelihood that all this will be seen as important: the crucial thing with a majority this big is to give all MPs grown-up jobs.

Not that any of this will necessarily determine the success or failure of this Government. Constitutional reform is the icing on the cake, but the cake itself is a question of getting the economic growth which, without a commitment to redistribution, is the key to increased public spending. Fail here and nothing will save us. This majority may well be enough to last one election, but the honeymoon does in the end depend on expectations which have to be fulfilled. The constitutional work we're now embarking on might distract attention from that for a time but in the end it is nowhere near as important.

# Chapter 7

# Foreign, defence and European affairs

*John W. Young*

Anyone looking at the international outlook of a socialist party during the twentieth century might expect to find evidence of foreign and defence policy being guided by working-class solidarity, an aversion to power politics, a deep commitment to disarmament, opposition to imperialism, a desire to establish strong international institutions, a dislike of co-operation with capitalist powers and a readiness to establish democratic control over external policy-making. And it certainly is possible, from time to time, to see such factors influencing Labour since its foundation. As early as 1911 the Party organised its own disarmament conference; in August 1914 some Labour MPs, led by Ramsay MacDonald, opposed war; and in 1919–20 many Labour members and trades unionists actively opposed Allied intervention against the Bolsheviks in Russia. With the advent of Bolshevism it was tempting for Conservatives to tar the Labour Party with the brush of revolutionary extremism, a task made easier when MacDonald's Government, in 1924, established diplomatic relations with the USSR. The result was the defection of the Liberals from supporting this, the first minority Labour administration. In the ensuing election campaign the Conservatives and the right-wing press, with the probable connivance of the intelligence services, exploited the 'Zinoviev letter' and the fear of Communist subversion in Britain against Labour. Labour's opposition to rearmament in the 1930s, its nominal rejection of Polaris nuclear missiles in the early 1960s and its sympathy for unilateral nuclear disarmament in the 1983 election suggested a Party which was averse to defence spending, uncomfortable with *realpolitik* and unwilling to accept the logic of deterrence, allowing the Conservatives to continue posing as the party of patriotism, realism and strong defence.

In fact, of course, it was Conservative Governments which presided over what, arguably, were the two most humiliating episodes for Britain's international standing in the twentieth century, appeasement under Chamberlain and the Suez crisis under Eden. The Labour Party has gone through radical periods, where international questions are concerned, when in opposition, as in the mid-1930s, in 1960–61 and 1979–83. But even then the victory of the radicals was less than total and proved short-lived. The pacifist George Lansbury was edged out of the leadership in 1935, Hugh Gaitskell was able to hit back against his critics and in 1983 the party's unilateralist and anti-European stance helped ensure its worst post-war election result. Labour in power has been far less ready to adopt radical policies abroad and, indeed, a consensus on the general lines of foreign and defence policy has generally been the rule for the front benches of the major parties. The great exceptions to this have been the Suez crisis (when Labour did not believe Nasser's behaviour was aggressive enough to justify a military response), Labour criticism of Conservative negotiations with the European Community in 1962–63 and 1971–72, and the differences on nuclear arms when Michael Foot was Labour leader. But on all occasions when Labour has been in power since 1945 it has supported an alliance with America against Soviet Communism, developed or maintained nuclear weapons, co-operated in European institutions and portrayed an image of Britain as a significant world power – all very similar to Conservative Governments. Many of the most intense debates on international issues have taken place, not between the two front benches, but between party leaderships and their backbench MPs. Just as Conservative leaders faced the pro-imperialist views of the Suez Group and the Monday Club or, more recently, vocal Euro-scepticism, so Ernest Bevin, as Foreign Secretary under Attlee, was criticised by the 'Keep Left' group, who wished to maintain co-operation with Russia and were critical of American capitalism; in the 1960s Harold Wilson's public support for American policy in Vietnam aroused the ire of the left and in the late 1970s Jim Callaghan's Cabinet faced pressures for nuclear disarmament.

Labour leaders have generally been careful to appoint 'reliable' individuals, with conservative views on foreign policy and defence, to the delicate positions of Foreign Secretary or Defence Secretary. Arthur Henderson, in charge of the Foreign Office in 1929–31, may have been popular with the left and unpopular with some of his officials, a keen advocate of disarmament and a strong supporter of the League of Nations. But he was never a unilateralist, his restoration of diplomatic contacts with the USSR did not result in a close relationship with Moscow and he had to compromise his views with the Atlanticism of MacDonald (in 1929 the first serving Prime Minister to visit Washington). Since 1945 all Foreign Secretaries, from Bevin to David Owen, have been on the right or in the centre of the Labour Party, and the ones who have raised controversy have done so for reasons other than their radical outlook on world affairs: the ill-fated Herbert Morrison seemed unfit for the job in 1951 and George Brown (1966–68) was too outspoken and inebriated. Denis Healey proved a dynamic, long-serving Defence Secretary in 1964–70 but he too was on the centre-right of the party, as were all other holders of the Defence portfolio. Even had Labour won the 1959 election all the signs are that its then foreign policy spokesman, Aneurin Bevan, would have proven less radical than his reputation suggested: the Marxist internationalist of the 1930s, still a critic of NATO, imperialism and rearmament in the early 1950s had, of course, told the 1957 Party Conference that it would be wrong to 'send a Foreign Secretary...naked into the conference chamber' by giving up atomic weapons.[1] How Robin Cook's policy is influenced by his left-wing, 'Old Labour' background remains to be seen.

Having made these preliminary points, it is appropriate to make comments separately about the foreign, defence and European policies of Labour Governments since 1945, whilst remembering that these three areas are closely linked together. It was a major feature of Labour's statements ahead of the 1997 election that defence policy must be integrated with the country's foreign policy and that in foreign, defence and European affairs it is essential to work closely with allies, whether it be the UN, Commonwealth, NATO or the European Union (EU). In rhetoric at least Labour sounded, as it has often done, more 'internationalist' than the Conservatives, better disposed to the Commonwealth and less willing to risk isolation in Europe. Past experience, however, suggests that, just as Conservative Governments have taken a full part in multilateral diplomacy, so Labour Governments are capable of being patriotic, self-seeking and cynical in their dealings with the outside world.

## Foreign and Commonwealth affairs

When Labour formed its first majority administration in July 1945 its ministers already had five years' experience of government and Bevin was already known as a defender of British policy in Greece, where a struggle for power was taking place between the Royalist Government and the Communists. In Britain, of course, it is always difficult for new Governments to differ radically from their predecessors in foreign policy. They inherit the same civil servants and previous treaty commitments. However idealistic, they find it impossible to escape from a world of insecurity, power politics and arms expenditure. Leaders of both main parties generally also share a common, pragmatic approach to policy-making, a need to safeguard Britain's financial and commercial interests abroad and a tendency to try to remove international problems by negotiation rather than to risk war. In 1945 all British politicians were affected by the need to restore national wealth and avoid another war, whilst absorbing the lesson of the 1930s that peace can only be secured at a price, involving substantial defence expenditure alliances and active diplomacy. It was immediately obvious that Bevin was carrying on policies begun by his Conservative opposite number, Eden, continuing co-operation with both the US and USSR while maximising British influence as head of a global Empire. But it is another major fact about foreign policy, even more than domestic policy, that events are forever changing, making long-term planning difficult and the precise course of policy unpredictable. Although Bevin came into office soon after the birth of the UN and with the hope that 'left can speak to left', he is best remembered for signing the North Atlantic Treaty in April 1949, a commitment which became the cornerstone of British security policy through the cold war and which was strongly supported by the Conservatives. Joseph Stalin's ruthless establishment of police states in eastern Europe and Germany, as well as the danger of Soviet expansion towards the British-dominated eastern Mediterranean and Middle East, made relations with Moscow difficult as early as 1946. On the other hand, despite serious differences with America (on the terms of a loan to Britain, the future of their atomic co-operation, or the fate of Palestine, for example) it proved possible to work closely with the US, which shared Britain's liberal-democratic outlook and fear of Soviet ambitions. More practically, Washington could offer financial support for Britain's occupation zone in Germany and offered, in 1947, to underwrite a western European recovery effort with the Marshall Plan.

Though sometimes criticised for his reliance on America, for his maintenance of the Empire in Africa and the Middle East, and for failing to match British resources to its commitments, Bevin is generally seen as a successful Foreign Secretary, perhaps the most successful since the war. Such failures as the hasty retreat from Palestine in 1948 can be excused because of the complexity of the local situation, whilst his physical decline in 1950 may help explain the problems which arose over the Korean war and German rearmament. In retrospect the successful foundation of NATO towers above all else, even if Bevin's role in that event is exaggerated. The Labour Government also scores highly on its conduct of decolonisation in India: whatever the bloodshed which surrounded partition, the British withdrew with timeliness and good grace, transforming the Commonwealth in the process into a multi-racial group, tolerant of Indian republicanism. Even if it was Churchill who coined the term, Britain's influence was based by 1951 on 'three circles': the US alliance, the Commonwealth and, through such institutions as the Brussels Pact and OEEC, links to Europe. On a global level Labour also backed a liberal world trade policy and the creation of the IMF and World Bank. Yet the fact remains that in 1951 the Government passed on global commitments which Britain could not sustain, defence spending so high that even the Conservatives reduced it and an American relationship so close that (again as Winston Churchill said) Britain had become the USSR's prime nuclear target in Europe. The criticisms of the 'Keep Left' group may have dissipated in 1947–48 as Stalin crushed the last vestiges of democracy in Hungary and Czechoslovakia, but by 1951 the Bevanites had emerged as critics of the rigidity of cold war politics, sceptical of the threat posed by the USSR and opposed to American hegemony.

One criticism which the left made of Bevin was that he had become a prisoner of his officials, unable to pursue a socialist foreign policy even had he wanted to. Such accusations were not new. They had first been levelled by Liberal radicals at Edward Grey in the Edwardian period. (Grey, like Labour Foreign Secretaries later in the century, was a moderate in his party, a supporter of strong arms and alliances, attacked by radicals for running the risk of war and for keeping policy-making in the hands of an undemocratic, secretive clique.) Foreign Office staff were themselves dismissive of the idea of the strong-willed Bevin as a civil service stooge: 'He never allowed himself to be bounced into anything against his better judgement', wrote one, adding '...it was misguided to try...'.[2] Yet Morrison, on succeeding Bevin, found the Foreign Office to have 'a sort of freemasonry about it which is stronger than...the civil service generally'[3] and the feeling has persisted on the left that the corruption of the party line by civil servants goes on, especially in a department as select, proud and long-standing as the Foreign Office. Thus, after visiting Tony Crosland there in 1976, Tony Benn wrote 'Anyone working there would be quite paralysed and incapable of challenging the existing authority in any way.'[4] Yet the evidence is that strong characters like Grey (in his pre-1914 attempts at *détente* with Germany), Henderson (on relations with Russia) or Bevin *were* quite capable of asserting themselves against officials at times and that the left could, on occasions, bring changes of policy. In 1977 it was David Owen who closed down the Foreign Office's propaganda arm, the Information Research Department (formed under Bevin forty years before) leading one of the Department's consultants to claim 'the Labour Government had destroyed the only active instrument of counter-subversion in the United Kingdom (as distinct from the passive observation of MI5), as a sop to the left.'[5] The atmosphere and the traditions of the Foreign Office may be intimidating to some, and all ministers must rely on their officials for opinions, but the full explanation of Labour Governments' lack of radicalism abroad must also take into account all the facts mentioned above – a pragmatic national character, the appointment of moderates to the Foreign Secretaryship, commitments inherited from previous Governments and the relentless kaleidoscope of world events.

When Labour returned to power in 1964, after 13 years in opposition, the 'three circles' were still intact and, with its presence in south-east Asia and the Persian Gulf, the country could still be considered a global military power as well as a commercial-financial one. Yet much had changed. Outside the Gulf, Britain's presence in the Middle East had dissipated after Suez. In 1959–61 the Conservative Colonial Secretary, Iain Macleod, had presided over a rapid acceleration of the decolonisation process in Africa. And in 1961–63 Harold Macmillan's Government had made its first vain bid to enter the European Community (EC). It is possible to see, in Conservative deliberations on Britain's place in the world around 1960–61, a self-conscious appreciation of the need to retreat from a global military-political presence to a European focus. But for Wilson's Government in 1964-70 there was a strong element of 're-learning' that same lesson. In 1964 Wilson and leading ministers like Patrick Gordon-Walker (Foreign Secretary) or Jim Callaghan (Chancellor of the Exchequer) were considered 'Commonwealth Men' as well as Atlanticists, and were doubtful about the need to move closer to the EC. True, in 1964–65 Labour began, for the first time since the 1930s, to gear defence spending to what the country could afford, rather than the commitments it had to defend. But there was still a strong belief in remaining 'East of Suez' not least because this pleased the Americans: already becoming embroiled in Vietnam, they had no desire to take over Britain's role of 'policeman' in Malaysia-Singapore or the Gulf.

Within a few years, however, the Government had seriously to refocus its policy overseas. The Commonwealth remained important to Labour, which continued to decolonise in Africa and the West Indies. But the Indo-Pakistan war of 1965 and the Unilateral Declaration of Independence by Rhodesia a few months later seriously divided the organisation, exposing it as a poor basis for British influence. Neither could much money be spared for the Overseas Development Administration established under Barbara Castle in 1964. More seriously, mounting economic pressures forced not only the devaluation of sterling in 1967 but the decision, announced soon after, to withdraw from bases east of Suez. This decision in turn undermined Britain's usefulness to Washington. Despite support for the Vietnam war, Wilson never became as close as he hoped to President Lyndon Johnson, yet Britain's very reliance on America – for Polaris missiles and the support of sterling – alienated France's Charles de Gaulle and ensured the defeat of Wilson's attempt to discuss EC entry in 1967. By 1970, Labour could claim to have taken some key decisions about Britain's future. The withdrawal from east of Suez, the reduced significance of the Sterling Area and the revival, in 1969–70, of possible EC entry were all important steps. Nonetheless they had taken place amidst an atmosphere of drift rather than decision. In contrast to Bevin's period, foreign policy-making under Wilson is not, in retrospect, recalled for any great foresight or success.

By 1974, when Wilson returned to the premiership, Britain's role in the world appeared even more to be at the mercy of events. Imperial decline, shrinking defence forces and, above all, industrial underperformance created a situation where the once leading power was increasingly at the mercy of a threatening international environment. Foreign Secretary Callaghan told the Cabinet in April 1974, 'our place in the world is shrinking: long-term political influence depends on economic strength and that is running out.'[6] For all that Britain was still a major commercial power, about the fifth largest economy in the world and a leading member of various international organisations including, since 1973, the EC. Despite the suspicion of the left, Callaghan, as Prime Minister in 1976–79, became the most trusted European ally of America's President Jimmy Carter. For a few years at least, East-West *détente*, which reached its height in the Helsinki Agreements of 1975, kept Labour united on cold war questions. And, following a difficult period under Edward Heath (who had restored arms sales to South Africa), there was a marked improvement in Commonwealth relations. The Rhodesia problem rumbled on, only being solved under Margaret Thatcher. But progress towards a settlement, based on majority rule, was made under Owen as Foreign Secretary (1977–79). Afro-Asian leaders were pleased with Wilson's support for a world commodity agreement to help developing nations – even if it came to nothing – and the Silver Jubilee celebrations proved that the British monarchy was more than a decorative institution, when it provided a focus for self-congratulation at the biennial Commonwealth Summit in 1977. Whatever its relative decline compared to its major industrial competitors, even in the uncertain 1970s, Britain still counted for something.

Under the Conservatives after 1979 there were dramatic changes in the world, not least the collapse of Communism, the break-up of the Soviet Union and the reunification of Germany. The Blair Government in 1997 arrived in office just as the last major Crown Colony, Hong Kong, was about to be given up; and it was the first Labour administration to come into office without having to concern itself with Anglo-Soviet relations. In the latter area at least, left-wingers would presumably provoke less embarrassment for the leadership, though there were still many areas – security in the Gulf region, the eastwards expansion of NATO (which may yet antagonise Russia), or the scale and focus of development aid, perhaps – where divisions within the Party were possible. What was certain was that events would crowd in on foreign policy-makers as they always do, making long-term planning as difficult as in the past. The expectations and hopes of 1997 would be reshaped as profoundly as those of 1945 and 1964. The range of problems on the international agenda had also expanded during Labour's lengthy period in opposition, with a much greater emphasis on combating crime or on environmental issues for example, making a coherent policy even more difficult. Then again it was not that the Labour Party promised much specifically in this area before being elected. The 1997 Labour manifesto was disappointingly thin on international questions other than the EU. A certain level of development aid was promised but with no timetable to achieve it. Reform of the UN was supported but it was unclear what the party's attitude would be on the main problem, the future shape of the Security Council, where Britain's possession of a permanent seat has been criticised by some other countries. Any idea that the seat could be given up was apparently ruled out by the manifesto's insistence that British influence must be revived and that the country remained a world leader – patriotic sentiments no different from the Conservative manifesto and underlined by Blair's only foreign policy speech during the election, in Manchester on 28 April. Pre-election speeches by the party's foreign policy team were a little more helpful. A readiness to strengthen UN peacekeeping, improve co-operation with the Commonwealth (after John Major's refusal to condemn French nuclear tests upset the last summit) and use economic pressure against Nigeria to ensure respect for human rights, all made Labour's rhetorical tone very different from the Conservatives. And Robin Cook tried to differentiate himself from the Conservatives by declaring '…the Government's aspiration is to stand alone while ours is to find partners.'[7] But, apart from the arms to Iraq affair, Labour policy on specific problems looked quite similar to the Conservatives', with support for the peace processes in Bosnia and the Middle East, for example, and hopes for a smooth transition to Chinese rule in Hong Kong, as well as a desire – not least from Blair himself – to work closely with Washington rather than consigning the 'special relationship' to the historical graveyard.

## Defence

In 1945 Clement Attlee's Government faced an unenviable situation on the defence front. The Royal Navy, still the largest in the world in 1939, was now only half the size of America's and, despite Britain's important contribution to its development, the Americans insisted on keeping sole control of the atomic bomb. Difficulties in Palestine and India, occupation duties in Libya, Ethiopia and Indochina and the need to garrison British colonies elsewhere, meant that the armed forces were scattered round the globe. But the worst threat was the USSR. The Red Army had been vital to the defeat of Germany but it was also the means by which Stalin dominated eastern Europe and, even after demobilisation began, it was far larger than western conventional forces in Europe. Actually western experts believed that post-war reconstruction, and the impact of its huge casualties, made the Soviets unlikely to launch war for at least ten years. But the Berlin Blockade (1948–49) and, more particularly, the coming of 'hot war' to Korea in June 1950, raised fears that another war *might* soon be possible. The Attlee Government took a number of key decisions in this period. One was to maintain substantial armed forces backed by the maintenance of conscription into peacetime. The traditional opposition of Labour politicians to such a policy had been undermined by memories of the 1930s when Britain's delayed rearmament (itself criticised by Labour at the time) left the country unable to deter Hitler. The outbreak of the Korean war brought a massive rearmament programme which threatened Labour's social spending and led to the resignation of Bevan and Wilson from the Cabinet. Secondly, of course, the Government proved ready to enter permanent peacetime alliances, another policy which had been highly controversial in the past. The foundation of NATO, and Bevin's role in it, was discussed in the last section. But NATO was preceded by a new Anglo-French alliance (the Treaty of Dunkirk, 1947) and the Brussels Pact of 1948 with France, Belgium, the Netherlands and Luxembourg (in 1955 this was expanded to Germany and Italy, becoming the Western European Union). Close co-operation with America also involved numerous US military and air bases being established in Britain and it included a close intelligence alliance, cemented by the highly secret UK/USA agreements. Finally, in another example of secret government (and another example of compromising past Labour beliefs) Attlee and a narrow group of ministers decided in 1947 to develop Britain's own atomic bomb. This was designed not only to deter a Soviet attack but also to maintain Britain's status as a great power and to help ensure the country's continuing importance to the US. The bomb was not, however, successfully tested until 1952, three years after the Soviets exploded one of their own, further emphasising Britain's vulnerability.

By pursuing a defence based on high spending, the Atlantic alliance and nuclear deterrence, Labour again can be said to have laid the foundations for British policy throughout the cold war. But as with foreign policy, the approach was attacked by the Bevanites in the early 1950s. They questioned the need to rearm former aggressors like Germany and Japan, argued that alliances and arms spending simply led to a spiral of fear (culminating in the danger of nuclear war over Cuba in 1962) and believed that totalitarian communism was best defeated, not by military deterrence, but by the evidence of a thriving, democratic western system, where money was spent on social reform programmes. In the mid-1950s concern mounted about the dangers of nuclear war, and the environmental effect of nuclear tests. The foundation of the Campaign for Nuclear Disarmament in 1957 was followed three years later by the Labour Conference vote against nuclear arms. Yet when a former Bevanite, Harold Wilson, came into office in 1964 his Government largely followed the path laid by Attlee. Healey argued that the Polaris programme was too advanced to reverse. The need to maintain NATO was reasserted after French withdrawal from the alliance's military arm in 1966. And, of course, the Government long tried to maintain a military presence in the Gulf and south-east Asia. Furthermore, even if Britain avoided a commitment to the Vietnam war, the defence relationship with America was as close as ever: US nuclear submarines now operated from Holy Loch, the Indian island base of Diego Garcia was secured by London for American use and the Cabinet quickly decided to abandon a number of military aircraft projects (notably the TSR-2), replacing them with cheaper US aeroplanes. The anti-communist focus of defence policy and the money to be made from arms sales also meant that, while largely fulfilling a UN arms embargo against South Africa's apartheid regime, the Government agreed to supply Pretoria with Buccaneer naval strike aircraft. There was one important early decision by the Government, however, which showed a readiness to limit overseas ambitions, protect the economy from overstretch and preserve social programmes rather than defence from spending restraints. This was the decision, in Labour's first defence review, to limit defence spending at 1964 prices to £2 billion per year. And, by the end of the Government, the decision to withdraw from east of Suez, plus Denis Healey's encouragement of a 'Eurogroup' within NATO, showed that the focus of defence planning was moving towards Europe. Labour also supported the 1967 Harmel Report by which NATO committed itself to a political role, that of achieving *détente* with the Communist bloc. By 1970 therefore, reduced expenditure, the end of a global defence role and the advent of *détente* all made for a very different atmosphere from the Attlee years, even if British defence spending was still higher than that of most other NATO members.

In the early 1970s, another period of opposition saw Conference resolutions against American nuclear submarine bases in Britain, but once back in office in 1974–79 Labour's defence policy was again dominated by Atlanticist thinking. Indeed 'the operational defence policy of the Government was more inconsistent with that of the Party than was the case for any administration since 1945.'[8] America's Holy Loch base remained and, indeed, the number of US military and intelligence installations in Britain now numbered over 100. The Cabinet stuck to its promise not to buy any new American nuclear missiles but nonetheless made a costly bid to update Polaris with the 'Chevaline' project. In 1977, as *détente* was called increasingly into question, Britain supported a NATO decision to increase defence spending by 3 per cent and discussions began on the modernisation of theatre nuclear weapons in Europe. Atlanticists argued that Soviet armed forces were being maintained at a threatingly high level, especially if Moscow honestly believed in *détente*. Soviet conventional forces were still large, their navy was rapidly expanding and mobile, multi-warhead SS-20 missiles were now being deployed in eastern Europe. But the left believed that the USSR had genuine security fears, not least given America's continued strategic nuclear superiority and the improved relations between Washington and (increasingly anti-Soviet) Beijing. Many on the left not only distrusted NATO calculations of the Warsaw Pact's military power but believed there was a moral case for giving up British nuclear weapons, especially since the economy was performing so badly. The debate over deploying the new 'neutron bomb' in Europe in 1977–78 increased the sense of moral unease among Government critics. But Carter's decision not to deploy the weapon intensified the fears of Atlanticists that NATO deterrence strategy in Europe was in trouble: the US might not, in the event of war, prove ready to defend Europe; and if the Soviets continued their current policies they could threaten to overrun western Europe (or at least West Germany) without risk of retribution.

Within months of Labour losing office in 1979 the international scene looked much worse. In December the Soviet invasion of Afghanistan brought an end to *détente* and heralded a massive increase in defence spending by the Carter administration. Shortly before the invasion, NATO finally agreed that within four years' Cruise and Pershing missiles would be deployed in Europe, unless the Soviets proved ready to negotiate limits on all theatre nuclear weapons: such a negotiation looked very unlikely after Afghanistan. Unrest in Poland, the triumph of the cold warrior Ronald Reagan in the 1980 American election and the decision of the Thatcher Government to replace Polaris with Trident missiles, all added to the sense of international danger and helped generate years of bitter division in the Labour Party over defence issues. The revival of CND, the establishment of 'nuclear free zones' and the evidence of popular unease in opinion polls created the impression that a determined anti-nuclear stance by Labour would win popular approval. Defence indeed became central to the Party's internal debates at this time, especially when the unilateral nuclear disarmer Michael Foot beat the Atlanticist Healey for the leadership. The formation of the Social Democratic Party was partly influenced by a desire to safeguard the nuclear deterrent; and, of course, it left the Party's Atlanticists, such as Healey and Roy Hattersley, much depleted in number. The 1983 election saw public differences between the unilateralist Foot and multilateralists Callaghan and Healey, and the manifesto – with its promises of removing US nuclear bases in Britain, reduced defence expenditure and international talks to liquidate Polaris – did not, in the end, win over the electorate. Instead Labour secured little more than a quarter of the vote. Despite this humiliating defeat, CND and unilateralism remained popular in the Party for some years, as did ideas for a 'non-provocative' (genuinely *defensive*) defence posture, the revival of *détente* and East-West talks on European security. The 1987 election manifesto was actually clearer on the intention to scrap Polaris than the 1983 manifesto had been and Labour was deeply opposed to Thatcher's Trident purchase. Although in the 1987 election Labour also promised to *increase* conventional arms spending, voters were no more impressed than in 1983, and the Conservatives again won a handsome majority, saddling Neil Kinnock with the image of a man bent on surrendering to any foreign opponent.

After 1987 the Party moved away from unilateralism. The late 1980s saw progress on *détente* between Reagan and Mikhail Gorbachev, the Intermediate Nuclear Forces treaty (removing Cruise and SS-20 missiles from Europe) and the decline, once more, of CND. With less fear of war and an increased determination to win the next election, Labour leaders pressed for a change in the Party's defence policy, the 1989 Conference accepting that Britain's nuclear weapons should only be removed as part of a multilateral disarmament process. The collapse of Soviet bloc Communism in 1989–91 was accompanied by triumphalism on the right. Deterrence it seemed had worked, Reagan's toughness had helped break Soviet power and NATO had become history's most successful alliance. In response socialists could have echoed Bevan by arguing that Soviet power *had* been vastly overestimated by the West, that NATO defence expenditure could have been better used on social programmes and that Communism was defeated, not by Reagan and Thatcher, but by the positive image of a freedom and social justice in the western societies which, if anything, had been compromised by the new right. But, as with the questioning of Bevin's policies in the 1940s, such arguments tended to be drowned out. The changes in European security did bring benefits for Labour, however: although NATO still believed in the validity of nuclear deterrence, the emphasis was now on the alliance's political role and in the 1992 election it was possible to urge a switch from defence to social spending without seeming unpatriotic. The 1990–91 Gulf war and the Bosnian civil war of 1992–95 showed that sizeable defence forces were still needed, but Labour was able to put the emphasis in 1997 on the need for a stronger UN peace-keeping machinery rather than for armaments as part of a balance of power contest. The 1997 manifesto showed some idealism in its encouragement of shifting arms producers to civilian manufacturing and its determination to ban landmines worldwide but the Party had very much returned to an Atlanticist mould in the statements of its front bench. Whilst nuclear disarmament was still an aim, Trident was to be retained after all – ahead of the new Government's much-trumpeted review of national security – NATO would remain central to British defence planning and America's continuing commitment to European security would be encouraged. Labour spokesmen like David Clark proudly recalled their Atlanticist inheritance from Ernest Bevin.[9]

## European integration

The idea that a European federation could be a practical political step was first suggested by the French foreign minister, Aristide Briand, in 1929 when he was looking for a peaceful way both to control German power and to match America's burgeoning economic might. The 'slump' and the rise of nationalism in Europe soon put an end to the idea, but it was MacDonald's Labour Government which had to react to the proposal and it did so with some striking parallels to Britain's post-1945 attitudes: a general feeling that European integration was impractical, a belief that British commercial interests were best solved by a *global* approach to free trade, a reluctance to alienate America and a wish to safeguard Commonwealth links. It was also a Labour Government which had to come to terms with the rebirth of European unity proposals after the Second World War. Bevin's policies in this area, especially the failure to take part in talks on the 'Schuman Plan' (for a supranational institution to control western Europe's coal and steel industries) are often criticised. But in fact there were positive aspects of British policy at the time. In 1945 Bevin was interested in proposals for a British-led western European bloc which could help control Germany in future, provide an outlet for trade and (alongside co-operation with the Commonwealth) help Britain to remain the equal of the US and USSR. Bevin also encouraged the Cabinet in 1946–47 to study a possible customs union with western Europe. And in 1947–48, as seen above, he led the west Europeans in accepting the Marshall Aid programme and establishing the Brussels Pact. He was, however, markedly less enthusiastic about proposals for a European assembly: for Bevin intergovernmental co-operation, in which Britain preserved its national independence, was infinitely preferable to supranationalism, where London would share decision-making with other powers. Britain was a founder-member of the Council of Europe, complete with an assembly, in 1949, but the powers of that body were strictly limited. Also, with their Commonwealth trade preferences, global commerce and relatively strong industrial sector, the British saw little reason to merge their economic future with the continent. In early 1949 Attlee's Cabinet agreed that it would co-operate in joint efforts at European economic recovery but only to the extent that this was compatible with Britain's ability to survive independently. Such a principle, alongside Bevin's increasingly Atlanticist outlook, made it difficult to join in the Schuman Plan, though Whitehall did expend considerable effort in studying the proposal. Having survived the war undefeated and unoccupied, Britain lacked the motivations of some continental states for 'pooling' their sovereignty: unlike France, the British did not have a deep-seated desire to control Germany by such a 'pooling'; and unlike Germany, they did not have a strong desire to replace a nationalist foreign policy with a European faith. Such factors reinforced Britain's psychological ambivalence towards Europe, an ambivalence born of geographical position, legal-constitutional differences and centuries free from foreign invasion.

By 1961 the Conservative administrations which followed Attlee had to come to terms with the declining value of Commonwealth trade, Britain's shrinking influence compared to the superpowers and the successful foundation of the European Economic Community. Certain Labour politicians too, foremost among them George Brown, believed Britain's future lay in Europe. But in a celebrated speech to the party conference in 1962 Gaitskell attacked Harold Macmillan's attempt to enter the EC as likely to end 'a thousand years of history'. Gaitskell himself was particularly concerned about the danger EC membership presented to the Commonwealth. Many Labour members were indifferent to the European issue but welcomed the chance to attack Macmillan's Government. So, Labour became identified with 'anti-Europeanism' even though, on a close reading of Party statements at the time, membership of the EC was not categorically ruled out. In the 1964 election it did not seem to matter anyway. In January 1963 de Gaulle had vetoed Macmillan's entry bid, accusing Britain of being too closely tied to America and unfitted for a European future, and none of the major parties saw a renewed application as practical politics. Harold Wilson, with his Atlanticism, pro-Commonwealth views and hopes of maintaining the 'world role' hardly seemed the likely man to lead Britain into Europe. And in the March 1966 election the Prime Minister castigated his pro-EC Conservative opponent, Edward Heath, for rolling 'on his back like a spaniel' before the French Government. Once again, however, Labour did not rule out EC membership in principle. Indeed Wilson's emphasis was always on the terms of entry. So long as the details were right – if Commonwealth interests could be protected, for example, and Britain retained its independent foreign policy – Wilson recognised that the EC offered access to a large market, where growth rates had recently been far better than those in Britain.

Before the end of 1966 Wilson's Government had begun to explore EC entry. The Prime Minister's inability to forge a close relationship with Johnson and the troubled state of the Commonwealth, due to the Rhodesia problem, encouraged the belief – as Macmillan had come to appreciate around 1960 – that Britain's future lay in Europe. The sterling crisis of July 1966 suggested that a 'go-it-alone' policy could only mean continuing decline; whilst the idea of a 'North Atlantic Free Trade Area' with the US and Canada, though seriously canvassed, was never practical politics. Big business, a majority in the opinion polls and key Cabinet ministers like Brown were in favour of entry, and the new intake of Labour MPs at the March 1966 election was also better disposed to Europe. The Prime Minister himself, pragmatic as ever, was no 'Euro-enthusiast' but he backed the idea of a European 'technological community' which might allow Britain, in co-operation with continental partners, to match US strength in such areas as the aerospace industry. The veto of Labour's application by de Gaulle in November 1967 was actually widely predicted in Government: for de Gaulle Britain was still over-reliant on the US, especially in the defence field. But an often-overlooked point is that Wilson kept the application 'on the table'. If Britain's future lay in Europe, then the country had little choice other than to keep knocking on the door. And other events in late 1967, the devaluation of sterling and the decision to withdraw from east of Suez, reinforced the impression that EC membership was essential. Another often overlooked point is that in 1969–70, after de Gaulle's resignation, it was the Wilson application which was taken up by the EC. True, formal negotiations for entry did not begin until after the June 1970 election. But in those talks Edward Heath's negotiations used the same briefs prepared by the Wilson Government.

In opposition in the early 1970s the European issue began to divide the Labour Party very seriously. For Wilson (supported by a substantial group of MPs) the main question, again, was a pragmatic one: determined to attack the Conservatives and with no strong emotional feelings on the issue, he again used the argument that what mattered were the terms of entry. Whilst, once more, never ruling out membership in principle (which, given his 1967 application would have been difficult), Wilson argued that the deal struck by Heath and the Community in 1971 was not good enough. Hence the promise by Labour in the 1974 election to renegotiate the Conservatives' terms, a promise which led in 1974–75 to some (largely cosmetic) changes in the financial arrangements for membership and better access for certain Commonwealth products. But other Labour MPs felt more strongly about the subject. Social democrats, especially, foremost among them Roy Jenkins, believed strongly in the principle of membership as a way to bolster British power in the world, secure better access to European markets and bring the country into line with post-imperial realities. Nearly 70 Labour MPs ignored the Party whip to vote in favour of membership in October 1971. Another diverse group, including left-wingers like Michael Foot but also rightists like Peter Shore, were opposed, in principle, to EC membership on a number of grounds: such a step would destroy the Commonwealth, undermine parliamentary sovereignty and impede the pursuit of socialist policies in Britain; it would make Britain part of a 'capitalist club' where working-class interests would be harmed by higher food prices (thanks to the Common External Tariff and Common Agricultural Policy, CAP) and unemployment caused by the need to deflate (in order to make Britain more competitive against Germany, France and the rest). It was largely to hold the Party together that Wilson, in 1975, held a referendum on EC membership, even allowing Cabinet colleagues to speak on opposite sides in the debate.

The referendum, a radical departure in British politics, but one justified by the constitutionally significant nature of the decision, had first been suggested by the anti-marketeer Douglas Jay in 1970 and was taken up enthusiastically by Tony Benn. Benn, a pro-marketeer in 1967, became a leading anti-marketeer in the 1975 referendum. But the outcome of the referendum was not as the 'antis' expected. Two-thirds of the electorate approved membership on the basis of Wilson's renegotiated terms, without the Prime Minister having to play a prominent public role. Instead, a well-financed and well-organised campaign by the 'pros', backed by most of the press, helped secure victory. The 'antis' often appeared a disorganised group from the extremes of British politics, with no convincing alternative to the EC if Britain were to remain a secure, influential power. The apparently decisive popular verdict did not, however, solve Labour's divisions in the way Wilson had hoped. Benn, Foot and other 'antis' remained in the Cabinet whilst, in 1977, Jenkins left to become President of the European Commission. The need for Callaghan's Government to rely on Liberal votes in the Commons in 1977–78 created a new complication because of the Liberals' pro-European approach. Controversy soon surrounded the growth of Britain's net contribution to the Community, which reached nearly £800 million in 1979, largely due to the expenses of the CAP from which Britain, as an industrial state, gained little. And the simple fact was that EC membership did not, as some had naively hoped, transform the country's economic prospects. Instead inflation, rising unemployment and the need for expenditure cuts made the 1970s a depressing and uncertain time. Neither were relations between Britain and its EC partners very close. The renegotiation process and the uncertainties of the referendum campaign hardly made the British popular on the continent, London caused a one-year delay to the first direct elections for the European Parliament, held in June 1979, and Callaghan avoided membership of the Exchange Rate Mechanism when it was launched the same year. Indeed, ridiculous as it may seem in retrospect, such was the continental view of British policy in 1979 that many EC leaders welcomed the advent of Margaret Thatcher (just as, in 1990, many welcomed her replacement by John Major).

After the 1979 election defeat, Europe, like defence, remained a major point of contention in the Party and helped bring the foundation of the SDP. European socialists despaired of Labour's policies and in 1983 the Party promised to negotiate withdrawal from the Community within the lifetime of a Parliament. Once again, however, the scale of defeat forced a change of thinking. So too, perhaps, did the failure of an attempt at fully fledged socialism (with nationalisation, higher social security payments and wage increases) in France under François Mitterrand. Already in the 1984 Euro-elections Labour shifted its approach to demanding reform of the EC from within, a line similar to Thatcher's and one which had done her no harm with the electorate. In the mid-1980s European economies were expanding, the proportion of British trade with the Community was increasing and talk of withdrawal looked increasingly unrealistic. In 1987 the Labour manifesto accepted EC membership alongside promises of reform (not least of the CAP). In the late 1980s, indeed, with a new drive for institutional reform in Europe, it was the Conservatives who became divided on the question. The single market, launched in January 1993, might be welcomed by Thatcherites as symbolising the acceptance of free enterprise values, but greater qualified majority voting, the social charter and talk of a common currency were not. Just as socialists feared the EC would impede their ability to pursue state intervention in the 1970s, so some Conservatives feared the EC would blunt the Thatcherite programme. The Trades Union Congress in September 1988 gave an enthusiastic welcome to the Commission President, Jacques Delors, who firmly backed greater social protection for ordinary people in the face of the single market. In 1992 and 1997 Labour's acceptance of the Social Chapter was one of the main areas in which the parties differed on international issues: in 1997, indeed, it was one of the few points on which there was a marked difference at all.

Robin Cook's promise of avoiding isolation in the EC was again meant to signal a different negotiating approach to the Conservatives. And Labour were readier to accept such new common policies as anti-racism. But in other areas of EC policy it was a case of similarities. In their general rhetoric Labour speakers denied Labour would be 'a pushover and a soft touch in Europe', still less accept a federal super-state.[10] And on details, like the Conservatives, Labour favoured the enlargement of the EC, suggested they would opt out of a common immigration policy and were unenthusiastic about close Community co-operation on defence. Most importantly perhaps, Labour spokesmen had made sceptical remarks about a European single currency, hinting that Britain would not enter such a currency when it was supposed to begin in 1999. But another, potentially disturbing similarity was the evidence of divisions in the Labour leadership over Europe, with Cook's scepticism about a single currency contrasting with the more positive views of the Chancellor of the Exchequer, Gordon Brown, while the precise views of the new Prime Minister were unclear.

## Conclusion

Whatever the hopes of the new Labour Government for a policy of partnership rather than isolation in Europe, and however sensible this is, there are plenty of signs that the Blair Government may not look too different from its Conservative predecessors. Thatcher, with her support for the single market (and the qualified majority voting needed to achieve it), and Major, with his desire to be 'at the heart of Europe', were not as Euro-sceptical as they sometimes claimed. Both believed that Britain must remain in the Community. The single currency (of which Cook had always been more sceptical than Gordon Brown, Blair's Chancellor of the Exchequer), VAT payments and fisheries policy are all areas where Labour might soon differ from its EC partners. And all Governments since 1973, including Heath's, have seen the electoral advantage of 'standing up for Britain' in the Community. More generally in foreign policy, the handover of Hong Kong and the peace process in Bosnia presents potential minefields, although it is more certain that America would remain committed to NATO and that Labour will be able to hold down defence costs. With less ideological baggage than Labour administrations in the past the Government might expect to tackle international issues flexibly, without arousing too much backbench ire, but divisions on the EC certainly exist in the Party and it was still possible to foresee criticism of moves which offend Russia. The main message of the past about international policy is that much is uncertain, events are rapidly changing and the unexpected often happens. As in other areas of policy-making, if Government ministers gain a good understanding of the problems they face, work well together (especially at the highest level, between Prime Minister and Foreign

Secretary) and minimise backbench criticism, some of the battle has been won. If no major military threat to Britain emerges to replace that of the USSR, if the world remains relatively peaceful and if, as is possible, the single currency proves stillborn it may be that the international challenges to the Blair Government will be far less significant than domestic ones. But the post-war Soviet challenge, Rhodesian UDI, or the decline of *détente* in the late 1970s all stand as reminders of how shifts abroad can impact on stability at home. In defence and foreign policy in particular, Governments need to steer between the impossibility of rigidity and the dangers of drift. At the next election it will be interesting to see how far the Blair Government's foreign policy has lived up to its idealistic rhetoric and how far it has merely continued older trends.

# Notes

I am grateful to Geoffrey Warner of Brasenose College, Oxford for his comments on this paper.

1 Labour Party, *Annual Conference Report 1957*, Transport House, 1957, p.182.
2 Ivone Kirkpatrick, *The Inner Circle*, Macmillan, Basingstoke, 1959, p.203.
3 Lord Morrison, *Herbert Morrison, an Autobiography*, Odhams, 1960, p.274.
4 Tony Benn, *Against the Tide; Diaries 1973–6*, Hutchinson, 1989, p.576.
5 Brian Crozier, *Free Agent*, HarperCollins, 1993, p.104.
6 James Callaghan, *Time and Chance*, Collins, 1987, p.326.
7 *House of Commons Debates*, Sixth Series, (H.C. Deb. 6s) Vol. 267, col. 148.
8 Dan Keohane, *Labour Defence Policy since 1945*, Leicester University Press, 1993, p.28.
9 H.C. Deb. 6s, vol. 267, col. 217.
10 H.C. Deb. 6s, vol. 287, cols. 497-502 for a statement by Joyce Quin in a December 1996 debate on Europe.

# Commentary

*Geoffrey Warner*

Labour Governments since 1945, regardless of some traditional Party shibboleths, or even the Party's actual policies while in opposition, have tended to pursue an essentially bipartisan foreign policy, not least because they were unable – even presuming that they were willing – radically to alter the external and internal environment in which foreign policy was made for the 50 or so years after the war. The first feature of this environment, of course, was the cold war between the West and the communist world. The second was the decline in the size of the colonial Empire and the relaxing of links with the Commonwealth. The third was the psychological ambivalence of the British towards Europe brought about primarily by the fact that in the second world war most of continental Europe was occupied and therefore, perhaps, less inclined to worry about giving up sovereignty; Britain still lives on a mythology that tells of how we stood alone, and this sort of mythology – or psychology – runs much deeper than mere trade patterns.

With the end of the cold war and the virtual end of empire, symbolised by the return of Hong Kong to the Chinese, one wonders whether there is, under a new Government, a real opportunity for a new departure. New Labour, new foreign policy? To the extent that New Labour has revamped its domestic policy pretty thoroughly, might it not do the same in the foreign and defence field? Well, mission statements and press briefings notwithstanding, there is little sign of it so far. This is largely due to the continuing influence of the third factor mentioned above: psychological ambivalence towards Europe.

Labour's record towards Europe was, under the Callaghan administrations, the cause for such dismay among continental Europeans that they actually welcomed the Thatcher Government in 1979, thinking that it was going to be the dawn of a new era. Something similar occurred when John Major replaced Mrs Thatcher in 1990. Now we have Tony Blair and his promise to pursue a policy of positive engagement. How likely, however, is he to deliver on his promises when the attempt to shadow the more (and sometimes the less) respectable versions of the Conservatives'

Euro-scepticism played such an important part in the long election campaign and the run-up to the Amsterdam summit, particularly over issues like immigration and foreign and defence policy? The language may be (though it is not always) softer, the approach might be better; but you can smile when you kick someone in the teeth just as much as you can growl at them. It is the substance as much as the style one has to look at if one wants to trace a real shift over the next few years.

The other side of this psychological ambivalence towards Europe is an exaggerated attachment to the so-called special relationship with the USA. This is clearly still present. Tony Blair spoke of Britain as a bridge between the United States and Europe at the Labour Party Conference in 1996 and the press indulged in an officially inspired orgy of self-congratulation on the strength of the special relationship during the visit of President Clinton to London in May 1997. Now, this has been a game which all British Governments have sought to play since 1945, and much good it has done them! A bridge is not needed, and is not wanted. It runs a very real risk of jeopardising our relations with our European partners and it does not do very much for Anglo-American relations either. The latter have not been notably better when Labour Governments have had the chance to work with Democratic Presidents. Relations were not always terribly good between the Truman and Attlee administrations over Palestine, the American loan, and the Korean rearmament programme. The relationship between Johnson and Wilson was not that good either, although we were told at the time that they got on splendidly. One wonders whether the purple prose about the personal chemistry between Clinton and Blair should not perhaps be treated with some caution. This is by no means a trivial point about personalities; it is also about policy. We might pause in particular to ask, for example, whether President Clinton's agenda on Northern Ireland is quite the same as our own.

Obviously, this is not to argue that a new Labour Government should be openly critical of the United States for the sake of doing so. But it does mean that there should be a clear reorientation of policy. Firstly, on the question of Security Council membership, surely it is not beyond the wit of the countries concerned to devise some system of a rotating seat on the Security Council for members of the European Union? Britain should be moving towards this rather than clinging on to our present position – a position which is clearly an historical accident in the sense that it represents our status and strength in 1945 rather than in 1997. Secondly, the new Government should not, in its much trumpeted defence review, rule out further Europeanisation of our policy in that area, for example, by seeking to participate in a mixed force on the Franco-German model. However, the Blair Government continues to rule out any expanded defence role for the European Union. The sacred cows of Britain's 'independent' nuclear deterrent and the need for a defence capability befitting a permanent member of the Security Council, continue to be paraded, when a Labour Government should be particularly aware that attempts to exercise responsibilities on behalf of someone or something else are apt to cause economic as well as political problems.

Ultimately, then, we cannot continue to function as a semi-detached member of a European Union which seeks to maintain a special link with an external power. We could get away with this when we still had some power left. We could get away with it during the period of the cold war because there was still some purpose behind it. But we cannot go on pursuing this policy. The sooner this Government starts educating the British people about the realities of the situation, the better. Unfortunately there is little sign yet of a determination to do so.

# Chapter 8

# Managing the Party and the trade unions

*Tim Bale*

Prior to Labour's election victory in 1997, the attempt to distance the Party from its supposedly strife-torn past was at the heart of its leader's modernising project. For some time Labour had tried to persuade voters to forget about its historical experience in office, to say nothing of the near suicidal internal conflict that engulfed the Party on its return to opposition after 1979. This had not, however, proved successful: the chaotic images of the Winter of Discontent regularly conjured up by the Conservatives were just too powerful, too entrenched. Instead, a new, rather audacious strategy was tried: rather than playing down its past difficulties, the Party would own up to them – and in spades. The encouragement of amnesia was replaced by the penitent's promise to have changed for the better, and for good. Almost as soon as Tony Blair became leader, he and his lieutenants more or less consciously began to 'paint a portrait of their own Party['s past] in which accuracy was sacrificed not to enhance but to belittle the original' in the hope that 'to engage in pre-emptive auto-strikes, acknowledging the truth of much of the tabloid version [of that past] and then demonstrating that "New Labour" had learnt its lessons and wiped the slate clean' would boost both the electoral chances of the Party and what they hoped was their ever-tightening grip upon it.[1]

So just as any improved version of a product must have an old, unimproved one from which it can be distinguished, New Labour needed old Labour – and in particular the Governments of Wilson and Callaghan. Of course, these had always been the subject of despair and scorn on the part of Labour's supposedly 'hard' left, but now the latter were joined by their sworn enemies on the Party's other extreme, many of whom were integral parts (or, had they been there, would have been vocal supporters) of the administrations in question. There was, however, a crucial difference between the hermetically sealed world of the left critique and the equally enclosed one inhabited by some of Blair's ex-SDP advisors. In the latter's version, old Labour's Prime Ministers were seen not so much as spineless in the face of the reactionary forces of organised capital, but rather as more or less willing prisoners of their own Party and more particularly its apparently innate inability to see that (to coin a phrase of which both Harold and Jim were, ironically, especially fond) 'the Government must govern'. Rather than being forced back to orthodoxy by the enemy without, as the left conspiracy theory would have it, we were expected to believe that it was blackmailed by the enemy within into 'beer and sandwiches' and 'tax and spend'. Little wonder, then, that improved management of the Party is seen by Labour's first Prime Minister in 18 years to be crucial to his – and of course his Party's – chances of staying in the job for some considerable time to come. But is the new orthodoxy about Labour's past good history? And will the lessons it purports to teach make for good politics?

## What is party management, and why is it important?

For all the talk of their terminal decline, political parties are still one of the British polity's most vital components.[2] They embody and transmit an ideological tradition, however fragmented and/or elastic that tradition may have become. They recruit people into politics at all levels, thereby providing an important link between civil society and the state. They aggregate a potentially bewildering range of interests and ideas into more or less coherent wholes which voters who are too busy (or too bored) to weigh up all the options in detail can simply support or reject. They provide and (ideally) sustain the parliamentary majorities without which any democratic administration would find it impossible to display the governing competence and argumentative superiority which are so vital, both in terms of running – and continuing to run – the country. When it comes to political success, then, considerations of party management are not extraneous or somehow sordid, the preoccupation of supposedly tiny minds more interested in so-called tactics than strategy. Rather, managing their party is the key to achieving every long-term and lofty goal a Government may have in mind.

But if a party is an essential resource, it is also – as the leaders of the outgoing Conservative Government cannot help but have realised – a potential liability.[3] Indeed nearly all of the plus points of party have their negative flip sides. A tradition can become a trap: the thoughts, words and deeds of one era may be completely inappropriate for another, but they may be a difficult habit to break. People who join a party may, in return for their efforts, demand more of a say in what goes on within it and what it comes to stand for than those who benefit from such efforts would really like; they may also demand favours which, if granted, may eventually rebound on those that grant them. Platforms designed to crystallise a certain approach to political problems may ignore inconvenient but nevertheless crucial details simply because they do not happen to fit the story the party wishes to tell voters at that particular time. Those who constitute the Government's legislative majority cannot (and perhaps, if we are serious about democracy, should not) be relied upon for blind loyalty, but as a result endanger its ability to deliver on any deals it makes with other forces, friendly or hostile, and imperil the unity which is assumed to be so crucial to electoral success.

## Who does the managing, who is managed, and are they sometimes the same?

Physical or material resources are difficult enough to manage; so too are the commercial companies set up to harness and exploit them. But the complex of people, institutional structures and symbolically transmitted ideas that is a political party is perhaps more difficult still. Nowhere is this more true than in the Labour Party.[4] For all its recent problems, the ideology and the morphology of the Conservative Party is still suited – as was intended – to control by a strong (or at least successful) leader. As a result, Tories find it fairly easy to differentiate between who does the managing and who (or what) is managed. For Labour, both as a whole and even within its various component parts, such a distinction is highly problematic. Labour is still a relatively egalitarian organisation, a Party which while it may seek leadership also distrusts it, a Party for whose members the very idea of management smacks of top-down control and betokens not simply a lack of consultation but a denial of fundamental rights.

The Labour Party is a federal institution. Power – a complicated phenomenon in any case – is located, either *de facto* or *de jure*, in a number of sites which can all lay claim to more or less legitimate authority.[5] While the annual Conference is theoretically supreme, for example, it is obvious that it can be and has been influenced, if not quite controlled, by the parliamentary leadership, the affiliated trade unions, and the combination of both which (along with other odds and sods like the Fabian Society and the Young Socialists) goes to make up the Party's National Executive Committee (NEC). Outside the Conference period control is supposedly vested in the NEC which, though it is strictly the custodian of Conference decisions and the conduit of constituency feeling, inevitably claims a degree of autonomy on the grounds that events and contingency alone dictate the need for at least some room for manoeuvre. And, while the NEC may lay claim to being the last court of appeal when it comes, for instance, to disciplinary matters, custom and practice grant the Parliamentary Labour Party considerable independence: the PLP is (and has been asserted to be so during various disciplinary crises down the years) 'a sovereign body' – a status which also affects the extent to which it can be bound by Conference decisions on matters of policy.

The distribution of power within these federated sub-sections is just as complicated and unstable as that which exists between them. For example, journalists, academics and politicians have over the years found it convenient to label the NEC as dominated by one side or other of Labour's socialist-cum-social democratic coalition. The reality, of course, has always been much more complex. Even when left-wingers (either elected to the constituency section or selected by represented trade unions) have supposedly been in control, they have found themselves subject to all sorts of pressures – particularly when Labour has been in Government – not to damage the leadership in the eyes of voters, markets, or other nations. By the same token, when the right has apparently had the whip-hand, it has often had to compromise (for example, on matters of discipline) in order to preserve some sort of unity or to adopt a critical stance (on matters of policy) in order to preserve its own credibility with the grassroots membership. This is to say nothing of the nuances in the relationship between the industrial and political components of the executive – or indeed of the way in which clashes of interest between different trade unions often make it more than a little misleading to conceive of the industrial wing of the movement as some kind of monolithic bloc.[6]

Every bit as complex is the institution that inevitably provides the most high-profile management challenge – the PLP. Labour's parliamentarians are members of an essentially collegial organisation. While only the naive would fail to take into account the informal strategies and the electoral imperative that afford the leadership more power in practice than it has on paper, it is still important to recall the importance attached by many MPs - and not only those thought of as left-wing – to the right of the PLP as a whole to decide on both policy and the policing of members' behaviour, not least via the supposedly sovereign PLP meeting which, though sometimes poorly and desultorily attended, has often – and certainly at times of tension – been a significant site of struggle.[7] Even accepting that formal structures are only a part of the story, the bulk of Labour MPs have (even if only potentially) more of a say on policy that their Conservative counterparts, whose ability in the Parliament of 1992–97 to 'blackmail' the leadership (for example, over Europe) was contingent on a small majority rather than the result of normatively supported procedure. And, whether or not the PLP meeting is visibly important in determining policy decisions, there is no doubt that, along with all its arcane rules and norms, it is crucial to their legitimation – far more crucial, for example, than a meeting of the Conservative backbench 1922 Committee. The meeting is also a means by which the leadership can be held to account: though in the short term this rarely means an immediate threat to somebody's tenure of office, the damage done to his or her standing in the long term can be serious. In addition, while the PLP has a Whips' Office just like its Tory counterpart, the final say in (disciplinary) disputes is not ceded to these officers (as it is with the Tories) but jealously guarded by the entire membership.[8]

These special characteristics of the PLP, however, only add to the key problem that faces anyone charged with managing things at Westminster – namely the fact that 'party discipline' is and always has been a misnomer.

As one seasoned political observer, still very much with us today, pointed out during one of the periodic (some would even say chronic) disciplinary crises that beset Wilson's 1966–70 administration, conformity within parliamentary party groups is ultimately normatively rather than coercively maintained.[9] True, MPs co-operate because they only have limited time and knowledge and therefore are often happy to delegate the power of decision to experts higher up. But for the most part, 'Members usually vote with their party because they want it to do well and are in agreement with it.'[10] In short, though more frequent than is commonly believed, breaking ranks is hard to do because it bespeaks rejection of norms of behaviour and communication that, for most MPs, are either articles of faith as important as their political preferences or facts of life to which they can conceive of no sensible alternative.[11] In Labour's case, deserting one's colleagues is to deny the traditional doctrine of standing by majority (and often in effect leadership) decisions which one analyst has labelled 'social democratic centralism'.[12]

But not all MPs play ball, and almost none will play ball all the time, especially if they feel they are being asked to support action which seems to go against what brought them into politics (and into their party) in the first place. Paradoxically, though, it is at these times, the times when 'discipline' is most sorely needed, that the essential inability to impose it – common to all parties – is starkly revealed. Whips may be able to make a recalcitrant's life logistically difficult for a short time. They may even deny him or her a few foreign trips. But they cannot afford, if that MP is one who shows promise, to stymie his or her career in the long term. Lurid tales of dark threats to reveal embarrassing secrets are also overplayed – such revelations, be they drawn from little black books, card indexes or even a computer database like New Labour's Excalibur, would damage the Government as well as the individual. Drastic action, such as withholding the whip or even expulsion, is just as unlikely. For a start, it would not be permanent unless the leadership could rely on the MP in question not being reselected by the local party to fight the next election. This is no easy thing to achieve – as the case of the Conservative, Neil Hamilton, proved. True, Labour's managers enjoy an advantage over their Tory counterparts in that they can ask the NEC to expel a dissident from the Party or withdraw its endorsement of him or her as a candidate, but historical instances of such requests are few and far between, while instances of NEC agreement to them are even rarer still. In any case, rebellious MPs are normally sensible enough to ensure they do not rebel alone, well aware that parliamentary arithmetic – as well as everything else – militates against the expulsion of a large enough group, especially one whose members can claim to be defending Conference policy and to be backed by their constituencies.

Talk of constituencies inevitably brings us to Labour's 'grassroots', namely the ordinary members whose potential power became evident in the (albeit evanescent) triumph of the left in the early 1980s, but whose potential contribution to the Party's electoral success – or failure, as in, say, 1970 – is, after years of being ignored, only just beginning to be fully acknowledged.[13] In some ways, such people personify the wider point that a party is a political project's greatest asset, but also its biggest liability. Managing this particular resource has always proved particularly difficult. Such is its disparate nature that simply communicating with it has, in the past at least, presented party leaders with a major headache. So too has its sheer variability. In terms of ideology, decades-worth of academic research has shown that CLPs refuse in reality to conform to the clichés employed by press and politicians (Labour as well as Conservative) alike: they are not – and never have been – uniformly or in any sense predictably 'more extreme' than the parliamentary elite, and they do not generally prefer doctrinal purity to electoral victory.[14] As regards organisation and activity, some areas have long had thriving local organisations, while in others meetings, if called at all, were rarely attended by more than a dedicated few. The situation is not made any clearer or easier by the fact that no-one has ever been quite sure (or at the very least agreed on) exactly what the Party at the grassroots is actually *for*. Should it be a mere 'vote-getting' organisation, or should it be so much more – on the one hand, a means of ensuring (through institutional devices ranging from emergency resolutions to representative office) that the parliamentary elite never becomes too divorced from the voice and the views of socialists at the sharp end, and, on the other, a way of guaranteeing Labour's project a continued supply of politically educated 'real people' who can act as its 'ambassadors in the community', spreading its message (almost by stealth or by accident) to friends, neighbours and colleagues in the workplace?[15]

One of the reasons why the CLPs are in some senses the Party's Cinderellas is that for Labour, unlike a number of its continental counterparts, individual membership was an afterthought rather than the main motive force in its foundation: the Labour Party was an 'indirect' institution, set up first and foremost to represent people not as individuals but as part and parcel of an interest, namely the trade union movement.[16] Accordingly, it was the latter that was afforded the greater say – a right reinforced, of course, by cash contributions (ranging from sponsorship of MPs to straight donations to the Party as a whole) that far outweighed anything Labour's constituency members (even if all those registered had paid!) could ever hope to come up with. Because of this – and because of the problems the trade unions have supposedly 'caused' previous Labour Governments – any discussion of how the Party can or should be managed is incomplete without consideration of the 'contentious alliance' above and beyond its formal institutional embodiment on the NEC. The industrial wing of what used routinely to be referred to as 'this great movement of ours' has always represented a particular management challenge because it exists both within and without the Party – at the same time part of it but also part of the environment in which it has to operate. And, as if that were not enough, it also has management problems of its own: indeed, it is arguably these, as much as anything else, that have been responsible for so many of the difficulties experienced by past Labour Governments.

## What went wrong in the past, why did it go wrong, and could it have been avoided?

While some would argue that we should remember that arguments did go on during the 1945–51 period, there is broad agreement that internal strife was far more serious during 1964–70 and 1974–79, though probably less agreement as to why – and hence on whether and how things could have been different. The superficial picture is familiar, if depressing: the PLP was riven by factional infighting and open dissent – and sometimes by leadership plots; ordinary party members in CLPs throughout the land became disaffected or simply disillusioned; the NEC became less a referee than yet another site of struggle, while the 'special relationship' between unions and Government proved unable to stand the myriad strains placed upon it. The reasons behind all this are less clear, and, predictably perhaps, people's ideas about them tend to depend less on objective assessments (assuming such things are ever possible) and more on their political presuppositions. While admitting that these are likely to leak through into any account, a balanced analysis of the question should, as well as dispensing with a few myths which seem to have grown up recently, strive to avoid dealing with it simply in terms of victims and villains.

To begin at the bottom, the discontent of CLP members, active or inactive, is understandable. It was not that Labour's leaders in the 1960s and 1970s failed to deliver socialism overnight – contrary to a view which seems to be popular among some of the more hard-line adherents of modernisation, most ordinary members did not expect such a thing, even if they really wanted it. It was that, in contrast to 1945–51, many of the very specific, largely reformist promises (or, dare we say, 'pledges') made in opposition – in order to outbid or to outflank the Tories, or simply to unite and mobilise the Party itself – were openly and in some cases even enthusiastically reneged upon. Either (like industrial planning agreements in the 1970s) they were never delivered at all or, if (as with the abolition of prescription charges in the 1960s) they did result in something during the Government's salad days, that something did not survive its fag-end. The Labour Governments of the 1960s and 1970s may well have been trying hard to preserve what they saw as the essentials of social democracy and also to safeguard its future as a governing force, albeit within a basically liberal capitalist international environment. But too often this involved them in dumping arguably peripheral but nevertheless emotively important policies overboard – and as a result losing members year-on-year. They could therefore provide none (or very few) of the classic incentives to party membership – material benefits, symbolic ideological satisfaction or continued comradeship. Consequently they were left relying on the fact that for many ordinary members there was no place else to go, and hoping that somehow they could break through into the sort of second full term in office that would head off the trouble that such a strategy was almost bound to cause.

When it comes to the trade unions, things are probably more complicated. For most of the 1964–70 period, for example, the Labour Government got (as it had done in 1945–51) what it asked for, at least in formal terms: trade union leaders co-operated with various measures of wage restraint and industrial restructuring (notably in the coal industry), and this despite the fact that the Government failed, with the important exception of action on pensions, redundancy and sick pay, to keep its side of the bargain – especially when it came to boosting growth, reducing unemployment and holding down prices (and dividends). What, however, they could not do, given their internal culture and pressures in the external environment, was ensure that their co-operation was translated into action at lower levels.[17] Restraint was undermined by the ability of lesser union officials to do deals with managements that were willing and able to break (often implicitly rather than explicitly) the so-called norms established by the Government, not least because they were desperate to avoid the sort of localised but crippling industrial action which – though often wildly exaggerated (especially when measured against both the reality and the record in other countries) – was again beyond the control of trade unionists at the top. The Government's frustration at the situation – combined with its perceived need to show foreign markets and governments, as well as domestic voters, that it was capable of 'tough action' (a recurring theme for all Labour administrations) – led to the attempt to put industrial relations on the less voluntaristic, more formalised and indeed corporatist footing called for by *In Place of Strife*. The attempt ended in failure and even ignominy.

It is important – though hardly novel – to emphasise that *In Place of Strife* was in fact undermined from within the Labour Government, not only by Jim Callaghan but also by Roy Jenkins, the so-called 'Iron Chancellor' whose mettle in this case was tried and found wanting by that supposed straw-in-the-wind, Harold Wilson, not to mention his apparently 'red queen', Barbara Castle. But it is even more important to understand why. Such big 'beasts of the jungle' as Callaghan and Jenkins were, it is true, probably thinking of their future prospects, but their willingness to sabotage (in the case of the first) and abandon (in the case of the second) the Government's proposal had just as much to do with their conviction that, even if it could be forced through Parliament, it simply could not be made to work in practice given relatively full employment and the trade unions' comparatively weak internal structures – a guess proved right by the various calamities which befell Ted Heath's Industrial Relations Act. The collapse during Labour's next period of office of the social contract and the consequent descent into the Winter of Discontent simply provide a more recent (and more lurid) example of the way in which relationships between Labour Governments and the trade unions are best explained not by blaming overmighty union barons but by focusing on their inability to control their members in the face of Government failure to provide a stable (and positive) economic environment. Such disputes not only illustrate the complexity of a situation that is all too often rather simplistically cast, but also remind us once again, firstly, of the way in which Labour's federal organisation facilitates the efforts of those who feel obliged (rightly or wrongly) to throw a spanner in the works and, secondly, of the extent to which Government success is dependent on managing the Party at the parliament- ary level.

This said, there are so many misconceptions about the role of the PLP – or certain sections of it – in supposedly 'undermining' the Labour Governments of the 1960s and 1970s that it is difficult to know where to begin.[18] To take the 1960s to start with, it is true that, especially after 1966, the Government began to experience persistent dissent from the left-wing Tribune Group, particularly with regard to its efforts to cut (or more properly reduce the rate of increase in) public expenditure. However, the group's hard core of around 25 almost always chose to abstain rather than actually vote against the Government, and – much to the relief, but also inevitably the irritation, of more loyalist Labour backbenchers – consciously ensured that its failure to support the Government would never precipitate a parliamentary defeat. And, while it is possible that such protests undermined the Government in the sense that they presented the public with the image of a divided Party, they also gave Wilson and his colleagues many a convenient opportunity to demonstrate that 'the Government must govern' and that their prime concern was with promoting 'common sense' and 'the national interest' rather than preserving the Party's supposedly 'sacred cows'.

In the 1960s, then, the organised left of the PLP was both an irritant and a useful cat to kick in times of trouble. It could only become truly dangerous if it were able to provoke and put itself at the head of extra-parliamentary dissent in the constituencies and/or the trade unions, or if, in the chamber of the Commons, its concerns were shared by Labour MPs of a different ideological persuasion. With regard to the first of these risks, the Tribunites' efforts to co-ordinate the 'outside left', though not insubstantial (especially when it came to Conference motions and NEC candidates) rarely amounted to as much as they would have liked or others feared. However, the second risk – that the Tribunites would be joined in protest (actual or potential) by other backbenchers who could normally be relied on to go (albeit grumbling and grudgingly) through its lobby on crucial divisions – was much more significant. Between 1964 and 1970 the European question may have been bubbling under rather than boiling over, but the Government had some sticky moments on other issues, not least on the defence of sterling, on race and immigration, on health service charges and of course on incomes policy and trade union legislation.

Historically, then, managing the Party at the parliamentary level has been a matter not just of handling the left – the preoccupation, even today, of so many commentators and Labour right-wingers – but also of heading off the discontent of their sometimes less prominent colleagues located nearer the centre or sometimes towards the other extreme of the Party's ideological spectrum. Accordingly, if Labour Governments were undermined, at least at the parliamentary level, by the organised left, they were also undermined by the 'soft' or 'unattached' left (who could often be persuaded to join the Tribunites in individual protests), by the supposedly 'solid' centre (ditto, but less often) and by the right. The last may have been hard-line traditionalists defending trade union privileges or protesting at the 'lax' punishments handed out to left-wingers. Or they may have been members of the self-styled 'radical right', who seemed to put aside the tolerance they displayed, for example, on racial questions when it came to calling for the Party to ditch not just their more left-leaning backbench colleagues but also Labour's leader, Harold Wilson, against whom they wasted so much of their (and his) energy plotting.

Though the feverishly plotted but always unrealised leadership coups which characterised the late 1960s were less of a feature of the 1974–79 Labour Government, the PLP proved even more difficult to manage than it had between 1964 and 1970. But this was not simply because the left grew more organised and more numerous. It was also because the intervening period of Conservative rule under Ted Heath had seen the collapse of some of the parliamentary conventions that had stood Governments of varying hues in good stead for almost a century: after what amounted to a watershed Parliament in terms of MPs' behaviour, it was clear that the defeat of the Government, even on a major issue, would not – as previously assumed – automatically lead to a dissolution; in addition, voting in the opposition lobby, rather than simply abstaining, became, if not de rigeur for the self-respecting dissenter, then at least a very real (and far more frequently exercised) option. The 1974–79 period simply put nails in the coffin, overturning, once and for all, for instance, the old adage that a small majority made for more acquiescent backbenchers.

This is not, of course, the same thing as saying that a large majority poses fewer problems. The devil does indeed make work for idle hands to do – as Wilson (after 1966) and even Attlee found.[19] The bigger the majority, the more difficult it is for the Prime Minister to find a job for everyone who, whether it is because they are talented, or because they could be troublesome, or simply because they embody a certain sex, place or interest, can claim to 'deserve' one. Similarly, the bigger the majority, the more dissident MPs there are likely to be – not necessarily as a proportion of the entire PLP, but that is not what matters: what matters to those thinking of rebelling is safety in numbers, and numbers in parliamentary votes are absolute, not relative. On the other hand, of course, the power of the so-called 'payroll vote' – a group comprising the Government's most senior Cabinet Ministers down to its most junior PPSs which if the worst comes to the worse can be relied on to toe the line to a man or woman – does depend very much on its size relative to the rest of the PLP, and this ratio is not something the leadership, who cannot really co-opt more than just over 100 MPs in this way, can do very much about.

For all this, however, there is an extent to which talk of the impact of large or small majorities, while fascinating (and in the case of the former obviously particularly relevant), can lead us to overlook two crucial lessons from Labour's Governmental past. Firstly, problems in the wider PLP are very often reflected in and a reflection of problems in the leadership itself. Those who are charged with leading the Party are rarely as united as they look on entering Government and quickly become even more estranged from each other as the stresses and strains of office begin to breed and feed departmental, personal and ideological rivalries. However dominant a Prime Minister may seem (and for those with short memories Harold Wilson for some considerable time towered over his colleagues even if they did not much like him), running the state cannot be done by one individual: in and of itself the possession of office sets up both powerful inter-dependencies and powerful animosities between those at the top.[20] And it is at the top that much of the damage to a Government's morale, capacity and credibility is done. Secondly, it is issues, rather than factions, which cause Governments the biggest headaches. While under the last two Labour Governments the Tribune Group may have constituted a cohesive dissident minority – even, to coin a phrase beloved of right-wing hardliners, 'a party within a party' – it only became truly dangerous when it rebelled on an issue that caused other MP's (often from all sides) to rebel as well. The ominous precedents are of course Europe, devolution and, to a lesser extent, public spending.

**What has changed over the years, what moves have been made to head off previous problems, and will they be successful?**

Sticking, to start with, with the PLP, it would appear that the importance and impact of the left has declined markedly from the mid 1980s onwards, not least because of the separation of the so-called hard and soft varieties that was one of the most significant (as well as earliest) achievements of the modernisation process begun by Neil Kinnock – a process obviously facilitated by a growing sense that many of the Conservatives' changes in areas like industrial relations and public ownership would be practically impossible to reverse.[21] However, reports of the death of the parliamentary left may well be rather premature. Certainly the existence of a significant number of Labour backbenchers, old and new, who may not be – to coin a recent phrase – 'on message' is not simply a story got up by the press, whose motives for mentioning such things probably has less to do with its traditional desire to stir up trouble for Labour Governments than with a need to inject some spice into what may seem rather a dull parliamentary prospect.

Pre-election research suggested the continued existence of a group of at least 30 persistent dissidents (by no means all members of the Campaign Group) colourfully called 'Blair's Bastards'.[22] True, the new Government's massive majority makes it very much more difficult for such a group to inflict actual defeat on the Government. On the other hand, of course, its ranks will be swelled while the size of the Government's payroll vote will never exceed more than 100 or so, and it may – on certain issues and in time – find itself more friends among the so-called lobby-fodder than may be imagined, not least because that amorphous group contains more middle-class professionals (many with local government experience) than ever before. These people may, of course, be attuned to the new managerialism and the need for discipline, but they are also used to having a say in the running of things – and used to putting over their views on the media – than ever before.

The new Government, however, can point to the efforts begun in opposition to stymie discontent before it has a chance to spill out into the officially public arena. Principal among these was the PLP's new 'Code of Conduct', designed to offer backbenchers more consultation on policy (via regular meetings of subject committees with ministers) in return for a commitment not to bring the parliamentary party into disrepute – a commitment, however, which backbenchers, jealous of their rights, managed at the last minute to get watered down by appealing to their long-held (and usefully ambiguous) right of conscience. Historical experience – particularly that of the Labour Government between 1966 and 1970 (the last time a significant change was made to the Code) – would teach us, however, that such formal agreements rarely deliver the goods – to either side. Ministers do not take kindly to having to explain themselves in advance to colleagues who, they imagine, can have no inkling of the range of problems faced by those in positions of real responsibility; backbenchers pretty soon wake up to the fact that they have no real say and their attendance – dependent anyway on the extent of general confidence in the Government and its electoral prospects – soon begins to dwindle. Meanwhile, while there are always those backbench hardliners who will call (and vote in PLP meetings) for a tough line to be taken with so-called troublemakers, they are more often than not outnumbered by colleagues who either disagree in principle with heavy-handed discipline or are simply unwilling to set a precedent which, should they at some later stage fall out with the leadership, might be used against them.[23] Indeed, it is perfectly possible to suggest that codes of conduct tend to provide not so much a solution for struggle as something else to fight about when things start to go wrong on the wider political or policy front.

As for those who have so often been blamed for things going wrong, namely the trade unions, they have undergone even more of a change than the PLP since Labour was last in Government. Membership has dropped precipitately: at eight million it stands at only 60 per cent of its 1979 peak. This is mainly due both to the relative decline of traditionally highly unionised sectors and the return of mass unemployment, but also has something to do with legal changes (the outlawing of the closed shop and secondary picketing, the introduction of compulsory ballots, the freedom of firms to withdraw recognition) which severely limited unions' room for manoeuvre with regard to industrial action and removed some (though not all) of their immunities from legal – and of course financial – redress.[24] Moreover, privatisation (and the defeat of the miners) removed a whole tranche of workers from the state's payroll, ensuring that industrial relations problems in those sectors affected would no longer be a direct concern of the Government. And, while the Conservative assault on union rights and privileges if anything made those unions all the more desperate to contribute resources to the return of a Labour Government, that desperation ensured that the leverage which financial support might have bought was even more limited than ever: the unions had to acquiesce as Labour's political leaders, on the one hand, abandoned (not least under Tony Blair) promises to dismantle Thatcher's reforms and, on the other, pressed on with their plans to lessen the role of the unions in the Party's internal decision-making processes – plans which, as the leadership 'let it be known' in the long run-up to the 1997 election, may well lead in the end to a complete divorce (either via the introduction of state funding for political parties or a new-found reliance on funds raised from individuals and corporations).[25]

However, it is by no means clear that these changes or planned changes will allow the current Labour Government to escape the 'trade union problem' encountered by its predecessors. For one thing, it is likely to face considerable wage pressure from public sector workers who have seen their pay squeezed in a series of tight public spending rounds under the Conservatives. Labour is pledged to be just as tough on public spending, and indeed will need to be, not least because the minimum wage, affecting as it will millions of low-paid workers in or under contract to the state sector, is likely to inflate its own wage bill in particular and possibly lead to the rush to preserve differentials in other sectors that caused such chaos in the 1970s. It may well be true that union leaders have seen their organisations suffer so much since 1979 (an election their own actions may have helped lose) that they will be content – at least for a while – with Labour delivering on its promises of a minimum wage (at whatever level), the European social chapter, a statutory right to representation and the removal of the red tape surrounding the 'check-off' system by which employees' union subscriptions are automatically deducted from their salaries and wages. It is also true, of course, that the abandonment of explicit (if not implicit) incomes policy will mean that not every strike – especially in the private sector – will be seen as a confrontation with the Government. On the other hand, memories are short – particularly when those at the top of the trade unions fear – as they feared in the 1960s and 1970s – losing the loyalty and respect of those below them. And, ironically, those below them now have, via the extensive use of balloting, a legitimate and legal way of rejecting pleas for moderation should they so choose – as we saw in the strikes in the rail and postal industries in the summer of 1996. Put at its most basic, then, there is little sign that British union leaders will be any more able to deliver on bargains made with the Government (as, for example, can their compatriots in Scandinavia and also perhaps Germany) than they were under previous Labour administrations.

One oft-touted solution to such a problem is to end the institutional link between Labour and the unions. The Party, it is claimed, should sacrifice what is still by far the largest single component of its funding (over 50 per cent) and perhaps a good number of its most active and organisationally capable members (who currently can join Labour at a reduced rate), in order to rid itself, firstly, of a reduced (and soon to be a minority) block vote at Conference – a vote which often comes in useful for the leadership by the way – and, secondly, of a highly insecure union grip on what is often an utterly impotent body, namely the NEC.[26] Even leaving aside the fact that such a break may well be politically costly and constitutionally difficult – if not impossible – to achieve, it is difficult to see why either the threat or the fact of a formal divorce between the industrial and the political wings of the Labour movement should bring the former into line. The end of the alliance would cut both ways. True, Labour Governments might be able to confront unions with a clearer conscience and without the nagging internal – or more accurately institutionalised – criticism which might undermine public confidence in any symbolically tough stance. But such criticism would still exist in some form within the Party, and, even if it were absent, such an absence is by no means a sufficient condition for success – things are just more complicated than that. More importantly, being cut adrift from the politicians may be something the unions, with their political funds thereby freed up for their own campaigning purposes and no feelings of family guilt to hold them back, could well get used to and, if push comes to shove, enjoy.

In other words, there is no guarantee that a change to its internal institutional arrangements – even one which would seem so obviously to constitute the symbolic culmination of the modernising project – would protect the new Labour Government and any successors from the pitfalls of the past. This applies with equal force to suggested changes to the Party's constitution – principally involving the NEC and Conference – first set out formally in the document produced in the new year of 1997 called (with, it turned out, justifiable confidence) *Labour into power: a framework for partnership.* In future, junior ministers will be obliged to attend local policy forums, open to all Party members, that would feed into appointed national policy forums with a two-year policy cycle, thereby downgrading the policymaking (or deciding) role of Conference, which would in turn become (it is hoped) more of a rally than the battlefield it has been in the past. In return for a number of seats on the NEC being reserved for ordinary CLP members rather than the parliamentarians (be they ministers, wannabees or never-will-bes) who currently dominate, union membership would be scaled down and the Cabinet (or Shadow Cabinet) given a set share of the seats. Depending upon one's point of view, the emphasis will be on control by the right kind (rather than the wrong – or should that be left? – kind) of parliamentarians, and the encouragement of participation by ordinary members on the grounds either that it encourages two-way dialogue and political education or, that it gives the appearance of influence but scarcely the reality.

A judgement as to the impact of such changes may well depend on one's faith in a wider concept that many on the centre-left of British politics are beginning to invest with almost totemic significance or at least (and inasmuch as they believe in such things any more) to see as the next 'big idea', namely 'stakeholding'. Even towards the left of the Party, there are some who set great store by its radical participatory potential,[27] realising that – as is the case with the 'new' Clause IV – it may be a surprisingly useful way of ensuring that Labour's leaders measure up to fine words.[28] On the other hand, there are those who suspect that there is neither beef nor mileage in the concept, and indeed that the whole thing is a very poor substitute for overarching ideas like socialism and democratic accountability. In practical – though paradoxical terms – it may be that both and neither are right. The idea of a stakeholding party, wherein all those with an interest in its vitality have an institutionalised (though not necessarily equal) say in the day-to-day running and future direction, represents (and who should say wrongly?) an attempt to replicate the success of those businesses which combine strong management with a genuine commitment to consultation with and loyalty to their human resources. Whether this can be achieved – or perhaps the exact nature of that achievement – will depend both on Party leaders and ordinary Party members.

While it is undoubtedly one of the most important, the relationship between the Labour Government and the people who collectively (albeit through millions of individual actions) helped to get it into office and to keep it there is one of the most difficult to analyse and predict. We know, not least through work done by Patrick Seyd and Paul Whitely (work which incidentally is ongoing), that Labour's members do not (if they ever did) conform to many of the stereotypes that abound about them: whether active or inactive they are not pathologically radical, nor do they value purity over power. We also know that many of them (like Labour's MPs) are male, middle-class, educated professionals, many of whom work in the public sector and are (or would like to be) local councillors. These characteristics present the leadership with both opportunities and threats. On the one hand, they are likely to mean a membership which can be persuaded by political education to accept compromise, especially in the interests of electoral success. On the other, they suggest that if such compromises involve, as they always have before, conflict with the public sector or with local government they are likely to provoke discontent among a group of people who are quite capable of making themselves heard and who also have better things to do with their time than defend a Government which has let them down.

## Past, present, future

It is nothing new to say that one of Tony Blair's big achievements before assuming office was to lower the expectations of his Party. Not only did he narrow down his promises to a few concrete and supposedly deliverable policies – something which, it is easy to forget, many of his predecessors also did – he also tried to make his supporters understand on a more profound level that this, for the moment, really was all there was, and that they should not imagine that he could or would do more on winning power. Quite how deeply this lesson has been learned will take time to tell. But even if it has been, it is unlikely to be enough to save Labour altogether from the internal conflict that has beset its predecessors in power. Nor will tough speeches to the serried ranks of the Government's massive parliamentary majority. Even the fact that the Government, at least on entering office, appeared to have neutered or marginalised those sections of the left press which in times past have proved a vital forum for dissent will not – given the ever-increasing importance of broadcast communication – guarantee silence.

This is not only because there will be new and as yet unforeseen challenges brought about, for example, by devolution, which opens up all sorts of possible power struggles between the metropolitan core and a newly powerful periphery. It is not even because things like 'parliamentary discipline' and 'the trade union problem' are simply misnomers, metaphors which obfuscate more than they illuminate. It is because, ultimately, discontent within the Party can only be avoided by a leadership which has the determination not only not to argue among itself, but also to avoid the temptation – as arguably no other Labour leadership in Government since, say, 1949 has been able to do – to see the Party, rather than the real world of which it is but a small part, as the problem. To govern successfully as a social democratic party in what is now more than ever a liberal capitalist economic environment is no easy task. But it is the enemies without rather than those within who make or break Labour Governments.

To learn anything else from Labour's Governmental history is to miss the main trick. Out of office – particularly if one has been there for too long – it is easy to become obsessed with managing the Party. In office, this obsession has to be forgotten. True, it can be so much easier – though not always wise – to demonstrate one's toughness to financial markets, foreign powers and even the domestic electorate by publicly repudiating those things closest to the heart of one's supporters and then forcing them to swallow the medicine. But the mark of a natural party of Government – as the Conservatives showed for so long after 1979 – is that, in pursuit of its most cherished objectives, it turns not in on itself but rather to those socio-economic forces which it really has to manage and, if necessary, to overcome. In short, a successful Government not only cannot avoid creating, but actually needs to create – and beat – symbolic enemies. If the new Labour Government takes the route followed in the 1960s and 1970s rather than in the 1940s and locates those enemies inside the Party and the trade unions, then it will inevitably face problems. If, on the other hand, it picks out – and picks off – other targets (the utilities are perhaps a good start), it may find its supporters rallying round rather than descending into the sort of in-fighting that caused its recent predecessors so many problems.

# Notes

1 Eric Shaw, *The Labour Party Since 1945. Old Labour: New Labour*, Blackwell, 1996, p.217.
2 See Paul Webb, 'Are British Political Parties in Decline?', *Party Politics*, Vol.1, No.3.
3 See Susan E. Scarrow, *Parties and their Members: Organizing for Victory in Britain and Germany*, Oxford University Press, 1996.
4 Peter Shore, *Leading the Left*, Weidenfeld and Nicolson, 1993.
5 Lewis Minkin, *The Labour Party Conference: a Study in the Politics of Intra-Party Democracy*, Manchester University Press, 1980.
6 Lewis Minkin, *The Contentious Alliance*, Edinburgh University Press, 1991.
7 The importance of the PLP meeting when Labour is in Government has been attested to by politicians from both ends of the the Party's ideological spectrum: see, for example, Woodrow Wyatt, *Turn Again Westminster*, Andre Deutsch, 1973 and Tony Benn, *Out of the Wilderness: Diaries 1963-1967*, Hutchinson, 1987, p.437. The cast-iron certainty that things have changed nowadays displayed by some (e.g. Austin Mitchell, 'Backbench influence - a personal view', *Parliamentary Affairs*, Vol.47, No.1) relies far too much on recent experience in opposition, not in office.
8 See Jack Brand, *British Parliamentary Parties: Policy and Power*, Clarendon Press, 1992.
9 Anthony King, 'The Chief Whip's Clothes', *Spectator*, 9 February 1968. See also the MPs quoted in King, *British Members of Parliament: a Self Portrait*, Macmillan, 1974, pp.56-63.
10 Philip Norton, *Dissension in the House of Commons, 1974-1979*, Clarendon Press, 1980, p.463.
11 See Robert J. Jackson, *Rebels and Whips: an Analysis of Dissension, Discipline and Cohesion in British Political Parties*, Macmillan, 1968.
12 Eric Shaw, *Discipline and Discord in the Labour Party: the Politics of Managerial Control in the Labour Party, 1951-1987*, Manchester University Press, 1988.
13 Patrick Seyd and Paul Whitely, *Labour's Grass Roots: the Politics of Party*

*Membership*, Clarendon Press, 1992.

14  See Seyd and Whitely, *Labour's Grass Roots*.

15  Patrick Seyd and Lewis Minkin, 'The Labour Party and its members', *New Society*, 20 September 1979.

16  See Angelo Panebianco, *Political Parties: Organisation and Power*, Cambridge University Press, 1988.

17  See Mary Douglas, 'Institutions of the third kind: British and Swedish labour markets compared' in Douglas, *Risk and Blame: Essays in Cultural Theory*, Routledge, 1992.

18  Much of the following is taken from Tim Bale, 'Sacred Cows and Common Sense: the Symbolic Statecraft and Political Culture of the Labour Party' (Ph.D. Dissertation: University of Sheffield, 1997), which concentrates on the 1960s, and Norton, *Dissension*, which is invaluable on the 1970s.

19  For Attlee see Jonathan Schneer, *Labour's Conscience: the Labour Left, 1945-51*, Unwin Hyman, 1988.

20  See various contributions to R. A. W. Rhodes and Patrick Dunleavy (eds), *Prime Minister, Cabinet, and Core Executive*, Macmillan, 1995.

21  Eric Shaw, *The Labour Party since 1979: Crisis and Transformation*, Routledge, 1994.

22  Philip Norton and Philip Cowley, *Blair's Bastards*, Centre for Legislative Studies, Hull, 1996.

23  Some would even suggest that the presence of 102 women in the PLP (out of a total of 119 in Parliament as a whole) makes it even more unlikely that macho posturing from hardline disciplinarians will go down well with the bulk of backbenchers; actually it is unlikely (as well as patronising to think) that attitudes on such questions can be simply 'read off' from someone's gender – as those who remember women like Sara Barker, Labour's National Agent in the 1960s, and Alice Bacon MP, who served on the NEC at the same time, will no doubt recall!

24  See David Marsh, *The New Politics of British Trade Unionism: Union Power and the Thatcher Legacy*, Macmillan, 1992; also Robert Taylor, *The Future of the Trade Unions*, Deutsch, 1994.

25  The distance between union leaders and the Labour leadership in the run-up to the general election of 1997 can be overstated. Leading trade unionists continued during that time to have what some might regard as 'privileged access' to Tony Blair via the Trade Union Liaison Committee (first set up after Labour's defeat in 1970) and a lesser-known body called the Contact Group. These lower-key, only quasi-official links may well continue in Government.

26  At the time of Labour's victory in 1997 unions controlled – potentially at least – 17 of the NEC's 29 members (12 union places plus the majority of votes for the five women members), but whether this potential can be realised (or whether it matters anyway) is of course a moot point:

Lewis Minkin's work demonstrates beyond doubt that there is simply no such thing as a monolithic trade union interest, nor are most union representatives keen to see the NEC in conflict with the parliamentary leadership.

27  See Peter Hain, Jean Corston and Derek Fatchett, 'A simple message to Conference', *New Statesman*, 27 September 1996.

28  Tim Bale, ' "The Death of the Past": Symbolic Politics and the Changing of Clause IV', in David Farrell *et al.* (eds), *British Elections and Parties Yearbook*, Frank Cass, 1996.

# Commentary

*Patrick Seyd*

There is no doubt that Party management is crucial. The Labour Governments of 1964–70 and 1974–79 ended in failure in this respect. The Party at the grassroots had been led to expect that their leaders would deliver on certain promises and commitments, and on the whole their hopes were shattered. The consequences were a decline in membership, an increasingly factionalised PLP and, in the 1970s, an NEC which set itself up as an alternative to the Cabinet. However, there are a number of reasons to believe that Party management will be a very different exercise under this new Labour Government.

One of the advantages that Blair has as Labour Prime Minister is that in opposition he lowered grassroots expectations. It is a mark of a new political realism to admit that governing is extraordinarily difficult; the recognition of this is one of the fundamental changes that have occurred within the Party. The expectations of the grassroots, after 18 years out of power, have altered significantly. In other ways, too, the contrasts between the Party in the 1960s/1970s and the present are considerable. The Party is now a one member one vote Party, the power of the activists has been diminished accordingly, and the NEC now has very extensive powers regarding election candidates. As far as the PLP is concerned, prediction is more difficult. Leaving aside the impact of the huge majority and the welcome increase in women MPs, it may be that the increasingly uniform social composition of the PLP – and the fact that so many of its members now have local government experience in the managing and distributing of services – will make it more cohesive; but a great deal may depend on the sort of serious parliamentary reform which will give backbenchers a more significant role. Also important, if faction-fighting does break out, will be the extent to which local parties will or will not support rebel MPs: the creation of a national register of Party members, and the opportunity that gives the Party leadership to make direct contact with the grassroots, could well be of some significance in this area.

When it comes to the trade unions, the bloc vote has been reduced and the sponsorship of MPs has been modified. More generally, the close

Party/union relationship of the 1960s and 1970s which helped to wreck the Callaghan Government, for instance, has disappeared and the 'fairness not favours' strategy of today has been electorally successful. However, there are both advantages and disadvantages in splitting the formal links. On the one hand, the Party can distance itself from particular interests and identify with the national interest. Furthermore, individual trade unionists might find their leaders less compromised in particular bargaining situations: they might be able to articulate more clearly their particular bargaining interests in disputes without feeling the need not to upset and embarrass the Labour Party. On the other hand, one of the great strengths of the link is that it institutionalises a means of working-class representation in what is predominantly a white, male, middle-class political elite.

On the grassroots, it is indeed useful to think in terms of assets and liabilities. They are assets in the sense that Labour had some 400,000 guaranteed voters before the polling stations even opened – a number which, though only a small proportion of the total electorate, should not be underestimated. More importantly, members are election campaigners. Notwithstanding the key seats strategy and the incredibly professional Millbank machine, the fact that the Representation of the People Act restricts local campaign expenditure means that parties are dependant on human resources. Furthermore, members (or even those individuals who are not officially members but who are sponsors) are a source of finance which is easily underestimated. Lastly, members are important as sounding boards and as political ambassadors. We need reminding that the bulk of the people in this country are totally uninterested in politics. Those 400,000 members are a means by which the Government can sound out ideas and get some sort of feedback on its intentions. How efficiently this is done – and how good members are at it – deserves further attention.

The last point relates to the 'Party into power' project which is attempting to change the culture of the Labour Party away from purely resolutionary politics. The debate now going on within the party as to the nature of its relationship with Government is of fundamental importance. There are two models of party being discussed. One is the electoral-professional model where human beings will be moved from constituency to constituency wherever the Millbank machine decrees. Another model is grassroots-based and is founded upon activist notions of political campaigning and education. Whichever model prevails, the attempt to create a two-year rolling programme for making policy is a serious attempt to change both cultures and structures, and may lead to a style of Party management which combines direction and democratic discussion.

# Commentary

*Peter Shore*

Nowadays, at least in terms of splits and so on, it sometimes seems as if the Conservative Party is becoming more like the old Labour Party, while the Labour Party is becoming more like the old Conservative Party. It is a remarkable reversal of roles and behaviour, particularly given the way in which the very structure of the Labour Party has always rendered it so prone to division and faction, with the constituency section of the NEC, for example, functioning for so long as virtually a left-wing fiefdom at the very heart of the Party. Now, of course, the solid block of left-wing members elected onto the NEC by activists has been reduced to a token Dennis Skinner, while the Party is also well on the way to reducing still further the weight of the trade unions, thereby ensuring that they are very much the junior rather than the senior partner in the relationship.

The people who have created New Labour have certainly analysed the past and, whether or not their analysis has been over-simplistic, they have obviously drawn the broadly correct conclusion that Labour Governments were very vulnerable because of the power of the Party outside Parliament which, at times in the 1970s anyway, claimed to be, if not an alternative Government, then at the very least a forum where Ministers inside the official Government could – despite Wilson's and Callaghan's best efforts – effectively abandon collective Cabinet responsibility and display their credentials for future leadership battles. The fact that they could do this, as well as the fact that they were able, albeit temporarily, to use the NEC after 1979 virtually to cripple the official parliamentary leadership by such measures as the electoral college and mandatory reselection, of course had as much to do with ethos as with institutional structures. Behind all this was the myth of betrayal that began with the betrayal of Ramsay MacDonald and continued with the feeling that successive Labour Governments were intimidated by what they found in the real world, by the forces that were ranged against them. This feeling was not entirely unjustified, but it has nonetheless had an unwarrantedly corrosive and destructive effect.

The architects of New Labour clearly have taken account of all this. They have changed the structure of the Labour Party, so that it is, in a sense, a much more manageable party now than it was in the past. It can deal much more easily with the trade unions, both in terms of their internal influence on Labour Party policy, and of their external influence through the TUC and in the real world of industry. There has been a great shift now to the ordinary Party member, who may well be less critical of a Labour Government than were the old general management committees of the CLPs. This has been achieved in no small part by the reduction of excessive expectations, symbolised perhaps by the ludicrously modest five manifesto pledges but also by the ditching of the old Clause IV, a move which has removed from the armoury of traditional critics of the left the gap between what Labour actually does in power and what Labour is supposed as a socialist party to do.

So Tony Blair has indeed learned some lessons and is in a much stronger position than his predecessors. But that does not mean he is going to have a quiet time! The power structure changes have been very important, but a price has been paid. There has been virtually no serious thinking or policy-making in the Labour Party now for years. Getting rid of the legacy of Bennism at its most extreme was what the last three manifestos managed to do. But they put nothing in its place – especially in the two great areas which are likely to determine the success or failure of the Labour Government in the future: namely the management of the economy and our relationship with Europe (two things which nowadays, of course, can't be separated). Whether a Labour Government can live with the EU capping of British Government borrowing is surely very doubtful. And whether a Labour Government can manage to handle the economy so that a substantial reduction is made in the levels of unemployment is another big question. We may well end up with the best-educated unemployed workforce in Europe, and that is unlikely to satisfy either the electorate in general or the Party in particular.

# Chapter 9

# Earthquake or watershed?
## Conclusions on New Labour in power

*Brian Brivati*

---

The arguments contained in the previous seven chapters suggest a set of connected but contrasting conclusions on New Labour in power. In particular there are differences of emphasis and argument in the various policy areas covered – the economy, welfare, education, foreign policy, European relations, constitutional reform and the management of the state – and some contrasts in perceptions of New Labour's approach to the broad ideological context of the Government, particularly in respect of politics and morality, the shifting notion of the nation state and the role of the state in determining political outcomes. However, three overarching conclusions can be drawn about the ideological and political position of the current Government in terms of the historical evolution of British social democracy. The first two are concerned with traditionally understood, primarily ideological, characterisations of the Government in relation to broad objectives and underlying convictions. In contrast, the third suggests a merger of these traditional concerns with a new emphasis on the presentation of ideas and electoral strategy, something I generally characterise as 'political competence', and therefore the creation of a new political position:

- The New Labour Government has substantially absorbed the lessons of the past and the changes of context of the last twenty years and in so doing has embraced the neo-liberal 'revolution' of the Thatcher years. In this sense, this is very much a New Labour Government, perhaps the foundation of a new political party – connected to old Labour by history and sentiment but not by objectives or even convictions.
- The New Labour Government has absorbed some of the lessons of the past and the experience of 18 years of opposition but has not changed as much, or as far, as the election result would suggest and we will gradually, over one or two terms, see a return to collectivism because of pressure from the bulk of the party which is still connected to an older set of values and because the Thatcher revolution did not extend as far as its champions suggest.
- The New Labour Government has adopted a British version of Clinton's triangulation in which the executive assumes a position that is separate

from the extremes of the parties in the legislature. Ignoring for a moment the obvious constitutional difference, the idea is that a new position has been created which is based on a substantially new ideological framework which means that this is a Government with a new political foundation, which is neither an old style collectivist one nor a new version of neo-liberalism, but holds a third position, equidistant from the other two. I want to suggest that, on balance, the third position is marginally more accurate, across a greater range of issues, than the first two options, but that the new party is not equidistant from these other two positions because it is closer to the old Labour tradition in some respects, reflecting the limits of the Thatcher revolution in, for example the resilience of the welfare state, and closer to the neo-liberal position in other respects, notably the question of state ownership. However, the emphasis on ideology as expressed in public policy outcomes is not the essence of the difference between this Labour Government and previous Labour Governments. The essence of the real Blair revolution – rooted in the Kinnock years – has been in the transformation of Labour's perception of political competence. (By this I mean the emphasis on the need to control and master the things that a Party, and a Government, can control, most importantly political communication.) In a sense this is also the real impact of the Conservative Governments of 1979–97 on the Labour Party: ideology has been merged with techniques for the gaining and holding of power.

### The context of New Labour in power

The success of this shift in the ethos of the Party means, on the face of it, that there is every likelihood of the Government successfully defending a record majority of 179. Recently the basis on which statistical analysis of elections is carried out has been criticised and the record of the pollsters in 1992 and 1997 has provoked a heated debate on this approach.[1] This uncertainty has to an extent broken the spell that pollsters and individual elections have had over analysis of political change. It suggests that results of general elections might actually be too 'tribal' a way of understanding the directions in which contemporary politics are moving; the changes in the broader context of the language and dominant ideas in politics are more significant. This slightly alters the question from 'why did Labour win the general election of 1997?' to 'what does Labour's victory mean?'

There are two possible answers to this question. The first is that the general election of 1997 was an 'earthquake election' and the arrival of Tony Blair's Government should therefore be seen as marking a new era in the way in which a broad range of issues are dealt with by government; reflecting, as Nick Ellison outlines in chapter 3, a great deal of new thinking. This was an election that turned Britain towards a substantially different future, it was another 1906 or 1945 or 1979, and as such it matters – above and beyond the 'tribal' sense of one party winning. The second is that the election was more a watershed – the election that marked the consolidation of a new political approach which began in the mid-1970s and was given shape by the Thatcher Governments of the 1980s. In which case this was an election which represented a fresh instalment of shifts that had already started and therefore what matter are the factors that shaped the new political arrangement and the way in which they have redefined the scope of government. The earthquake vs. watershed question catches something of why individual elections might matter, but, equally, why they might not.

It is difficult to define and impossible to measure the impact of political ideas on elections in isolation from other factors or from the way in which those ideas are communicated.[2] However, there is a clear sense in which political parties have a conception of how to deal with problems and that this sense is more often derived from an ideological response, albeit sometimes rather instinctive. For much of the post-war period, the Labour Party's explanation of the best way of dealing with problems – through state or collective action – was more intellectually coherent than the Conservative's adherence to a watered down version of the free market which appeared to embrace the Attlee settlement while trying to roll it back from within. In the later period, the new right's capturing of the Conservative Party gave the Tories a clear mechanism for dealing with problems through the free market and deregulation. The point is not that these ideas inspired complete agreement in detail and general thrust across both political parties, but that in the market place of ideas Labour went from being a seller to being a buyer, reversing the previous pattern.

These shifts in the balance of ideas suggest that, as David Marquand has put it, the precursor to a political victory is a victory in the battle of ideas. With respect to the nature of the conflict between Labour and Conservative or collectivist and neo-liberal ideology, the authors and commentators in this volume are divided. Some argue that rather than the Labour Government being tuned to the economic conditions established by the neo-liberalism of the Thatcher years, the Government remains, in terms of welfare policy for example, wedded to much older notions of the state. Other contributors argue that this 'settlement' in fact reflects the limits of the changes which took place in the 1980s and the extent to which many things remained unchanged by the so-called Thatcher 'revolution'. Moreover, Labour's perception of the state, Gerard Alexander argues in chapter 5, has anyway been much subtler than usually understood, the Party has been interested in constitutional change, has been prepared to contract out cultural services and so on. Therefore not only has the shift away from collectivism not been as pronounced as is commonly supposed, but in those areas in which private mechanisms for service delivery have replaced public ones, the real challenge is to regulate those mechanisms to ensure the desired outcomes rather than return to state operation. This, it seems to me, is the heart of the debate on the meaning of the New Labour Government.

Lord Fraser of Kilmorack, a Conservative Party strategist, once said that 'Elections are won and lost by a mood and everything that happens, the most unpolitical things that happen from one election to the next one, influence that mood.'[3] What makes up this mood? What is the relationship between a shift in the hidden continental plates of British politics and the outcomes of elections: sometimes a great deal, the record suggests, and sometimes very little. The response of the opposition to shifts in the political landscape tends to translate into the electoral cycle, but with varying degrees of delay. There is no hard and fast rule by which one can predict the response of, for example, centre left parties in a era of high inflation to a change in approach to macroeconomic problems, but there is significant evidence that oppositions have adapted their ideology to what they perceive to be hegemonic shifts in the terms of political discourse. The obvious cases are the response of the Conservative Party to the rise of state-led collectivism, from the mid-1930s to the mid-1950s, expressed in electoral terms most clearly at the election of 1945 and the response of the Labour Party to the rise of neo-liberal solutions to economic management from the early 1970s to the mid-1990s, expressed in electoral terms in the series of Conservative victories from 1979.

### The international context

It is clear that in certain respects external factors limit the range of options that Blair's Labour Government has for moving back towards collectivism or indeed giving substance beyond presentation to the new triangulated position. In terms of the international context, the room for manoeuvre that exists for shifts in political economy is limited, given the constraints of international co-operation, commitments abroad in terms of defence, Empire or Commonwealth attachments and the broad global ideological 'map' of interstate relations, but there are also, possibly, real opportunities. Labour claimed in its 1950 manifesto that 'Britain has regained her moral position in the western world and has won the confidence of many millions in Africa and Asia', a record which the party was happy to fight on, despite growing disunity within its ranks on issues like Europe. Within weeks of the election Attlee had disowned a pamphlet written by Denis Healey which was hostile to the movement for European unity. More significantly perhaps, the perception of foreign affairs in the 1950 election was securely in the sense of moral leadership as part of the cold war alliance. Constraints on action were seen as being the need to support the United Nations and keep the United States on side rather than constraints of power. The real test and the engulfing of the Government in foreign affairs crisis came after the election with the beginning of the Korean war. It is not until this time that the international context combines with domestic political issues to undermine the position and unity of the Government.

Explanations for the reduction in the size of Labour's majority must come from elsewhere in 1950. In 1951, the dispute inspired by the Korean war did contribute to the disunity of the Government and generally sap confidence, but Labour's landslide majority was not undermined in the period 1945–50 because of the international context of the Government.

The situation was markedly different in 1966–70. The seeds of Labour's division of the early 1970s were sown in the indecisiveness on the question of relations with Europe, and the international pressure produced a series of both currency and balance of payments crises which characterised the post-1966 Government. Moreover, foreign policy was an increasingly contentious issue between the Government and the movement. Disputes centred on the beginnings of the Rhodesia crisis, the issue of arms sales to the apartheid regime in South Africa, deep division in the Commonwealth on this and other issues, and sustained and violent opposition to support for American policy in Vietnam. Partly as a result of the divisions within the Commonwealth, Wilson relaunched a bid for British entry to the EEC and while accompanying George Brown on a tour of European capitals to discuss the bid, entered one of his periodic phases in favour of entry. The key difference from the period of the first bid for entry in the early 1960s was that the economic case for joining looked much less attractive and therefore was more immediately divisive than it had been earlier. Wilson's tactical switches, and the depth of division in the party, contributed to the profound problem of confidence in the Government. Heath's clear alternative, despite his own problems on party unity on the issue, was an electoral advantage. The international context in the period 1966-70 worked powerfully against Labour.

### The impact of the ending of the cold war

In the context of the Labour victory in 1997, as John Young discusses in chapter 7, the absence of the cold war was much more significant than it had been in 1992: defence did not feature on one day of the election, nuclear weapons were not mentioned, unilateralism was not thought about. One of the major electoral ghosts for Labour in the 1980s had been completely laid to rest. The collapse of the Soviet Empire was also presented as part of the triumph of individualism, which drowned collectivism as an organising idea for the state. Despite the recent recovery of some eastern European Communist parties, 1989 suggested that collectivism was an historical artefact from the twentieth century. It is hard to pin down the impact of the collapse of the Soviet Empire on the Labour Party's internal policy debate, but it clearly, in a perhaps abstract sense, undermined the collectivist case within the Party: it removed the sense of conviction, in for example the debate on Clause IV, that the resonance of the commitment to state ownership was anything more than a symbol. Moreover, the ending of the cold war and the introduction of a moral agenda for the conduct of foreign policy, when coupled with the further symbolism of the handover of the last substantial colonial outpost in Hong Kong, all suggest that in the international context the case for the third position, the new political position, is strong simply because of the movement of history.

The other context of the international dimension is the impact on the ability of the Government to act. In comparison with earlier periods the amount of decision-making power that is now out of the hands of the British Government is highly significant. It is not clear if this represents a unique opportunity to be electorally judged on the more tightly defined criterion of competence or whether this simply leaves more open the scope for being the victim of externalities or regional authorities. There are some external factors that are highly contested and therefore unproven in their impacts on a Labour Government. This will be the first Labour administration to deal with global capital markets operating at such speed and intensity; globalisation in a number of significant sectors might also have long-term economic impacts, and Rio-style agreements will constrain certain forms of economic activity. In presentational terms the media are more fractured and sectioned than in the 1960s and 1970s, so the communications challenge is correspondingly enhanced.

Labour is creating other kinds of external challenges – external to the traditional Westminster model – by its renewal of the British constitution, as discussed in chapter 6 by Vernon Bogdanor and Edward Pearce. Scottish and Welsh devolution, the operation of subsidiarity to county and local government in the English regions, elected mayors and the renewal of other intermediate institutions, will be part of a reshaped British state. This will result in a perceived spread of power, contrasting sharply with both 1945–51 and 1966–70, in which central government clung to power and therefore were held responsible to an extraordinary degree for a whole range of things beyond their control (a situation that might, of course, have come about earlier if the Government of 1974—9 had had greater luck). For the current Government, the electoral gamble has to be that the electorate will recognise the level of competencies for different decisions and that the Government will not be blamed if international or internal factors adversely affect key groups of voters.

## Confidence and communication

Part of the ability of a Government to maintain its level of support over the lifetime of a Parliament is determined on the one hand by the confidence it inspires in the electorate and, on the other, the extent to which it does well those things that are within its control. Of the three layers of confidence in government – intellectual self-confidence, voter confidence in the Government and the communication of confidence to the electorate, the medium through which the first and the second interact – it is the last that is perhaps both most difficult to measure and most difficult to achieve over the lifetime of an administration. It is also, arguably, the area that has advanced the most in the last 50 years.

In simple terms there is no better measure of the cultural distance between 1945–51 and 1997 than a comparison of the 'images' of Attlee and Blair – in practically every meaningful sense they relate differently with the media. The 1945 Labour Government inherited much from the wartime coalition, including the level and extent of its propaganda operation. It is not that the Attlee Governments did not communicate their policies throughout the Parliament, they did and Tom Wildy has shown they did so effectively at times,[4] particularly in promoting the public understanding of the new welfare system; it is that this was not seen as a central part of all government activity, even at times when political communication was paramount. Dennis Kavanagh relates how Attlee in the 1950 general election was asked by a deferential television interviewer 'if he had anything he wished to say on the eve of the election campaign. Attlee replied "No" and after an awkward pause that was the end of the interview.'[5] This illustrates both Attlee's indifference to the notion of the centrality of communicating and the diffidence of television. Wilson in 1966 and 1970 is perhaps a halfway house to the Blair of 1997.

The 1966 campaign was well fought in television terms but Labour in the 1960s was not overwhelmed by campaigning. In 1964 the campaign committees that had been in operation continuously since 1962 were not enshrined in the heart of government. Wilson's successor developed the trends of communication being important to the perception of the Government. Callaghan had come to the top in politics when the ability to communicate effectively through television was becoming essential. When Michael Foot and AJP Taylor were dropped from 'In the News', the BBC's top current affairs show in the 1950s, Callaghan was brought in. He developed an ebullient, jocular style which often worked effectively and insisted on strict conditions for interviews, stopping those he was not happy with and ensuring that the tapes were suppressed.[6] This private petulance was also a sign of someone not intimidated by the medium and Robin Day has described the most difficult interviews he had to do as ones in which Jim Callaghan 'decides to mix it'. Despite this early skill with television he was to be resoundingly outflanked by the Thatcher team in the 1979 general election when they took the use of the medium to new heights and Callaghan's approach suddenly appeared dated. A development that Tony Blair must be careful of; there has been a tendency for innovators in political advertising and presentation to leapfrog each other.

Most of the attention in electoral literature of the 1980s focused on voter perception of economic expectations. The economic model of election results rests on the presumption of improving economic performance, but it need not be rational, based on the real indicators of economic performance, as against a perception of economic failure, like the winter crisis of 1947 or Black Wednesday; it should also be seen as being connected to the broad role of political ideas or explanations of how to deal with problems rather than just a narrow conception of economic well-being. One of the underlying judgements that needs to be made is the extent to which politics is, simply, 'the economy, stupid'. In terms of 1997, some commentators, like Ivor Crewe, are already suggesting that the lessons of the American experience had been too well learnt, and that Labour was fighting the British general election of 1992 and the American Presidential election of the same year. It is not yet time to suggest that Churchill was wrong when he stated that:

> It is no longer a case of one party fighting another, nor of one set of politicians scoring off another. It is the case of successive Governments facing economic problems and being judged by their success or failure in the duel.[7]

It might be that by isolating one set of factors, the economic, some commentators have ignored others that might override these considerations in certain instances. It might also be that the economic confidence factor has simply coalesced with a series of other factors in contributing to Labour's landslide.

Indeed, the economic expectations model has, in fact, evolved somewhat and the key recognition about expectations of improvements in personal well-being has been supported by questions of the extent to which the Government is seen as being more competent to manage the economy. David Sanders highlights the impact of Black Wednesday on voter perception of the Conservative Party's management in a recent *Political Studies* article:

> Until the middle of 1992, the competence series is above the zero line – reflecting the clear lead which the Conservatives had apparently enjoyed for most of the period since 1964. Note, however, what happened at the time of Britain's ignominious exit from the ERM in September 1992. The competence graph (as well as the popularity graph) plunges downward and continues to trend downwards thereafter.

Labour eventually overtakes the Conservative Party on this measure.

### A defining crisis: the IMF 1976

The clearest earlier example of a defining moment, on a par with Black Wednesday, was the IMF crisis of 1976. In assessing the decision to call in the IMF it is important to understand the separate and competing pressures that the Labour Government and Callaghan in particular were under.[8] It is arguable that such a combination of economic, political and Party pressures will not be repeated with the same intensity again because of the ending of the cold war, the evolution of the European Union and the trade union legislation of the Thatcher administrations. However, in 1976 the EEC was still relatively marginal to economic management. The autumn of 1976 was dominated by the British tradition of a sterling crisis (following similar occasions in 1947, 1949, 1951, 1955, 1957, 1964, 1966, 1967, 1972 and 1975).[9] The cold war was still dominating international politics so the question of nuclear defence remained a central concern. Trade unions were still unregulated and capable of paralysing the country in opposition to an incomes policy which in turn was a response to the highest inflation in British history. On top of this was the overarching political constraint of the lack of a parliamentary majority. In such a circumstance, Cabinet government itself was placed under enormous pressure. Callaghan also had party management to consider and the need to keep the Labour Party together was a constant constraint. Few if any of these particular factors will present a challenge to Blair or his Government.

Callaghan's main strengths were his conduct of Cabinet business and his standing internationally. His main weakness was his inability to grasp the changing nature of the Labour Party and his preference for a short political fix over a lasting political solution. The sterling crisis, which was Callaghan's first real test as Prime Minister, resulted from an international loss of confidence in the pound, caused in part by the deposit and then gradual withdrawal of £2,500 million by petroleum producing states.[10] Moreover, inflation was running at 25 per cent when Callaghan took over and despite a package of public expenditure cuts adopted in July 1976 the pound continued to spiral downwards. It became increasingly likely that the IMF would have to be approached to restore international confidence. The decision to ask for a loan from the IMF, which entailed a review of the Government's books and recommendations of changes in policy, was a defining moment in the post-war history of the Labour Party. Despite the fact that the July package of public expenditure cuts was already in place, the left charged that Labour had abandoned its programme in response to the demands of international capitalism. In turn, the new right charged that the bankruptcy of the neo-Keynesians was revealed by the humiliation of Britain applying for aid of this kind and that in so accepting the need to reduce public expenditure the Labour Government in fact accepted the monetarist arguments.

These accusations affected the intellectual self-confidence of different sections of the Government. Callaghan's speech to the Labour Party conference illustrated the depth of the revaluation of Labour's broad approach to political economy that had been building, in response to the

AES discussed in chapter 2, since the early 1970s. The speech was a manifesto for good housekeeping. Callaghan was warning his Party and the country that the current situation was not sustainable:

> For too long, perhaps, ever since the war, we postponed facing up to fundamental choices and fundamental changes in our society and in our economy. That is what I mean when I say we have been living on borrowed time. For too long this country ... has been ready to settle for borrowing money abroad to maintain our standards of life ...The cosy world we were told would go on forever, where full employment would be guaranteed at the stroke of the Chancellor's pen ... I tell you in all candour that that option no longer exists, and that, insofar as it ever did exist, it only worked on each occasion by injecting a bigger dose of inflation into the economy.[11]

Edmund Dell maintains that this had been the message of Governments for years[12] but in the context of the cuts in public expenditure, the radical content of the 1974 manifesto and the increasingly right-wing tone of the Conservative opposition under Margaret Thatcher, the impact of the speech was politically profound and lasting, even if its long-term impact on the economic policy of the Government – given Denis Healey's mildly reflationary budget of 1978 – was limited.

In terms of the communication of confidence, the case for the third new political position is again rather strong. The Blair Government's attachment to the notion of constant campaigning and high presentation values, from town meetings, to MPs' constituency weeks, to the place of Peter Mandelson at the heart of the Government, suggests two things. First that, as with Harold Wilson, the political presentation of the Government is centred on the Prime Minister, but that unlike the past, the presentational values extend to every Minister and every policy. There is a question of the extent to which this is sustainable once problems develop, but the intention is clear. Second, that, though this may sound paradoxical, power is the central currency and objective of the Government. The latter is clearly a direct Thatcherite inheritance and marks a significant shift in the Labour Party's character towards that of the Conservative Party. The open question at this moment remains the extent to which basic New Labour ideological positions will be sacrificed to the pursuit of power. Moreover, the balance of forces in the Blair Cabinet is such that over the lifetime of the 1997 Parliament, the Prime Minister's position, already dominant, will be further strengthened as old Labour wets are replaced by New Labour drys.

This concentration of power in the office of the Prime Minister will be successful so long as the things that the Government have power over continue to be well handled. The timing of elections is the most obvious piece of electoral mechanics that the governing party controls. The power of the Prime Minister in this respect has not altered since 1950 or 1970, or the success of October 1974 after Heath's failure in February 1974. All the evidence of Blair's leadership so far is that he will enjoy the power that this decision gives him but that he will consult. Attlee had a great deal of advice – some commissioned, some not – thrown at him from the spring of 1949 onwards. In the end he hung on and reduced his room for manoeuvre. In 1970 the timing in part was dictated by a patient waiting game by the Prime Minister for a recovery in his own authority and this came, according to Ben Pimlott, with a firm Government response to trouble in Northern Ireland and a long delayed economic response to the devaluation of the pound. When this recovery was translated into good local election results, and a string of polls showing Labour pulling ahead of the Conservatives, Wilson asked his inner Cabinet to approve a June 18 polling date: ' "Everyone agreed?" he asked. "Right: then no one can be able to claim the virtue of hindsight".'[13] So far so good.

The first miscalculation was that the trade figures for May showed a £31 million deficit, £18.5 million of which came from the purchase of two jumbo jets. This dented the image of the renewed improvement of the economic situation and suggested that another international trade crisis was on the way. The Chancellor, Roy Jenkins, considered a cosmetic adjustment to the official statistics, but, in conversation with the Prime Minister, rejected the idea. Jenkins commented in his memoirs that 'it was not a question of morals but of sense'.[14] If the civil servants had talked against the change in methodology then the correction might have proved counter-productive. That they had got themselves into this position and that the opposition from the Head of the Government Statistical Service stopped them from getting out of the situation are both highly illustrative. Part of the mechanics of electoral politics – controlling that which you can control – is summed up in this decision. Attlee and Cripps would not have discussed it: the figures would have been put out. Jenkins and Wilson discussed it, saw no real problem with the changing of the figures to leave the jumbo jets out, but could not guarantee that the presentation of the figures could be properly handled. A similar instance from the 1974–79 Government illustrates the direction of change further. Denis Healey took a 2.2 per cent increase in retail prices in May-August 1975 and claimed that inflation was running at only 8.4 per cent. In the 1980s the Conservative Governments regularly manipulated the unemployment figures. And what of Mandelson and Blair, faced with the Jenkins-Wilson choice, or a Healey situation on a key indicator like inflation or growth? It is difficult to imagine them resisting the urge to put the best presentational spin possible on the figures but it is also possible to see the management of government statistics becoming an even more central part of permanent campaigning.[15] This emphasis on news management may also help, in the long term, with the tendency, highlighted by Jim Tomlinson in chapter 2, of Labour history to be written as a story of perpetual failure.

What will not be necessary, unless the number of by-elections reaches unprecedented proportions, will be the kind of majority management that so hampered the ambitions of the Labour Government of 1974-79, to the point at which staying in power become an end in itself. The position was made even worse because the small majority the Labour Party had gained at the general election of October 1974 was slowly eroded in by-elections, the resignations of Roy Jenkins and David Marquand who went to the European Commission and the defection of left-wing MPs on issues of nationalism or in opposition to public expenditure cuts. At the beginning of the 1976–77 session Callaghan had pinned his hopes on nationalist support for the devolution bills in order to maintain a majority. However, in February 1977 the motion for a guillotine was defeated by a backbench revolt. Without the limitation of the time for debate, the Leader of the House, Michael Foot, judged that the bills would not be passed in reasonable time and they were therefore postponed until the next session. (The bills were finally passed in February 1978.) The nationalists thereafter opposed the Government. The defeat in 1979 was widely expected, but if a last-minute plan by Michael Foot and others in the Cabinet to delay polling had taken place, things might have been different. Callaghan rejected the idea and the party went down to defeat. An examination of the Labour Party's own NEC analysis of each election between 1945 and 1979 reveals a number of dynamics at work in the mechanics of electioneering. The Cabinet discussions surrounding the timing of the elections in 1950 were rather farcically – to our contemporary eyes – connected with the movements of the King and in 1978 with a serious miscalculation by the Prime Minister.

Tony Blair is apparently freed from virtually all the factors that contributed to the defeat of the 1979 Labour Government, and the reforms in the structure and discipline of the Labour Party may make the re-emergence of such problems in the 1997 Parliament less likely, though Tim Bale in chapter 8 suggests that dissent will still be a significant factor particularly if the Labour leadership over-reacts to disciplinary problems, as it has done throughout the post-war period. Given the majority and the change of circumstances, however, such dissent is unlikely to be a defining electoral issue. A general reading of the political literature of the period suggests that Labour has learnt a great deal in opposition but things can still go very wrong. One of the dangers might be that the lessons have been learnt so well and that campaigning has become such a central part of Government policy, that when good timing and the campaign itself are added to the equation, Labour will begin to believe it has learnt a science of election winning. The past suggests that there is no science, but that there are a set of key things that a Government can do to maintain their position: communicate effectively, campaign hard, time the election correctly, keep the party united and the Government energised.

The historical record implies that the Labour Party is not particularly good at doing these things and that the real meaning of 'New Labour' might be the ability to co-ordinate across these five fields in order to win. My argument is that there was not enough work in these areas in the period between 1945–51 and 1966–70, at the right point in the electoral cycle, and that this was not all down to external factors or in some sense inevitable because of an ageing Government: it was not events, dear boy, events. That works as a explanation of electoral results only if everything else is in place. My central point is that not enough of those things that politicians can plan were planned well and tuned to the electoral cycle in the periods 1945–50, 1966–70 and most particularly, though in a very different political context, in 1974–79, and that Blair and Mandelson's challenge is to minimise the number of these that slip away. This will be difficult, because historically the Labour Party is the least straightforwardly malleable of the major parties; moreover, for it to happen, policy debate will have to be virtually absent from the Government towards the end of the cycle.

A glance over their shoulders will show the new Cabinet that the electoral challenge has by no means been wiped out by the 1997 result. Increasing the overall size of a landslide majority would be unprecedented. Labour has increased its majority twice, in 1966 and October 1974, but this was from a much lower base. Maintaining the share of the vote will also be difficult but might not, as in 1951, or for the Conservatives between 1983 and 1987, be translated into seats. Timing the next election correctly and, more significantly perhaps, the one after that – assuming a cut in majority in between – and generally having the electoral system work in Labour's favour, have all proved immensely difficult since 1945. Indeed, this led Richard Crossman to believe that the point of the Labour Party was to come into power in times of crisis and then depart soon afterwards. A sentiment entirely lacking, after 18 years of opposition, from New Labour.

## A new political ideology?

The current Labour Government will be, unless there are some extra-ordinary events, the Government which will take Britain into a new millennium. The campaign which elected it was dominated by soundbites and spin doctors, by issues that echoed the last campaign and by a feeling that somewhere the issues and ideas that will matter in the next century were trying to emerge. The Conservative Government which was defeated left a country with stable prices and falling unemployment but an electorate that had little faith in its ability to govern. The symbolism of the times, which featured in the pre-election campaign more than in the actual period of most intense campaigning, the convergence of change in global and local politics, makes the next five years a critical period. The coincidence of interesting and symbolic times makes the moment an odd one – it has the potential to be unique and in some sense defining, something which the Salisbury Government which took us into the twentieth century failed even to attempt to be, unless one counts imperial humiliation as indicative of what was to come.

Since the middle of the 1960s, the nature of contemporary capitalism has been undergoing a period of change after a time of relative stability from the later 1940s. Individual life patterns in work, relationships, housing and life expectancy, national challenges from the European agenda, the changing global economy, our evolving international position and a backward body politic, global challenges from the environment, the structural inequality between northern and southern hemispheres and the movements of people this provokes, are intertwined at each level of change with rapidly advancing technology. The beginning of a new century provides an opportunity to re-examine our institutions and our politics, and the beginning of a new millennium demands that we consider fundamental questions of national identity, national wealth and the kind of society and world we wish to live in.

This is not about a moment at which we begin to see a life after politics, seductive though such terms might appear.[16] Rather it is a moment at which a set of trends, born in the affluence and technology of the 1950s and 1960s, mature and their profound and permanent impacts on the pattern of our individual and collective lives reach full growth. Election 1997 in the United Kingdom is thus a convenient peg on which to hang the realisation of change and of the level and extent of continuity, but means little in a broader context of the political evolution of Britain. The conflict and the gap in our democracy is the extent to which there is so little connection between the maturity of the revolution in our private experiences and the solidity of our political institutions in the face of these changes. We know our lives are different – our emotional lives more atomised, our experience of the world more crowded and our ability to be self reliant more constrained – from those of our parents. We do not know how to communicate this through our existing democracy. Given this combination of factors and the length of its periods in opposition since the war, it would be extraordinary if the Labour Government had not attempted to articulate a new political position that incorporated the political lessons of the last 50 years, even if the policy lessons remain more disputed.

A number of writers were suggesting before the election that the tide of opinion had turned towards a new form of political ideology. Foremost among these were Will Hutton and David Marquand. The latter has suggested that the central question of the *Unprincipled Society* – where now for the left? – might have been answered by a combination of stakeholding capitalism, a resurgence of moral collectivism and the focusing of debate across the spectrum on community. Thus ideas coming from the left and the recognition of the failures of the new right project of the 1980s might be coalescing in a new paradigm. This is more than just Labour's big idea, this is the beginning of the political language of the twenty-first century. Perhaps if that is the case then election 1997 was an earthquake and its tremors will be felt for the next two or three elections in both results and the way Governments affect the lives of individuals. I am not sure.

The essays in this volume suggest a somewhat mixed conclusion. In terms of ideas, the international context, what people expect of politics and what politicians think they can do, 1997 was a watershed which enshrined neo-liberal concepts of a limited state and the support of market over planned economics at the heart of Labour's approach. But in the context of the cold war, the new spread of power in the British state and the responses to the disputed impacts of globalisation (see Jim Tomlinson, chapter 2), a new political territory has been mapped out. Where the earthquake has undoubtedly occurred and where the agenda of this Labour Government is indicative of the future, is in the comprehensive rejection of Conservative constitutionality in state structures and the Conservatives' definition of sovereignty. In both these respects, however, it would be a mistake to see a rejection of Conservative definitions as in any way a return to the collectivism of the previous Labour Government. Labour's thinking in these areas seems set to be genuinely new, partly because of force of circumstances and partly because of the real Blair revolution: the merger of ideology and the pursuit of power and its position at the forefront of the doctrine and ethos of the New Labour Party.

# Notes

1 See for example, Helena Catt, *Voting Behaviour, A Radical Critique*, Leicester University Press, 1996.

2 For a full discussion of this see Anthony Seldon's chapter in Seldon and David Marquand (eds), *The Ideas that Shaped Post-war Britain*, HarperCollins, 1996. Though some new analysis suggests that at the micro level of policy the notion of Conservative acceptance of the consensus was virtually non-existent and that the content of Labour's 'socialism' has been misunderstood, see Harriet Jones and Michael Kandiah (eds), *The Myth of Consensus, New Views on British History, 1945-64*, Macmillan, Basingstoke, 1996.

3 Peter Hennessy, *Never Again*, Cape, 1992, p.66.

4 Tom Wildy, 'The Social and Economic Publicity and Propaganda of the Labour Governments of 1945-51', in *Contemporary Record*, Vol. 6, No. 1, 1992, pp.45-71.

5 Dennis Kavanagh, *Election campaigning. The New Marketing of Politics*, Blackwell, 1995, p 12.

6 Michael Cockerell, *Live from Number 10*, Faber and Faber, 1988.

7 Quoted in Peter Hennessy, *Muddling Through*, Victor Gollancz, 1996, p.298.

8 H.M. Drucker, 'Leadership selection in the Labour Party,' *Parliamentary Affairs*, Vol. XXIX, No. 4, pp.378-95.

9 Kathleen Burk, 'The Americans, the Germans and the British. The 1976 IMF Crisis', *Twentieth Century British History*, Vol. 5, No. 3, 1994, pp.350–69, and Kathleen Burk and Alec Cairncross, *Goodbye Great Britain: The 1976 IMF Crisis*, Yale University Press, 1992.

10 Alec Cairncross, 'Economic policy after 1974', *Twentieth Century British History*, Vol. 3, No. 2, 1992, pp 199-208.

11 Quoted in Richard Cockett, *Thinking the Unthinkable, Think-tanks and the economic counter-revolution, 1931–1983*, Fontana, 1995.

12 Edmund Dell, *A Hard Pounding, Politics and Economic Crisis, 1974-76*, Oxford University Press, 1991 pp.236–37.

13 Ben Pimlott, *Harold Wilson*, HarperCollins, 1992, p.554.

14  Roy Jenkins, *A Life at the Centre*, Macmillan, 1991, p.299.
15  Denis Kavanagh, 'The timing of elections: the British case', in Ivor Crewe and Martin Harrop (eds), *Political Communications: the General Election of 1987*, Cambridge University Press, 1989, p.8.
16  Geoff Mulgan (ed), *Life after Politics*, Fontana, 1997.

# CUSP

*Kingston University Centre for the Study of Society and Politics*

The roots of the moral activist sensibility lie deep in the history of western civilisation. (David Marquand)

Surrogacy...has reduced children to consumer products...It is quite incompatible with the respect a decent society ought to have for children and motherhood. (Peter Garrett)

The state whose rulers come to their duties with the least enthusiasm is bound to have the best and most tranquil government, and the state whose rulers are eager to rule the worst. (Plato)

If I had written a letter to my MP would all these cameras be here? (Daniel 'Swampy' Hooper).

The impact of state action and technological advance on traditionally private areas of life is a central preoccupation of our age. New moral, political and ethical dilemmas arise from changes in fertility and parenthood, in the perception of private conduct and public accountability and over the balance between collective and individual needs in public policy. The boundary between the public realm and what we defend as the private is constantly moving.

In response to these challenges, CUSP aims to stimulate innovative research and discussion using personal experience and a historical perspective by exploring:

- private behaviour and the state: the effects and limits of government policy on the individual; the changing relationship between government and the family; the state's responsibility for health and education; the impact and control of technology on personal choice.
- individual rights and collective policy: the conflict between personal freedom and a morally activist political culture; the contemporary notion of a limited state and the decline of public service; the changing balance between collective intervention and market mechanisms.
- government and the governed: the connection between public and private conduct; the interaction between popular movements and culture and government action; the influence of masculinity and femininity on

politics; the meaning of personal integrity, faith and conviction in the practical exercise of power.

The Centre is an innovative project in university and public life designed to examine these themes in a series of research projects, publications, seminars and lectures and an imaginative use of the internet. Our intention is to break down the conventional barriers between academic, political and journalistic analysis. We will invite contributors to the Centre's work from a spectrum ranging from mainstream political to popular or even anti-parliamentary activity, from 'quality' to 'tabloid' media, from soap opera to National Opera; and we will exploit the knowledge and experience of other specialists to broaden the Centre's basis of academic analysis.

For further information contact Ruth Winstone, Director, CUSP, Kingston University, Faculty of Human Sciences, Penrhyn Road, Kingston upon Thames, SU1 2TN.

# ICBH

*Institute of Contemporary British History*

History is the collective memory of a society. The Institute of Contemporary British History was founded in 1986 by Peter Hennessy and Anthony Seldon to encourage the study of the most recent part of that memory. The ICBH's aims are:

- the study and better understanding of post-war British history in schools and throughout higher education;
- the use of historical experience in government and business decision-making;
- the development of oral archives and resources for post-war British history;
- research into post-war British history, especially in neglected areas;
- interdisciplinary contacts for those working on contemporary Britain;
- the dissemination of information about, and the preservation of, archives and sources on post-war British history.

The ICBH is strictly non-political, and has a balanced and authoritative board of trustees and academic advisors to guarantee its standards. As an independent registered charity it relies on donations, research grants and income generated from its publications and conferences to fund its continued existence.

ICBH activities include academic conferences, for example on Britain and the Cold War; an academic journal, published quarterly, *Contemporary British History*; sixth-form conferences and an A-level journal, *Modern History Review*; research projects, for example on the Cabinet Committee system; oral history seminars - a recent series has examined British policy in Northern Ireland up to the Anglo-Irish Agreement; and books of all sorts, from school textbooks to collections of essays, academic monographs, and a comprehensive annotated bibliography on post-war British history.

For more information about ICBH's work, and how to become a Friend of the Institute, write to: Paul Nicholson, Administrator, ICBH, Room 357, Senate House, London WC1E 7HU or email icbh@sas.ac.uk.

# Index